SERIAL KILLERS

SERIAL KILLERS

INSIDE THE MINDS OF THE MOST MONSTROUS MURDERERS

CHARLOTTE GREIG

Picture Credits

AP/Worldwide: 118, 203

Corbis: 15, 29, 96, 106, 111, 158, 195, 228, 252

Getty Images (Hulton): 101

Rex: 188

Topfoto: 21, 24, 32, 67, 70, 75, 76, 132, 153, 162, 168, 300

This edition published in 2017 by Arcturus Publishing Limited
26/27 Bickels Yard, 151–153 Bermondsey Street,
London SE1 3HA

AD005860UK

Printed in the UK

Contents

Introduction

For most of us, the crazed mind of the serial killer is a closed book, one that we may be curious to open, perhaps, but one that we know will fill us with terror. What do we expect to find there? Unimagined horrors, unspeakable desires, inexplicable compulsions and inhuman cruelty – at best. At worst, we may encounter some stirrings of recognition in ourselves, some acknowledgement of our own curiosity about death and dying. However much we may deny it, we are fascinated by what serial killers do, how they do it and why they do it. We want to know about the different ways in which the human body can be destroyed, dismembered and ritually abused; about how victims suffer; about the links between sex, pain, torture and death. Most of all, perhaps, we want to know about the psychology of the serial killer, the individual who acts upon the darkest of human impulses and lets them surface into reality.

The Lone Killer

Mass murderers have existed since the beginning of recorded history. In some eras, they were kings, queens and princes: think of Vlad the Impaler, 'Bloody' Mary I of England or the mad Ottoman ruler Murad IV. Hideously cruel methods of torture and killing that we now consider completely inhuman were part of everyday life in many ages and civilizations, from the Aztecs and the Barbarians to early Polynesian cultures and medieval Europe. In modern times, state-sanctioned atrocities on a grand scale have been committed, for example in Nazi Germany and, more recently, in Rwanda. However, the phenomenon of the serial killer, who generally works alone and in secret, usually killing victims one at a time, is a different one. These are the murderers that we find particularly disturbing, the 'ordinary' people who could be our next-door neighbours or office co-workers, the individuals who may have a troubled family history but who, on the face of it, have no more reason to kill than the rest of us. These are the murderers who baffle and terrify us, precisely because they seem so ordinary and so much – on the surface – 'just like us'. However, when they are finally caught they are revealed to have tortured and killed a string of innocent victims, often in the most gruesome ways imaginable.

The 'Ordinary' Killer

Our list of serial killers contains many apparently ordinary people. Ted Bundy, for example, was an attractive, self-confident man who escaped the law for many years precisely because he seemed so unlike the accepted image of a lonely, psychotic killer. Nevertheless, Bundy killed scores of young women and girls, the youngest aged 12. Before clubbing his victims to death, he raped them and bit their bodies ferociously, often leaving marks all over them. (It was the bite marks that finally led to his conviction, when an impression from his teeth matched the marks on the bodies.) Meanwhile in Britain, ex-policeman Dennis Nilsen, a closet homosexual, murdered a string of men he brought home, storing body parts in his home in a bizarre way that was later described by his biographer Brian Masters as 'killing for company'. His victims were mostly young drifters, one of them a skinhead with 'cut here' tattooed on his neck – an instruction Nilsen unfortunately took literally. It was only when his flat started to get crowded, and Nilsen took to boiling the body parts and flushing them down the toilet – thus blocking the drains – that he was finally caught.

In the same way, it was only when police visited the home of serial killer John Wayne Gacy and smelled the awful stench coming from the crawl space under his house that his ghastly spate of horrific murders was uncovered. Like Bundy and Nilsen, Gacy blended in well with his surroundings, seldom giving any indication of the horrors of his personal life. Gacy was a well-respected building contractor who lived in a middle-class neighbourhood and was active in politics, performing as a clown at children's parties and charity events. Unbeknown to his neighbours, however, he had for years been luring boys as young as nine to his house, sodomizing them, torturing them on a homemade rack and finally garrotting them before dumping their bodies outside. In a chilling finale to his murderous career, when he was on death row he continued to function as an enterprising businessman, selling his paintings of skulls and clowns, which became collectors' items and reached high prices.

Historical Figures

In the past, of course, many serial killers had no need to hide behind the façade of a conventional way of life. Historical figures such as the 16th-century Hungarian countess Elizabeth Bathory were in a position to do what they liked; in Elizabeth's case what she liked was torturing servant girls to death. She would pierce them with pins, needles and branding irons, burn their vaginas with lighted candles and then attack them in a frenzy, tearing their breasts to pieces. During the torture sessions, she would also bite chunks of flesh from the girls. One victim was forced to cook and eat her own flesh. After these orgiastic rituals of torture and murder, the bodies of the girls would be left to rot, or dumped outside the castle walls for wolves to eat. This continued for years, without anyone intervening. It was only when Elizabeth started to torture daughters of the nobility instead of mere peasant girls that the king decided to put a stop to her activities and ordered a night raid on the castle, catching her in the act. Even then, instead of being executed like her servant accomplices, Elizabeth was given a special dispensation and, despite the fact that she had killed hundreds of victims, ended her days imprisoned in her castle rooms.

Anonymous Killers

Perhaps even more terrifying than these monsters of depravity, whether historical or modern day, are the ones who got away. The most infamous of these is, of course, Jack the Ripper. The fact that his victims were so brutally murdered, that he apparently issued taunting messages to the police and that his identity to this day remains unknown, continues to make this one of the most disturbing, and fascinating, cases of all time.

Jack the Ripper claimed his first victim in 1888 – a prostitute in London's East End known as 'Polly', though her real name was Mary Nichols. Her throat had been cut and there were vicious stab wounds to her stomach and genitals. About a month later, prostitute Annie Chapman was found disembowelled, her entrails laid across one shoulder. In a pattern that was to prove horribly familiar, parts of the body, in this case the bladder, vagina, womb and ovaries, were missing. The murders continued, each one more gruesome than the last; in the case of victim Catherine Eddowes, a kidney was removed and then half of it sent to the police with a letter bragging that the killer had eaten the other half. Finally, with the murder of Mary Kelly, the Ripper reached new depths of violence and madness: her dead body was disembowelled and her hand had been inserted into her stomach. In addition, her liver had been placed on her thigh, while her breasts had been cut off and laid out beside her severed heart, kidneys and nose. Strips of flesh were hung from nails around the room in which she was murdered. A post-mortem discovered that Kelly had been three months pregnant, but the Ripper had taken her womb and foetus with him.

Jack the Ripper was never found, and speculation about him (or, according to one theory, her) abounded, casting a long shadow over the inhabitants of London for many years. Every time a fresh murder was committed, people would fear the hand of the Ripper; murders that had happened before the Ripper's reign of terror were also re-examined. Currently, the case is still open, and the list of suspects continues to grow as the evidence is repeatedly sifted, in the hopes of one day solving the mystery.

Human Evil

Even when we know exactly what crimes a serial killer has committed, a mystery still remains: the mystery of why any human being should brutally kill at random in a compulsive way, one victim after another, according to what often appears to be some kind of deranged logic. While we may be able to solve the puzzle of a particular series of crimes, or even begin to construct a coherent picture of the mind of a murderer, the existence of human evil in the form of the serial killer remains a conundrum that we can never fully understand.

Angels of Death

Angels of death are some of the most disturbing of all serial killers. These are the murderers who, on the face of it, seem to be the carers in our society: housewives, grandmothers, nurses, doctors – in short, pillars of the community. They are well-respected family men and women who spend their lives taking care of others. They seem such unlikely perpetrators of murder that their evil crimes often go undetected for years, leaving them to kill dozens, even hundreds, of victims.

The most famous angel of death is the British family doctor Harold Shipman. Over the course of two decades, he murdered around 200 elderly female patients, possibly more. His patients saw him as a dedicated man who went out of his way to care for them. In reality, however, he was a deranged murderer who secretly dispatched his elderly but often perfectly healthy victims with killer doses of morphine.

As well as professional carers such as doctors and nurses, there are also informal carers – mothers, grandmothers, housekeepers and so on – whose kindly exterior belies an evil, twisted mind. These people seem like models of respectability, but in reality take pleasure in killing their victims, often in cruel ways. An example of this type is the first known female serial killer of modern times, Belle Gunness, whose catalogue of murders included her children, husbands and lovers. Another is Nannie Doss, who murdered a series of husbands by poisoning them with arsenic-laced coffee and prunes stewed in rat poison.

What characterizes the angel of death is the mismatch between the pose of a caring, kind person, concerned with looking after others – and the reality – a psychotic, ruthless murderer who takes pleasure in causing suffering and death.

CHARLES CULLEN

The usual cliché about serial killers is how normal they always seemed before their ghastly secrets were uncovered. Not so Charles Cullen. Few people could have appeared more out of step with their surroundings. Cullen worked for 16 years at hospitals in New Jersey and Pennsylvania, during which time he admitted to killing as many as 40 patients, but that could be just the tip of the iceberg.

Police suspect he could have given drug overdoses to as many as 400 elderly patients, which would make him the worst serial killer ever in North America, but due to lack of evidence this figure may never be confirmed.

Danger Signs

Charles Cullen was a shy and unhappy child. The youngest of eight children, he was born in West Orange, New Jersey on 22 February 1960. His father, a bus driver, died when he was only seven months old and two of his siblings passed away while he was still young.

The danger signs were there from an early age. When he was 9, Cullen tried to take his own life by swallowing the contents of a

Charles Cullen

chemistry set. Later he told police he had tried to commit suicide on at least 20 separate occasions (though it would only have taken one attempt had he shown the same shabby expertise he used to despatch his mainly aged victims).

In 5th grade, he revealed the depth of his adolescent angst with an unpublished book called *Infinity Years Will Never Know* about growing up in a world devoid of meaning, and he began compulsively reading and re-reading Dostoevsky's *Crime and Punishment* which details the mental torment of a student who commits murder.

At the age of 17, he suffered a crushing blow when his mother was killed in a car crash. Cullen's behaviour became increasingly off-kilter. Bullied at school, he went to a party where he laced his tormentors' drinks with rat poison. It was a practice run for what was to follow.

Dropping out of high school, Cullen joined the US Navy in April 1978, enlisting as a ballistic missiles technician. He came through the stringent psychological test for submariners with flying colours and was assigned to a Poseidon missiles unit on board the nuclear submarine U.S.S. *Woodrow Wilson*. Here he was christened with the nickname 'Fish-belly white' due to the deathly pallor of his complexion. His bunkmate, Marlin Emswiler, acknowledged Cullen had no friends. 'Charlie hung out with Charlie. Kept saying he wanted to become a nurse because he liked helping people.'

One day, Cullen was discovered by crew members at the missile control panel of the nuclear submarine, wearing a green surgical gown, surgical mask and latex gloves pilfered from the ship's medical cabinet. He was transferred to the U.S.S. Canopus, and discharged from the Navy in March 1984 after yet another suicide attempt.

One-Word Answers

He was now free to follow his morbid medical bent. He gained a degree from the Mountainside School of Nursing, Montclair, NJ which he left in 1987. He married his wife, Adrienne, in that year and began his first nursing job at the St Barnabus Medical Center, Livingston, NJ.

A colleague recalled his inability to deal with normal social situations. 'You'd ask him, "Are you married" or something like that, and get one-word answers.' In 1988 he killed for the first time. His victim was 72-year-old judge John Yengo, who was injected with a drug called Lidocaine. The death was recorded in newspapers of the time as being 'a case of Stevens-Johnson syndrome', a rare allergic reaction. In 1992, Cullen was fired, probably for randomly contaminating bags of intravenous fluid with insulin. No one seems to be quite sure.

Due to the shortage of nurses and the fact that, for legal reasons, honest work appraisals were seldom passed on between medical companies, Cullen never had trouble finding work. Over the next 11 years, he had nine separate jobs. Like many 'angels of mercy', he discovered a taste for working 'graveyard shifts' on cardiac and intensive-care wards where he was left without supervision and where people died all the time. The atmosphere of trust in hospitals allowed him plenty of leeway.

In 1993 his wife Adrienne, from whom he was now estranged, filed for a restraining order against him: she claimed he had spiked drinks with lighter fluid, left his daughters at a babysitter's for a week and shown cruelty towards their two Yorkshire terriers, zipping one up in a bowling bag. His debts mounted steadily as he took to drink and his life fell apart.

Bizarre Behaviour

Psychologists say Cullen killed to relieve stress and this does seem to be borne out by the facts. Accused of domestic violence, he murdered three elderly women by giving them overdoses of the heart medication digoxin. Faced with a lie detector test to show he had not neglected his children or abused alcohol in their presence, he killed 85-year-old Mary Natoli.

After a social worker recommended all visits to his children be supervised, he killed Helen Dean, 91, who was recovering from surgery for colon cancer. Her son Larry recalled a thin male nurse entering the room and telling him to leave. When Larry returned, his mother said, 'He stuck me,' and showed him an injection mark on her thigh. Next day she grew ill and died.

Cullen's behaviour grew more bizarre. Neighbours talked about him chasing cats down the street at dead of night, muttering to himself and making faces. He harassed and stalked a fellow nurse when she turned down his offer of an engagement ring after just one date.

In every hospital where he worked Cullen aroused suspicions. He was fired from one for stealing vials of medicine. At St Luke's Hospital, Bethlehem, Pennsylvania, a group of nurses reported their suspicions that Cullen has been using drugs to kill patients. The case was dropped.

At Somerset Medical Center, NJ, computer records showed Cullen was accessing the records of patients he was not assigned to as well as requesting medications that patients had not been prescribed. When Jin Kyung Han, a 40-year-old cancer patient, went into cardiac arrest, doctors were surprised to find high levels of digoxin in her system despite the fact they had taken her off the drug.

Cullen was fired from Somerset on 31 October 2003 for falsifying his job application, but he remained under surveillance. On 12 December he was arrested and charged with the murder of Father Florian Gall, a 68-year-old Roman Catholic priest who died from a digoxin overdose, as well as the attempted murder of Han. The floodgates opened and Cullen confessed to a catalogue of murders, but not to all of them. He had blocked most of the fatalities from memory... or so he said.

On 2 March 2006 Cullen was sentenced to 11 consecutive life sentences for the murder of 22 and the attempted murder of three persons in New Jersey; this will make him eligible for parole after 397 years in jail.

NANNIE DOSS

Many serial killers have been driven by perverted ideas of sex. Nannie Doss may be one to have been driven by a perverted notion of romance. When investigators asked this mild-looking grandmother about the four husbands she had murdered (among at least ten victims in all), she explained her actions by saying: 'I was looking for the perfect mate, the real romance of life.'

Nancy 'Nannie' Doss was born in the rural town of Blue Mountain in the hill country of north-west Alabama in 1905. She had a tough childhood. Her father James Hazle was an authoritarian farmer who worked his children as if they were hired farmhands and beat them if they failed to keep up with his demanding pace of work. Despite, if not because, of her father's strictness, Nannie became a wilful teenager, known for her promiscuity. In 1921, aged 16, she married a co-worker at the Linen Thread Company, Charles Braggs, and they had four children in quick succession. Nannie jumped into the relationship to escape her domineering father but found herself living with her new husband's equally domineering mother. When Charles himself turned out to be a drunk and a womanizer, Nannie responded by going back to her wild ways.

The marriage clearly was not built to last and it came to an end with what appeared to be a double tragedy. In 1927 the couple's two middle children both died in separate episodes of suspected food poisoning. At the time no one suspected foul play, but soon afterwards Charles Braggs ran off, taking their eldest daughter with him. He later claimed that he was frightened of his wife and had made a point of not eating anything she prepared.

Another 'Tragedy'

With her husband gone, Nannie took a job at a cotton mill to support herself and her remaining daughter, Florine. In due course she moved across the state line to Georgia and remarried, to a man named Frank Harrelson. Harrelson turned out to be another alcoholic ne'er-do-well, although the relationship persisted until 1945 when another apparent tragedy struck. Once again a child died. This time it was Florine's daughter, Nannie's granddaughter. Florine had left her infant son with her mother while she visited her father. Three days later the baby was dead. The suggestion was that he might accidentally have swallowed rat poison.

Three months later, Nannie claimed her first adult victim. Frank Harrelson came home drunk and abused her one time too many. The next day, she put rat poison in his corn liquor. Several agonised days later he was dead, and, once more, no one suspected a thing.

Fortunately for Nannie, she had recently insured Frank's life and she now used the payment to buy a house in Jackson, Mississippi, where she lived until 1947. At this point, Nannie answered a lonely hearts advertisement – romance magazines and lonely hearts columns were Nannie's favoured reading matter – placed by a man named Arlie Lanning from Lexington, North Carolina. Two days after they met, they were married. However, once again Nannie's new husband proved to be a disappointment. Arlie was another drunk, and after three years Nannie had had enough of him.

In February 1950 Nannie served Arlie a meal of stewed prunes and coffee. He had terrible stomach pains for two days, and then died. Nannie told the neighbours that his last words were: 'Nannie,

Nannie Doss

it must have been the coffee.' Of course, he may have been wrong: it may have been the arsenic in the coffee, but then again it could have been the prunes that had been stewed in rat poison. The doctor, needless to say, did not suspect murder, not even when their house – which would have gone to Arlie's sister in his will – mysteriously burned down, leaving Nannie with the insurance payment.

As soon as the insurance cheque cleared, Nannie left town. She visited her sister Dovie – who promptly keeled over. In 1952 Nannie signed up to a new innovation, a dating agency called the Diamond Circle Club. Through the agency Nannie met Richard Morton from Emporia, Kansas. Yet again he proved a disappointment, not a drunk this time, but a fraud and a womanizer. He was not to be her next victim, however: that was her mother Louise, who came to stay in January 1953, fell ill with chronic stomach pains and died. Three months later, Richard

Morton went the same way. Yet again the doctors failed to ask for an autopsy.

During her brief marriage to Morton, Nannie had continued corresponding with her lonely hearts, and immediately after the funeral she went to Tulsa, Oklahoma, to meet the likeliest new prospect, Samuel Doss. They were married in June 1953. Doss was not a drinker or womanizer: he was a puritanical Christian and a miser. Once again, Nannie's new husband failed to meet her romantic ideal. A little over a year later, in September 1954, shortly after eating one of Nannie's prune cakes, Samuel was admitted to hospital with stomach pains. He survived and was released from hospital 23 days later. That evening, Nannie served him a perfectly innocent pork roast, which he washed down with a cup of coffee laced with arsenic. He died immediately, and this time the physician ordered an autopsy.

They found enough arsenic to kill 20 men in Samuel's stomach. The police confronted Nannie, unable to believe that this 50-year-old grandmother could be the killer. She unnerved them by giggling at their questions; then, when they refused to let her continue reading her romance magazine, she confessed to killing not just Samuel but her previous three husbands as well.

The news was an immediate sensation. The press dubbed Nannie the 'Giggling Granny' and she was put on trial for murder. She was duly sentenced to life in prison and, after serving ten years of her sentence, died in 1965, aged 60. Further investigation revealed that Nannie's four husbands, two children and granddaughter were not the only victims; Nannie's mother, two sisters, a nephew and a grandson had also died of arsenic poisoning.

BELLE GUNNESS

Belle Gunness can lay serious claim to being the first female serial killer of modern times. She was the archetypal black widow killer, a woman who repeatedly attracted husbands and other suitors, and promptly murdered them for their money. While others, like Nannie Doss, were relatively timid murderers who would wait years for the chance to poison their latest husband, Belle was happy to despatch most of her suitors almost immediately and, if they did not care to take a drop of cyanide, she was quite willing to terminate their prospects with a blow from an axe or hammer. After all, at a strongly built 280 pounds, there were not too many men able to overpower her.

Belle Gunness may also have a second claim to fame. There are very few serial killers who have succeeded in evading the law even after being identified. The Hungarian Bela Kiss was one; Norwegian-born Belle Gunness was another.

Belle Gunness was born Brynhild Paulsdatter Storset on 11 November 1859 in the Norwegian fishing village of Selbu. Her parents had a small farm there and Belle's father also moonlighted as a conjuror. Allegedly Belle, in her youth, would appear alongside him as a tightrope walker and it is certainly true to say that she walked a tightrope for the rest of her life.

Foster Mother

In 1883 her older sister, Anna, who had emigrated to Chicago, invited Belle to join her in the United States. Belle jumped at the chance of a new life and soon arrived in Chicago. The following year she married a fellow immigrant, Mads Sorenson. They lived together happily enough for the next decade or so. They failed to conceive children but instead fostered three girls, Jennie, Myrtle and Lucy. The only dramas to strike these hard-working immigrants were the regular fires that dogged their businesses. Twice their houses burned down and, in 1897, a confectionery store they ran also succumbed to fire. Thankfully, each time they were well insured.

Insurance also served Belle well when, on 30 July 1900, Mads Sorenson died suddenly at home, suffering from what was officially listed as heart failure, but strangely showing all the symptoms of strychnine poisoning. Amazingly enough, he died on the day that one life insurance policy elapsed and another one started, so his grieving widow was able to claim on both policies.

Grieving Widow

With her $8,500 windfall, Belle decided to start a new life. She moved her family to the rural town of La Porte, Indiana, a place popular with Scandinavian immigrants, and soon married again,

Belle Gunness

this time to Peter Gunness, a fellow Norwegian. Sadly, this marriage was not to last as long as her first. In 1903 Peter died in a tragic accident after a sausage grinder allegedly fell on his head. If some observed that it looked as if a hammer blow might have caused the head wound, the grieving – and pregnant – widow's tears were enough to quieten them. Once again there was an insurance payment, this time for $4,000.

Belle never married again, though not, it appears, for want of trying. She placed regular advertisements in the Norwegian language press' lonely hearts columns. Describing herself as a comely widow, she advertised for men ready to support their amorous advances with a solid cash investment in their future lives together. She received many replies and several of these suitors actually arrived in La Porte, cash or bankbooks in hand. They would be seen around town for a day or two, tell their loved ones they were preparing to marry a rich widow and then they would disappear.

They were not the only people around Belle to disappear. Her foster daughter Jennie also vanished – Belle told neighbours that she had gone to a finishing school in California. Farmhands seemed to go missing on the Gunness farm on a regular basis. As far as the community as a whole was concerned, however, Belle Gunness was a model citizen who had had some very bad luck.

This view seemed to be compounded once and for all when, on 28 April 1908, Belle's house caught fire. Fire-fighters were unable to stop the blaze in time and the bodies of two of Belle's three children were found in the rubble, along with an adult female body assumed to be that of Belle herself – though identification was difficult as the body had been decapitated. The beheaded body was clear evidence that this was no accident but murder.

The police immediately arrested an obvious suspect, local handyman Ray Lamphere, who had had an on/off relationship with Belle, but had lately fallen out with her and threatened to burn her house down.

That might have been the end of the matter if investigators had not continued digging around the site, looking for the corpse's missing head. They did not find the head but they did find 14 other corpses buried around the farm, mostly in the hog pen. Among those they were able to identify were two handymen, foster daughter Jennie and five of the hopeful suitors. The remainder were mostly presumed to be other unidentified suitors.

No Ordinary Widow

It was horribly clear that Belle Gunness was no ordinary widow but a vicious serial killer. More alarm bells rang when it was discovered that some of the bodies recovered from the fire had cyanide in their stomachs. Rumours immediately began to spread that the adult female corpse was not Belle. These were partially quashed a couple of weeks later, when her dental bridge and two teeth (looking suspiciously untouched by fire) were found in the rubble. Some accepted this as definitive evidence that Belle was dead. Others saw it as simply a final act of subterfuge. The prosecution of Ray Lamphere went ahead, but the jury expressed its doubts as to whether Belle was really dead by finding the handyman guilty only of arson and not of murder.

Sightings of Belle Gunness began almost immediately and continued in the ensuing years. Most of them were obviously wrong, and to this day, the true story of the United State's first known female serial killer remains shrouded in mystery.

HAROLD SHIPMAN

With a total of over 200 suspected murders to his name, Harold Shipman is the most prolific serial killer of modern times. His grisly tally of victims puts him well ahead of Pedro Lopez, the 'monster of the Andes', who was convicted of 57 murders in 1980. (Lopez claimed to have killed many more, but the exact number of deaths was never verified.) Until Shipman's crimes came to light, Lopez had the dubious distinction of topping the serial killer league; at present, however, it is a British family doctor, rather than a penniless Colombian vagrant, who has become the world's number one murderer.

Mother's Favourite

The sorry tale begins in 1946, when Harold Frederick Shipman was born into a working-class family in Nottingham. Known as Fred, the boy had an unusual childhood. He had a brother and sister, but it was clear that he was his mother's favourite. She felt that Fred was destined for great things, and taught him that he was superior to his contemporaries, even though he was not especially clever and had to work hard to achieve academic success. During his schooldays, he formed few friendships with other children, a situation that was exacerbated when his mother became seriously ill with lung cancer. The young Shipman took on the role of carer to his mother, spending time with her after school waiting for visits from the family doctor, who would inject her with morphine to relieve her from pain. It is possible that the stress of this experience during his formative years may have pushed him into mental illness, causing him to re-enact the role of carer and doctor in the macabre fashion that he later did.

By the time Shipman was 17, his mother had died of cancer, after a long and painful illness. He enrolled at medical school, despite having to resit his entry exams. Although he was good at sport, he made little effort to make friends. However, at this time he met and married his future wife Primrose; the pair went on to have four children, as Shipman began his career as a doctor in general practice. To many, he seemed kind and pleasant, but colleagues complained of his superior attitude and rudeness. Then he began to suffer from blackouts, which he attributed to epilepsy. However, disturbing evidence emerged that he was in fact taking large amounts of pethidine, on the pretext of prescribing the drug to patients. He was dismissed from the practice but, surprisingly, within two years he was once again working as a doctor, this time in a different town.

Pillar of the Community

In his new job, the hard-working Shipman soon earned the respect of his colleagues and patients. However, it was during his time at Hyde, over a 24-year period, that he is estimated to have killed at least 236 patients. His status as a pillar of the community, not to mention his kindly bedside manner, for many years masked the fact that the death toll among Shipman's patients was astoundingly high.

Over the years a number of people, including relatives of the deceased and local undertakers, had raised concerns about the deaths of Shipman's patients. His victims always died suddenly, often with no previous record of terminal illness; and they were usually found sitting in a chair, fully clothed, rather than in bed. The police had been alerted and had examined the doctor's records, but nothing was found. It later became clear that Shipman had falsified patient records, but at this stage the doctor's calm air of authority was still protecting him against closer scrutiny.

Then Shipman made a fatal mistake. In 1998 Kathleen Grundy, a healthy, active 81-year-old ex-mayor with a reputation for community service, died suddenly at home. Shipman was called and pronounced her dead; he also said that a post-mortem was unnecessary, since he had paid her a visit shortly before her death. When her funeral was over, her daughter Angela Woodruff received a badly typed copy of Mrs Grundy's will leaving Shipman a large sum of money. A solicitor herself, Mrs Woodruff knew

Harold Shipman

immediately that this was a fake. She contacted the police, who took the unusual step of exhuming Mrs Grundy's body. They found that she had been administered a lethal dose of morphine.

Surprisingly, in murdering Mrs Grundy, Shipman had made little effort to cover his tracks: either to forge the will carefully or to kill his victim with a less easily traceable drug. Whether this was through sheer arrogance and stupidity, or through a latent desire to be discovered, no one knows. However, once the true nature of Mrs Grundy's death was uncovered, more graves were opened, and more murders came to light.

During his trial, Shipman showed no remorse for the 15 murders he was accused of. (There were known to be others, but these alone were more than enough to ensure a life sentence.) He was contemptuous of the police and the court, and continued to protest his innocence to the end. He was convicted of the murders and imprisoned. Four years later, without warning, he hanged himself in his prison cell.

Today, the case of Harold Shipman remains mystifying: there was no sexual motive in his killings and, until the end, no profit motive. His murders did not fit the usual pattern of a serial killer. In most cases, his victims seem to have died in comfort, at peace. It may be, as several commentators have pointed out, that he enjoyed the sense of having control over life and death, and that over the years he became addicted to this sense of power.

What is clear is that, in finally taking his own life, Harold Shipman ensured ultimate control: no one would ever fully understand why he did what he did.

Crazed Cannibals

The definitive fictional serial killer Hannibal Lecter received the nickname 'Hannibal the Cannibal' because of his fondness for eating his victims, whom he generally washed down with a good Chianti. He is a terrifying creation, because the notion of the crazed cannibal is a powerful image of utter disdain for any kind of human morality, a breaking of the ultimate taboo.

Cannibalism is without doubt an ancient human custom, but it is one that the modern world now regards with revulsion. However, it still occurs. There have been well-known instances of air crash victims facing a ghastly choice between eating human flesh and starving to death. Even though we can understand those who choose to live by eating the flesh, we feel that their actions somehow transgress the limits of what it is to be human.

There have also been mass outbreaks of cannibalism during the great famines of the twentieth century: in Russia during the period of Stalin's forced collectivization, in Germany after the First World War and in China. Each time, starving people were reduced to eating the bodies of the dead – in some cases, even the bodies of their own children.

Some cannibal serial killers, like the German Joachim Kroll, grew up during these times of ferocious poverty. Others, however, like Jeffrey Dahmer, seem to be responding to a deep, animal urge to annihilate their victims through ingestion. The details of their activities after killing these victims are often more disturbing than accounts of the actual murders themselves, which perhaps shows that the taboo against cannibalism is almost more deeply entrenched than the taboo against murder.

JEFFREY DAHMER

Jeffrey Dahmer is among the most troubling of all serial killers – an apparently regular guy who turned into a psychopathic murderer, necrophile and cannibal.

Dahmer was born on 21 May 1960, the son of Lionel, a chemist, and Joyce, a homemaker. Joyce was highly strung, while Lionel worked long hours; the pair argued a great deal but to all appearances this was still a normal family household. However, at an early age, Jeffrey developed a fascination with dead animals. Then, aged six, following a hernia operation and the birth of his younger brother

Jeffrey Dahmer

David, he became withdrawn. He remained solitary and friendless throughout his childhood. In his teens, his fascination with dead creatures intensified. He would cycle around looking for road kill, which he would carefully dismember. By the time of his high-school graduation, he had also become a heavy drinker.

Jeffrey's parents did not appear to notice his troubles, as by this time they were locked in an acrimonious divorce. During the summer of 1978, just as Jeffrey was due to graduate, they both moved out of the house, leaving Jeffrey there alone. His response was to pick up a hitchhiker, Stephen Hicks, take him home, have sex with him and then, when Hicks tried to leave, to hit him on the head with a bar bell, strangle him, dismember his corpse and bury it nearby.

Alcoholic

Jeffrey's father Lionel had by this time moved in with his second wife Shari, who pointed out to her new husband that his son was an alcoholic. Lionel responded by giving Jeffrey an ultimatum: to stop drinking or to join the army. Jeffrey refused to stop drinking, so his father saw to it that he enlisted in January 1979, aged 18. Dahmer appeared to enjoy army life, but he was soon discharged for habitual drunkenness. Soon after, he moved into an apartment in his grandmother's basement and his life continued its downward spiral.

In 1982, Dahmer was arrested for indecent exposure, and then again in 1986. Each time his father paid for lawyers, and for his second offence Dahmer was given a suspended sentence and counselling. The counselling clearly had little effect, however, as he went on to kill three times during the next year.

First Victim

His first victim that year was Steven Tuomi, whom he met in a gay bar. He murdered Tuomi in a hotel, put the body in a suitcase, took it home, had sex with it and then dismembered it. Next, Dahmer murdered a 14-year-old Native American boy called James Doxtator, who hung around the Milwaukee gay scene. After Doxtator came a Mexican youth named Richard Guerrero. (Dahmer's career of savagery categorically disproved a previously held theory that serial killers only murder within their own race.)

At this point Dahmer's grandmother, bothered by his drunkenness and the terrible smells coming from his apartment, evicted him. Dahmer moved into his own flat in Milwaukee in September 1988. The next day, he lured a 13-year-old Laotian boy there, offering to pay him for a nude modelling session. He drugged the boy and fondled him but did not become violent. The boy's parents reported Dahmer to the police. He was sentenced to a year in prison for sexual assault. While waiting for sentence, however, he killed his next victim, Anthony Sears.

Dahmer served ten months in prison before beginning his final killing spree. Between June 1990 and July 1991, he murdered another 12 men. In the end he was committing a murder almost every week, and his treatment of his victims was becoming ever more bizarre. He was obsessed with the notion of creating zombies – half-humans who would be his playthings. To this end he drilled holes in his victims' skulls while they were still alive, and dripped acid into their heads. (Unsurprisingly, none of his victims survived.) In at least one case, he also tried cannibalism. He kept his victims' body parts in his refrigerator, and placed their skulls on an altar in his bedroom.

Most disturbing of all was the case of Konerak Sinthasomphone, the brother of the Laotian teenager he had previously molested. Dahmer drugged Konerak, but the boy managed to escape from the apartment. Two young black women found Konerak and called the police, but when they arrived on the scene, Dahmer persuaded the police that the drugged and bleeding Konerak was his boyfriend. Incredibly, the police returned the boy to Dahmer, who promptly took him home and murdered him.

In the next few weeks, a frenzied Dahmer went on to kill his last four victims. On 22 July 1991, his final intended victim, an adult black man, Tracy Edwards, escaped from the apartment, a pair of handcuffs trailing from his wrist. Edwards managed to flag down a police car and then led the police back to the apartment, where they were horrified to find a human head in the refrigerator.

Dahmer's killing spree was finally over. As details of the story emerged in the press, the full picture of Dahmer's horrific crimes shocked an America that had become wearily accustomed to tales of murder and perversion. By 22 August 1991 Dahmer had been charged with 15 counts of murder. His trial began on 30 January 1992. He pleaded guilty but insane. The jury found him sane and he was sentenced to 15 consecutive life sentences.

ALBERT FISH

Albert Fish – the model, at least in part, for Thomas Harris's fictional killer Hannibal Lecter – is perhaps the most bewildering of all serial killers. At the time of his arrest in 1934 he was 64 years old, a slightly built, mild-mannered old man with grey hair and a shabby suit, as innocuous-looking an individual as one could hope to meet. However, under the placid exterior there lurked a man of extraordinary violence; according to psychiatrists, Fish had tried and enjoyed every perversion known to humanity, including eating the flesh of the young children he had savagely tortured and murdered.

Braggart

Just how many children this seemingly benevolent old man killed we will never know. There are no more than four whose deaths can certainly be attributed to Fish, though at least a dozen killings, plus a large number of rapes, seem probable. Fish himself – an early example of the serial killer as braggart – claimed to have killed hundreds, with at least one murder in every state. The psychiatrist who examined him most closely believed that Fish probably committed at least a hundred rapes.

So what kind of background produced this monster? Albert Fish was born on 19 May 1870. His father Randall Fish was a boat captain, operating on the Potomac River. Albert's given name was Hamilton Fish, apparently in honour of a family link with Washington's eminent Hamilton family. So this was a respectable, relatively well-off world that Albert Fish was born into. All this changed, however, when his father died in 1875. His mother had to find a job and put Albert, aged five, into an orphanage. It was there, in response to teasing from the other boys, that he started to call himself Albert. More seriously, it was here that he acquired a lifelong taste for sadomasochism, after the regular bare-bottom whippings he received. He became a persistent bedwetter who regularly ran away from the orphanage. When he was nine, his mother removed him.

Drifter

Albert left school at 15. He soon found he was a very able painter and decorator and he followed this trade for the rest of his life, drifting from town to town as he did so. By 1898 he had married, settled in New York, and fathered six children. Fish himself claimed that he committed his first murder during this period, killing a man in Delaware in 1910. However, most people, including his children, dated his descent into madness from the time his wife left him, running off with a boarder in 1917. Thereafter he appeared to suffer from hallucinations: he would take the children to a summer house in Westchester where he would climb a hill, shake his fist at the sky and declare himself to be Christ, before asking his children to beat him on the buttocks. He became obsessed with pain, driving needles into his groin and inserting fabric into his anus before setting it on fire. Eventually his oldest son had had enough of his father's demented behaviour and threw him out of the family house.

Fish was regularly arrested, sometimes for vagrancy, sometimes for petty theft and sometimes for indulging in one of his favourite perversions, sending obscene letters to women. Each time he would be examined, pronounced peculiar but harmless and tossed back into the community. Exactly how many murders and rapes he committed during the 1920s and early 1930s we will never know.

However, it was one case in particular that ensured both his notoriety and his downfall. At the beginning of June 1928 he noticed an advertisement in the newspaper from one Edward Budd, an 18-year-old looking for a job in the countryside. Fish answered the advert, arriving at the impoverished Budd household in the guise of Frank Howard, a farmer from Long Island who was looking for a willing worker. Despite 'Mr Howard's' rather shabby appearance, he was a well-spoken man and the Budd family were happy to believe in him as a benefactor, especially when he handed out dollar bills to the other children. On meeting the rest of the family, Fish decided against abducting the burly Edward and instead focused his attention on 12-year-old Grace. He persuaded the family to let him take her to a children's party that his sister was holding.

That was the last the family saw of her. Fish took Grace to the deserted summer house in Westchester. There he strangled her, dismembered her body and over a period of nine days ate as much of her body as he could, before burying her bones behind the house.

A huge manhunt was launched but without success. It was only the determination of one man, Detective Will King, that kept the case alive. Even so, he might never have got his man if Fish had not succumbed to the urge to brag about his crime. In 1934 he sent the Budds a letter telling them exactly what had happened to their daughter. This vile act led to his downfall. The envelope Fish used had a distinctive logo that eventually led Detective King to a New York flophouse. There he finally came face to face with Albert Fish. On being challenged, Fish lunged at King with a straight razor but King overpowered and arrested him.

On arrest, Fish began an extraordinary, rambling, obscene confession. As well as the Grace Budd murder, he was also responsible for the killings of four- year-old Billy Gaffney in 1929 and five-year-old Francis McDonnell in 1934. The only question was whether his defence of not guilty by reason of insanity would be accepted. Fish was, as several psychiatrists pronounced, fairly obviously mad.

The jury, eager for his heinous crimes to be punished, rejected the insanity defence and found Fish guilty. He was sentenced to death by electrocution, a fate he positively relished. He was executed at Sing Sing Prison on 16 January 1936. It took two attempts to kill him. Legend has it that the electric chair failed the first time due to being short-circuited by the large number of nails that Fish had embedded in his body over the years.

STEPHEN GRIFFITHS

A psychology graduate and PhD student in Applied Criminal Justice Studies, Stephen Griffiths is destined to be remembered as 'The Crossbow Cannibal'. The gruesome moniker didn't come from the popular press, but from the man himself. On 28 May 2010, wearing a black shirt and jeans, he stood in a packed magistrates' court and boldly gave the name in place of his own.

The declaration was met with gasps from a crowd that had no idea what it was he had done with the three women he was accused of murdering. When asked by the court clerk for his address, the Crossbow Cannibal replied, 'Here, I guess.' These short lines were part of a three-minute performance that ended with the 40-year-old confirming his date of birth.

Stephen Shaun Griffiths was born in Dewsbury, West Yorkshire on 24 December 1969 – like all children, he couldn't wait for Christmas Day, went the family joke. The eldest of three children, Shaun, as he was known, was a slender child. The Crossbow Cannibal's first moniker was 'The Stickman'.

Unlike his siblings, Griffiths was introspective and quiet. 'You could never get a read on him,' remarked one uncle. 'He was very much a loner.'

Griffiths didn't seem to care much for football or any other interests of most boys his age. This is not to say that he didn't attract attention. One former neighbour recalls that as a child the future murderer had a habit of killing and dismembering birds: 'It looked as if he was enjoying what he was doing. He wasn't dissecting them bit by bit, he was ripping them apart.'

In trouble

When Griffiths was still very young, his parents split up. He moved with his mother, sister and brother to the nearby city of Wakefield. There he attended the exclusive and expensive Queen Elizabeth Grammar School, the alma mater of serial killer John George Haigh, 'The Acid Bath Murderer'.

He was a diligent student, but outside school Griffiths was often in trouble with the law. In his early teens he was caught stealing from a garage. At the age of 17, he slashed a supermarket manager with a knife when he was stopped for shoplifting. Griffiths received a three-year sentence for that attack, some of which was spent at a high-security mental hospital. One doctor diagnosed Griffiths as a 'sadistic, schizoid psychopath'. Another recorded that the youth had a 'preoccupation with murder – particularly multiple murder'. Griffiths told his probation officer that he believed he would one day become a serial killer.

Within three years, Griffiths was back in prison, this time for holding a knife to the throat of a young girl. He could give no reason for his actions.

Not long after his release, the future Crossbow Cannibal got into trouble again, this time for possessing two airguns and carrying a knife in public. Despite his years of incarceration, further run-ins with the law and wildly unpredictable, anti-social behaviour, Griffiths managed to earn a degree in psychology from Leeds University. He was accepted at the University of Bradford, where he began six years of work on an academic thesis, 'Homicide in an Industrial City', comparing modern murder techniques in Bradford to those used during the second half of the 19th century. Griffiths incorporated some of his research in 'The Skeleton and the Jaguar', a website he established that focused largely on serial killers.

He spent a good amount of time online, frequenting social networking sites. Griffiths would identify himself as 'Ven Pariah... the misanthrope who brought hate into heaven', under which guise he would post his disturbing thoughts. 'Humanity', he once wrote, 'is not merely a biological condition. It is also a state of mind. On that basis, I am a pseudo-human at best. A demon at worst.'

His relationships with women tended to be abusive and short-lived, yet he fathered at least one child. Griffiths was arrested numerous times for domestic violence, and once appeared in court for leaving threatening messages on the voicemail of a former girlfriend.

Sinister habits

From his teens on, Griffiths was one of those people the media describes as being 'known to police'. In 2008, attention increased after local librarians reported that he'd been borrowing books on human dismemberment. This warning sign coincided with problems at the building in which he rented a small bachelor flat. Male neighbours were being threatened, while the females increasingly became the focus of untoward attention. Two women reported that a once friendly and polite Griffiths had become extremely hostile after his sexual advances were rejected.

The building management became so concerned that it installed closed-circuit cameras and a panic button for its caretaker. An unnamed senior manager with the company that owned the building was convinced that it was only a matter of time before Griffiths committed murder... which, of course, he did.

It's likely that the true number of women murdered by Stephen Griffiths will never be known. Ultimately, he would admit to just three, the first being 43-year-old Susan Rushworth.

A sex trade worker who struggled with heroin addiction, she was last seen alive near her home during the dying minutes of 22 June 2009. In the months that followed police made numerous appeals to the public, hoping for some hint as to the missing woman's whereabouts.

What the authorities didn't know, but perhaps suspected, was that Susan Rushworth was long dead. It's almost certain that she was killed by Griffiths on the evening of her disappearance.

On 26 April 2010, another prostitute, 31-year-old Shelley Armitage, disappeared while working the streets of Bradford city centre. No one noticed at first; two days passed before she was reported missing.

Less than a month later, on 21 May, a Friday, Suzanne Blamires also vanished from the streets of Bradford. The mystery behind the disappearance of this 36-year-old sex trade worker would last only a weekend.

We know that Blamires accompanied Griffiths to his flat, most likely willingly. We also know that she tried to leave. The same security cameras that had been installed in Griffiths' apartment building by concerned management captured her sudden and swift end. Grainy footage shows Blamires fleeing Griffiths' flat with the PhD student in pursuit. He knocks her unconscious, and leaves her lying in the corridor. Moments later, Griffiths returns with a crossbow, aims and shoots a bolt through Blamires' head. Before dragging the woman back into his apartment, he raises his crossbow to the camera in triumph. Moments later, Griffiths returns with a drink, apparently toasting the death. Still later, the murderer can be seen carrying a series of bin bags out of the building.

The first person to view these images was the building caretaker. He called the police – but not before first selling the story to a tabloid newspaper.

Griffiths was arrested within hours. Asked to confirm his identity, he replied, 'I'm Osama Bin Laden', later adding cryptically, 'I've killed a lot more than Suzanne Blamires – I've killed loads. Peter Sutcliffe [the Yorkshire Ripper] came a cropper in Sheffield. So did I, but at least I got out of the city.'

Authorities searched his home and the immediate area for any sign of Blamires and the other missing women. The small flat was lined with shelves holding hundreds of horror films and books on serial killers, terrorism and genocide. It wasn't strictly true that Griffiths lived alone; he kept two lizards, which he fed baby rats that he bred for just that purpose.

The first body was discovered not by the police, but by a member of the public in the River Aire. Cut into at least 81 separate pieces, the corpse was not complete. Police divers would recover a black suitcase containing the instruments Griffiths had used to carry out the dissection. As would become clear in the coming days, Griffiths had consumed several pounds of flesh from his victims. The remains would be identified as belonging to Blamires. Identification came without the aid of DNA testing – her head, with the crossbow bolt, was found in a rucksack. At some point Griffiths had embedded a knife in her skull.

The bathtub 'slaughterhouse'

During police interrogations, the man who had rambled continuously on the internet proved oddly reticent. When asked why he felt the need to kill, Griffiths was initially flummoxed. 'I don't know,' he said. But then he added: 'Sometimes you kill someone to kill yourself, or kill a part of yourself. I don't know, I don't know – it's like deep issues inside of me.'

The investigating officer pressed on; 'So, why did you feel the need to kill any of the girls?'

'I don't know,' Griffiths eventually responded. 'I'm misanthropic. I don't have very much time for the human race.'

Griffiths gradually opened up about the murders, providing police with macabre details. He described his flat's bathtub as a 'slaughterhouse', saying that it was there that his victims were dismembered. He used power tools on the first two bodies, boiling the parts he ate in a pot.

Blamires was cut up by hand, and her flesh was eaten raw. 'That's part of the magic,' he said, explaining his predilection for human meat.

While Griffiths did not share many details of the actual killings, police had video evidence.

There was, of course, the death of Suzanne Blamires, which had been captured by a security camera, but the horrific images paled next to those of Shelley Armitage.

Griffiths had filmed his second victim's death using his mobile phone, which he subsequently left on a train. The device was bought and sold twice before police managed to track it down. The footage it held was described by one veteran detective as the most disturbing he'd ever viewed.

Armitage is shown naked and bound with the words 'My Sex Slave' spray-painted in black on her back. Griffiths can be heard saying: 'I am Ven Pariah, I am the Bloodbath Artist. Here's a model who is assisting me.'

Only Susan Rushworth was spared the indignity of having her death caught on camera. Investigators believe that she was killed with a hammer.

On 21 December 2010, three days before his 41st birthday, Griffiths pleaded guilty to the murders of Susan Rushworth, Shelley Armitage and Suzanne Blamires.

He was handed down a life sentence. (Bizarrely, he had insisted on being represented by the Bradford law firm Lumb & Macgill, who acted for serial killer Peter Sutcliffe in the early 1980s.)

Since being taken into custody, Griffiths has repeatedly attempted suicide. He also went on a hunger strike, reportedly losing 40 lb (18 kg). Behind bars, Griffiths is less the Crossbow Cannibal, and more the Stickman.

ED KEMPER

Edmund Kemper, 'the co-ed killer', was a disturbed child who grew up very tall, very bright and very dangerous. He earned his nickname by killing six young women whom he picked up hitchhiking. There may well have been more victims, but Kemper very carefully avoided leaving any clues. However, he eventually lost all sense of caution when his killing rage turned on his own mother. This time, there was only one obvious suspect.

Troubled Childhood

Edmund Kemper was born in Burbank, California, on 18 December 1948, one of a cluster of serial killer baby boomers. Something else he had in common with other serial killers was a troubled childhood. His father, known as E.E., was a Second World War hero and gun collector; his mother was named Clarnell. The couple split up when Ed was nine and his mother took him, along with his sister, to live in Helena, Montana. Ed reacted badly to the break-up and began to manifest some of the warning signs of serious disturbance. He killed the family cat by burying it alive in the back garden, then he dug it up, cut off its head and mounted it on a stick, keeping it in his bedroom as a trophy. He also took to mutilating his sister's dolls. Once he confided in his sister that he had a crush on a female teacher. Joking, his sister asked him why he did not kiss her. Edmund answered, in all seriousness, that if he did that 'I would have to kill her first'.

It was not just Edmund's behaviour that was disturbing: his size was also a problem. Both his parents were very tall and, as he reached his teens, Edmund became far taller than his peers, although despite his size, he was also unusually afraid of being bullied. His relationship with his mother deteriorated until she could take no more. Branding him a 'real weirdo' she sent him to live with his father. His father could not handle him either and in turn sent him, aged 15, to live with his paternal grandparents on their California farm. This arrangement worked tolerably well for a while, country living at least providing Edmund with plenty of opportunity to shoot animals and birds; but on 27 August 1964 Kemper moved from animals to humans. He shot dead first his grandmother and then his grandfather.

Kemper was promptly arrested and, when he explained his actions by saying 'I just wondered how it would feel to shoot Grandma', he was judged to be mentally ill and placed in a secure hospital at Atascadero. Five years later, in 1969, Kemper, who was by now 6 feet 9 inches tall and 300 pounds in weight, managed to persuade doctors that he was a reformed character, and he was paroled to his mother's care.

Customized Car

This was, to put it mildly, a mistake. His mother, Clarnell, had now relocated to Santa Cruz, a college town in the San Francisco Bay area. For the next two years Kemper bided his time. He applied to join the police, but was turned down on the grounds that he was too tall. Undeterred, he became a regular drinker at a police bar called the Jury Room, where he befriended numerous detectives. He also worked odd jobs and bought himself a car, similar to those used by the police as undercover vehicles. He started using the car to pick up young female hitchhikers, gradually getting the hang of learning to put them at ease. Next he customized the car, making it impossible to open the passenger side door from the inside. In retrospect it is obvious that he was just waiting for his moment.

The moment finally arrived on 7 May 1972, when he picked up two 18-year-old students, Mary Ann Pesce and Anita Luchessa, who were hitching to Stanford University. He drove them down a dirt road, stabbed them both to death, and then took them back to his apartment. There he sexually assaulted the bodies and took photographs of them, before cutting off their heads, putting the bodies in plastic bags, burying them on a nearby mountainside and throwing the heads into a ravine.

It was four months before he killed again. This time the victim was 15-year-old Aiko Koo.

He strangled her, raped her corpse, and then took her body home to dissect. He had her head in the trunk of his car the next day when he went for a meeting with court psychiatrists – who were pleased with his progress and declared him officially 'safe'.

They could, of course, hardly have been more wrong. Another four months went by and Kemper murdered another student, Cindy Schell. By this time he had acquired a gun that he used to shoot Schell dead after forcing her into the trunk of his car. Now following a pattern, he raped, beheaded and dissected her before disposing of the corpse. He buried her head in his mother's garden.

Less then a month passed before Kemper struck again. This time, it was two more hitchhikers, Rosalind Thorpe and Alice Lin. They hardly had time to get into the car before he shot them both dead. He put both bodies in the trunk and left them there while he went to have dinner with his mother, returning to the car afterwards to decapitate them, then taking Lin's headless corpse inside to rape.

Kemper's madness was now a long way out of control. At this point he apparently contemplated trying to murder everyone on his block. Instead, though, he decided to stay closer to home. Over the Easter weekend, 1973, he murdered his mother with a hammer, decapitated and raped her, and tried to force her larynx down the waste disposal unit. In a muddled attempt to cover up his crime, he then invited one of his mother's friends over, Sally Hallett. He murdered Hallett, and then, on Easter Sunday, he got in his car and started driving west.

By the time he reached Colorado he realized the game was up. At this stage, he telephoned his friends on the Santa Cruz police force and told them what he had done, where and when.

Kemper's confession left no room for legal manoeuvring, except on grounds of insanity. The jury eventually decided that he was sane and found him guilty on eight counts of murder. Asked what the appropriate punishment would be, Kemper reportedly said 'death by torture'. In fact he was sentenced to life in prison, a sentence he is still serving.

Fuelling the court's belief that here was a sociopath not a psychopath, Kemper understands and enjoys his notoriety. He has given regular interviews (including one shared with John Wayne Gacy that was broadcast live). Asking himself the rhetorical question, 'What do you think when you see a pretty girl walking down the street?' Kemper provided this for an answer: 'One side of me says I'd like to talk to her, date her. The other half of me says, "I wonder how her head would look on a stick." '

In the light of this history, it is unsurprising that Kemper does not expect to be released. In 2016 newspapers reported that he had no intention of attending his next parole hearing.

JOACHIM KROLL

Joachim Kroll, the 'Ruhr Hunter', was in some ways the archetypal serial killer. He was a nervous, sexually inadequate loner who preyed mostly on young girls and teenagers. What made him unusual was that his killing spree did not burn itself out in a frenzy, but went on at a steady pace for over 20 years before he was finally caught.

Joachim Georg Kroll was born on 17 April 1933 in Hindenburg, towards the east of Germany near the Polish border. His childhood was dominated by the terrible years of the Second World War and its aftermath, a time of great poverty and widespread starvation in Germany. Kroll's father was taken prisoner by the Russian Army during the war and never returned. In 1947, Kroll and his mother fled Russian-occupied East Germany to live in the heavily industrialized Ruhr area of West Germany.

Mother's Death

The event that seems to have tipped the shy, withdrawn Joachim Kroll into madness was the death of his mother in January 1955. Just three weeks later, on 8 February, Kroll killed for the first time, raping and stabbing to death 19-year-old Irmgard Srehl in a barn near the town of Lüdinghausen.

Just how many people he went on to kill over the next two decades will never be known. The only murders that can be traced to him are those he confessed to after his eventual arrest, and he was not sure that he remembered all of them. However, we do know that his next victim was 12-year-old Erika Schuleter, whom he raped and strangled in Kirchellen.

In 1957, Kroll moved to Duisburg, an industrial city in the Ruhr, where he lived until his eventual arrest. On 16 June 1959 he marked his new territory with the rape and murder of Klara Frieda Tesmer in the Rheinwiesen district of the city. Little more than a month later, on 26 July, he raped and strangled 16-year-old Manuela Knodt in Essen, another major Ruhr town. This time, however, Kroll took his perversion one step further. He cut slices from her buttocks and her thighs, took them away and ate them. The police later arrested a compulsive confessor named Horst Otto for this murder.

Taste for Human Flesh

Then came a three-year gap before, sometime in 1962, Kroll raped and strangled Barbara Bruder in the town of Burscheid. That same year, on 23 April, Petra Giese was abducted from a fair in Dinslaken-Brückhausen, raped and strangled. Once again, he cut off the girl's buttocks to eat. From now on this was a regular trademark. Kroll had clearly acquired the taste for human flesh. Little more than a month later, on 4 June 1962, he indulged himself once again. This time the victim was 13-year-old Monika Tafel, who was found dead in a cornfield in Walsum with portions of flesh once again removed from her buttocks. This rash of murders provoked an uproar, and the people of the town of Walsum soon identified Walter Quicker, a 34-year-old paedophile, as a suspect. He hanged himself soon afterwards.

Lovers Lane

Kroll appears to have lain low for the next three years, perhaps scared by the intensity of the investigation in Walsum. Then, on

22 August 1965, he crept up on a couple parked in a lovers lane in Grossenbaum-Duisburg. He stabbed the man to death, but before he could attack the woman she escaped.

Another year passed and then, on 13 September 1966, Kroll strangled Ursula Rohling in a park in Marl, north of Duisburg. Ursula's boyfriend Adolf Schickel was the suspect this time, and he too soon killed himself. Three months later, Kroll returned to Essen and abducted his youngest victim yet, five-year-old Ilona Harke. He took her by train and bus to a woodland area called the Feldbachtal. There Kroll raped her then, in a variation that he later put down to simple curiosity, he drowned her.

The following year, on 22 June, Kroll lured ten-year-old Gabrielle Puetman into a cornfield and showed her pornographic pictures. She fainted but was saved by the arrival of passers-by. Kroll managed to escape from the scene.

Innocent Victims

Once again, he waited before raping and murdering his next victim. This time it was an older woman, 61-year-old Maria Hettgen, whom he raped and strangled in her home on 12 July 1969. Two years later, on 21 May 1970, he raped and strangled 13-year-old Jutta Rahn as she walked home from school. Her neighbour, Peter Schay, was suspected and spent 15 months in prison for the crime.

This time, six more years went by before Kroll raped and strangled another schoolgirl, Karin Toepfer, in Dinslaken-Voerde. Then, on 3 July 1976, he took his final and youngest victim, four-year-old Marion Ketter, whose disappearance provoked a widespread investigation by neighbours and police.

At this point, it seems that Kroll was crying out to be caught. A local resident in the block of flats where he lived complained to him that his toilet was blocked; Kroll apparently replied that the reason for this was that it was 'full of guts'. The neighbour did not know what to make of this, but a call to a plumber soon showed that Kroll was not joking. The child's lungs and other organs were blocking the pipe. The police were immediately called to Kroll's apartment, where they found bags of human flesh in the refrigerator, and a child's hand boiling on the stove, along with some carrots and potatoes.

Kroll was arrested and promptly confessed to his whole 20-year history of murder. Three years later, the case finally came to court and, after three more years of drawn-out proceedings, he was finally found guilty on eight counts of murder and one of attempted murder. He was duly sentenced to nine terms of life imprisonment. On 1 July 1991, he died of a heart attack in prison.

Demon Lovers

Serial murder is for the most part a lonely business, a sickness dreamed up in the depths of an isolated, damaged soul. The stereotype of the serial killer is a crazed loner operating in the shadows, so it is peculiarly disturbing to encounter serial killers who act as a team, who have managed to find others to share in their perversion. While there are instances of serial killer teams being simply friends (Kenneth Bianchi and Angelo Buono, or Leonard Lake and Charles Ng, for instance), the most common type of team killers is a pair of lovers. It is appalling to contemplate a kind of love so perverse that it leads couples to share in murder for their own sexual gratification.

Take, for example, the case of Douglas Clark and Carol Bundy. While we can imagine that a man like Clark might be drawn to rape and murder, it almost defies belief that he could bring home the severed head of one of his victims and that his lover, Carol Bundy, could first apply make-up to the dead woman's face and then look on approvingly as Clark committed an act of necrophilia with the head.

Less bizarre, but perhaps even more shocking, is the case of Paul Bernardo and Karla Homolka, in which Homolka deliberately drugged her own 15-year-old sister so that Bernardo could rape her; or that of British killers Ian Brady and Myra Hindley, in which Hindley would lure young girls into Brady's clutches, then take part in torturing them before Brady murdered them. It is this perversion of love – and in particular the reverse of what we conventionally see as the civilizing influence of the woman – that makes the disturbing stories of these demon lovers so profoundly unsettling.

DOUGLAS CLARK AND CAROL BUNDY

Doug Clark and Carol Bundy appeared to make an unlikely couple. Doug was a good-looking man from a well-to-do family, a 32-year-old charmer with a string of girlfriends pining after him. Carol was a divorcee with thick glasses and a weight problem. Five years older than Clark, she had recently split from an abusive husband and was working as a nurse. Underneath, however, the pair had a great deal in common: both were sexually driven, both lacked a moral compass and together they embarked on a rampage of sexually motivated murder.

'King of the One Night Stand'

Douglas Daniel Clark was born in 1948, the son of a Naval Intelligence officer, Franklin Clark. The family moved repeatedly during Doug's childhood, due to his father's work. He later claimed to have lived in 37 countries. In 1958, his father left the navy to take up a civilian position as an engineer with the Transport Company of Texas: some sources suggest that this was in fact merely a cover for continuing intelligence activities. Either way, it did not put a stop to the family's nomadic lifestyle.

They lived in the Marshall Islands for a time, moved back to San Francisco, and then moved again to India. For a while Doug was sent to an exclusive international school in Geneva. Later, he attended the prestigious Culver Military Academy while his father continued to move around the world. When he graduated in 1967, Doug naturally enough enlisted in the air force.

At this point, however, Clark's life began to unravel. He was discharged from the air force and for the next decade he drifted around, often working as a mechanic, but really concentrating on his vocation as a sexual athlete: 'the king of the one night stand' as he liked to call himself. The 70s was the decade when casual sex first became a widespread, socially acceptable phenomenon – at least in the big cities – and Doug Clark, a smooth-talking, well-educated young man, was well placed to take advantage of this change in the nation's morals.

Nowhere was this lifestyle more prevalent than Los Angeles, and eventually Doug Clark moved there, taking a job in a factory in Burbank. One of the bars he liked to frequent and pick up women was a place in North Hollywood called Little Nashville, where, in 1980, he met Carol Bundy.

Bundy was 37 years old. She had had a troubled childhood: her mother had died when she was young, and her father had abused her. Then, when her father remarried, he had put her in various foster homes. At the age of 17, Bundy had married a 56-year-old man; by the time she met Clark she had recently escaped a third marriage to an abusive man, by whom she had had two young sons. Most recently, she had begun an affair with her apartment block manager, a part-time country singer called John Murray. She had even attempted to bribe Murray's wife to leave him. Murray's wife was not pleased at this and had told her husband to have Bundy evicted from the block. However, this had not ended the infatuation and Bundy continued to show up regularly at venues where Murray was singing. One of these was Little Nashville.

Clark, an experienced manipulator of women, quickly saw the potential in seducing the overweight and transparently needy Bundy. He turned on the charm and won her over immediately. Before long, he moved into her apartment and soon discovered that this was a woman with whom he could share his increasingly dark sexual fantasies.

Prostitutes

He started bringing prostitutes back to the flat to have sex with them both. Then he began to take an interest in an 11-year-old girl who was a neighbour. Carol helped lure the girl into sexual games and posing for sexual photographs. Even breaking the paedophile taboo was not enough for Clark, however. He started to talk about how much he would like to kill a girl during sex and persuaded Carol to go out and buy two automatic pistols for him to use.

The killing began in earnest during June 1980. In June, Clark came home and told Bundy about the two teenagers he had picked up on the Sunset Strip that day and subsequently murdered. He had ordered them to perform fellatio on him and then shot them both in the head before taking them to a garage and raping their dead bodies. He had then dumped the bodies beside the Ventura freeway, where they were found the next day. Carol was sufficiently shocked by this news to make a phone call to the police admitting to some knowledge of the murders but refusing to give any clues as to the identity of the murderer.

Refrigerated Remains

Twelve days later, when Clark killed again, Bundy had clearly got over her qualms. The victims were two prostitutes, Karen Jones and Exxie Wilson. Once again, Clark had picked them up, shot them and dumped the bodies in plain view, but this time he had decided to take a trophy: Exxie Wilson's head. He took the head back to Bundy's house and surprised her by producing it from her fridge. Almost unbelievably, she then put make-up on the head before Clark used it for another bout of necrophilia. Two days later, they put the freshly scrubbed head in a box and dumped it in an alleyway. Three days after this, another body was found in the woods in the San Fernando Valley. The victim was a runaway called Marnette Comer, who appeared to have been killed three weeks previously, making her Clark's first known victim.

Clark waited a month before killing again. Meanwhile Bundy was still infatuated with John Murray. She would go to see him singing in Little Nashville, and after a few drinks her conversation would turn to the kind of things she and Clark got up to. These hints alarmed Murray, who implied he might tell the police. To avert this, Bundy lured Murray into his van after a show to have sex. Once they were inside the van, she shot him dead and decapitated him. However, she had left a trail of clues behind her: Bundy and Murray had been seen in the bar together and she had left shell casings in the van. Bundy herself was unable to take the pressure. Two days later, she confessed to her horrified co-workers that she had killed Murray. They called the police and she began to give them a full and frank confession about her and Clark's crimes.

Clark was immediately arrested and the guns found hidden at his work. Bundy was charged with two murders: Murray and the unknown victim whose killing she confessed to having been present at. Clark was charged with six murders. At his trial he represented himself and tried to blame Bundy for everything, portraying himself as an innocent dupe. The jury did not believe him, and he was sentenced to the death penalty, while Bundy received life imprisonment. Ironically enough, it was Bundy who met her end first, dying in prison on 9 December 2003 at the age of 61. Clark, meanwhile, continues to fight his conviction.

PAUL BERNARDO AND KARLA HOMOLKA

On the surface, Paul Bernardo and Karla Homolka seemed the most unlikely of serial killers. They were a middle-class young Canadian couple, both good looking and fair-haired. However, these ostensibly model citizens conspired together in the rape, torture and murder of at least three young women, including Karla's own sister, Tammy. At her trial, Karla blamed all the crimes on her abusive husband Paul. Subsequent evidence showed that she herself was just as deeply implicated. However, it is probably true to say that without Bernado, Homolka would never have killed – while Bernardo almost certainly would have done, whether or not he had had a lover to aid and abet him.

Abusive Father

Paul Bernardo was born in the well-to-do Toronto suburb of Scarborough in August 1964, the third child of accountant Kenneth Bernardo and home-maker Marilyn. At least that is what Paul believed when he was growing up; it was only when he was 16 that his mother revealed him to be the offspring of an

Paul Bernardo

affair she had had. By this time, it was abundantly clear that all was not well in the seemingly respectable Bernardo household. Kenneth was physically abusive to his wife and sexually abusive to his daughter; meanwhile, Marilyn had become grossly overweight and remained virtually housebound.

Karla Homolka

Nevertheless, up to that point Paul appeared to be a happy, well-adjusted child, who enjoyed his involvement in scouting activities. It was only when he became a young man that he revealed a darker side to his nature. He was good looking, charming and, not surprisingly, popular with women. However, his sexual appetites turned out to be anything but charming. He would beat up the women he went out with, tie them up and force them to have anal sex. This behaviour carried on through his time at the University of Toronto, a period during which he also developed a money-making sideline in smuggling cigarettes into the US. After leaving college, he got a job as an accountant at Price Waterhouse. Not long afterwards, in October 1987, he met Karla Homolka at a Toronto pet convention.

Karla Homolka was born on 4 May 1970 in Port Credit, Ontario, the daughter of Dorothy and Karel Homolka. She had two sisters, Lori and Tammy. Like Bernardo's, this was a middle-class family, but in this case it seemed to be a genuinely happy one. Karla was a popular girl who attended Sir Winston Churchill High School and then became a veterinary assistant, working at an animal hospital, which was where she met Paul Bernardo.

Dark Fantasies

Unlike most of his previous girlfriends, Karla was not repulsed by her new boyfriend's sexual sadism. Instead, she joined in enthusiastically, encouraging him to go ever further into his dark fantasies. Before long, this meant going out and finding women to rape. Over the next few years, Bernardo carried out well over a dozen rapes around the Scarborough area. How far Homolka was involved is not entirely clear, though one victim reported seeing a woman lurking behind the rapist, filming the event.

The police took a long time to deal with the case. In 1990, they finally released a photo-fit sketch that produced an immediate identification of Paul Bernardo. A blood test was taken from Bernardo, revealing that he had the same blood group as the rapist. Further tests were called for. Unbelievably, it took the police laboratory three years to carry out detailed tests, which proved conclusively that Bernardo was the 'Scarborough Rapist'. By that time, however, he was also a murderer.

As time went on, raping strangers was no longer enough for Bernardo. He developed a fantasy about raping Karla's 15-year-old sister Tammy. Once again, Karla was a willing accomplice. She decided to drug Tammy, using anaesthetics stolen from the veterinary clinic where she worked. On 24 December 1990, Karla got Tammy drunk and administered a drug called Halothane to her. Both Paul and Karla then raped Tammy and videotaped the entire episode. They did not initially intend to kill Tammy but the anaesthetic caused her to choke on her own vomit, and she died on her way to hospital. The official cause of death was suffocation. Karla's grieving parents put the tragedy down to an accident, caused by Tammy having drunk too much.

Marriage of Minds

Karla grieved briefly but was soon engrossed in planning her wedding that summer. A few weeks beforehand, she lured one of her friends, a teenager named Jane, round to the house and gave her the same treatment she had doled out to her sister. This time, though, Jane survived the experience, awaking from her drugged sleep confused and sore, but unaware that she had been raped by both Karla and Paul. This lapse of memory undoubtedly saved her life.

The couple's next victim, 14-year-old Leslie Mahaffy, was not so lucky. Paul abducted her on 15 July 1991 and the couple raped and tortured the girl over a 24-hour period, filming the event, before Paul finally killed her. Her body was found soon afterwards, dismembered and encased in cement on Lake Gibson. The same day that Mahaffy's body was found, Paul and Karla were married in a lavish affair at Niagara.

Four months later, on 30 November 1991, 14-year-old Terri Anderson disappeared. She may well have been murdered by Bernardo and Homolka, but the case remains unproven. Their final victim was 17-year-old Kristen French, abducted from a church parking lot on 16 April 1992. This time, the couple kept their victim alive for three days, raping and torturing her. They finally murdered her when they realized they were due to attend an Easter dinner at Karla's parents house.

This was the last murder the couple committed. By the summer of 1992, Bernardo had started to take out his rage on Homolka and in January 1993 she left him. The following month, the police lab finally ran the test on Bernardo's blood sample and discovered that he was the Scarborough Rapist. As Bernardo's name had also come up in the investigations into the murders of Mahaffey and French, the police finally put the whole case together. Homolka successfully painted herself as just another victim of the dominating Bernardo, and agreed a plea bargain whereby she would plead guilty of manslaughter and receive a 12-year prison sentence in return for testifying against Bernardo.

Willing Partner

Homolka's trial duly began in June 1993. She once again played the abused wife and received the agreed sentence. However, two years later, when Bernardo's trial began and the prosecution revealed the new evidence of Bernardo's videotapes, the judge and jury were able to see, in all too graphic detail, how willing a partner Homolka had been in the rape and torture of Mahaffey and French. Bernardo did his best to put the blame back on to Homolka, but the videotapes were utterly damning, and he received a life sentence in prison. Controversially, Homolka was released from prison in July 2005 and was reported to be living in Montreal in 2011, married and the mother of three kids.

IAN BRADY AND MYRA HINDLEY

Britain has had other prolific serial killers than Ian Brady and Myra Hindley, but none has attracted so much attention or become so clearly the embodiment of evil as this couple, the so-called 'Moors Murderers' who brutally tortured and killed at least five children in the early 1960s. At the heart of the horror was the role of Myra Hindley, as, up to that time, only men were known to carry out serial sex murders of children. That a woman should have joined in seemed so utterly against nature that Hindley became Britain's number one hate figure, reviled even more than the principal agent of their crimes, Ian Brady.

Ian Brady was born in Glasgow, Scotland, on 2 January 1938. His mother, Peggy Stewart, was unmarried at the time and unable to support her child. She gave her baby, aged four months, over to the care of John and Mary Sloane, a couple with four children of their own. Peggy continued to visit her son for a while, though not revealing that she was actually his mother. The visits stopped when she moved to Manchester, England, with her new husband, Patrick Brady, when her son was 12 years old.

Ian was a difficult child, intelligent but a loner. In his teens, despite having passed the entrance examination to a good school, Shawlands Academy, he went completely off the rails. He became fascinated by Nazi Germany and by Adolf Hitler in particular, missed school frequently and committed burglaries. By the age of 16, he had been arrested three times. He was only saved from reform school when he agreed to leave Glasgow and go to live with his natural mother Peggy in Manchester.

When he arrived in Manchester, in late 1954, he made an effort to fit in, taking his stepfather's name. He worked as a market porter, but within a year he was in trouble again. He was jailed for theft, and while imprisoned seems to have decided on his future career: professional criminal. With this in mind, he studied book-keeping. On his release, he found work as a labourer while looking for a suitable criminal enterprise. Unable to find anything, he put his new skill to more conventional use and got a job as a book-keeper with a company called Millwards Merchandising. A year later a new secretary arrived to work there: Myra Hindley.

Baby-Sitter

Myra Hindley had a slightly more conventional upbringing than Brady. She was born in Manchester on 23 July 1942, the oldest child of Nellie and Bob. During the war years, while Bob was in the army, the family lived with Myra's grandmother, Ellen

Maybury. Later, when Bob and Nellie had trouble coping in the postwar years, Myra went back to live with her grandmother, who was devoted to her. Throughout her school years Myra was seen as a bright, though not overambitious, child with a love of swimming. In her teens, she was a popular baby-sitter.

Leaving school at 16, she took a job as a clerk in an engineering firm. Soon afterwards, she got engaged to a local boy, Ronnie Sinclair. However, she broke off the engagement, having apparantly decided that she wanted more excitement in life. That wish was all too horribly granted when she took a new job and found herself working with Ian Brady.

Hindley soon fell for the sullen, brooding Brady. It took him a year to reciprocate her interest, but once they became lovers, he realized he had found the perfect foil for his increasingly dark fantasies. Brady had spent much of the previous few years obsessively reading. Particular favourites were Dostoyevsky's *Crime and Punishment*, Hitler's *Mein Kampf* and the Marquis de Sade's *Justine*, among other, less elevated books on sadomasochism. Brady increasingly saw himself as some kind of superman, beyond the bounds of good and evil. The devoted Myra lapped all this up. During their first years together she transformed herself with hair dye and make-up into the Aryan blonde of Brady's fantasies. She gave up seeing her friends and devoted herself utterly to her lover.

In 1964, Brady introduced Hindley to the next stage in their relationship: a life of crime. His first notion was a bank robbery. The dutiful Myra joined a gun club and obtained two weapons for him. However, before the robbery could be carried out, Brady changed his mind. It was not robbery he wanted to commit but murder.

First Victim

The couple's first victim was 16-year-old Pauline Reade. The couple waylaid the teenager on the way to a dance on 12 July 1963. They lured her on to Saddleworth Moor, where Brady raped her and cut her throat. They then buried her there.

Having got away with the crime, on 11 November Brady decided it was time to kill again. The victim this time was a 12-year-old boy, John Kilbride, whom they abducted from Ashton-under-Lyme. Seven months later, in June 1964, another 12-year-old, Keith Bennett, was abducted from near his home in Manchester. Both boys were raped, murdered and buried on the moors.

After six more months they struck again, on Boxing Day, 26 December 1964. This time they took a girl: ten-year-old Lesley Ann Downey. With Hindley's assistance, Brady took pornographic photographs of Downey, which he planned to sell to rich perverts.

Ian Brady and Myra Hindley

The couple, now entirely engrossed in their evil, even made an audio tape of their torture of the terrified little girl. Finally, Brady raped her and either he or Hindley – depending on whose account you believe – strangled her, before they buried her on the moors with the others.

Brady took to boasting about his exploits to Hindley's brother-in-law, David Smith. Angered when Smith did not believe him, Brady made Hindley bring Smith to their house on 6 October 1965, just as he was about to dispatch his latest victim, 17-year-old Edward Evans. Smith was not impressed but horrified and went to the police the next morning. They raided the house and found Evans' body there. Further investigation soon led them to start digging on the moors, where they discovered the bodies of Downey and Kilbride. Next, they found a box containing the photos and the tape documenting Downey's murder. At trial both Brady and Hindley tried to pin the blame on David Smith, but the sensational evidence of the tape led to them both being convicted of murder.

Brady and Hindley received a life sentence each. Hindley protested her innocence for a long time, but eventually came to accept partial responsibility. Brady accepted his guilt and later confessed to five other murders, which remain unproven. In 2002, he wrote a book on serial killers that caused controversy in Britain on its publication. That same year, Myra Hindley died in prison. In 2017, Ian Brady took the location of his final victim, Keith Bennett's body with him to the grave.

CHARLES STARKWEATHER AND CARIL FUGATE

The case of Charles Starkweather and Caril Fugate is a fascinating if shocking one. Charles Starkweather, a rebellious 19-year-old, modelled himself on James Dean. Caril Fugate was his underage girlfriend. Together, they went on an unprecedented killing spree, murdering family members, friends, strangers and anyone else who got in their way. Eventually, the law caught up with them and they were found guilty of a string of murders. Starkweather was sentenced to death; being only 14 at the time of her conviction, Caril Fugate's sentence was commuted to life imprisonment. Just why the pair suddenly showed such unbelievable brutality to a series of innocent victims, leaving a trail of bloodshed behind them wherever they went, remains to this day something of a mystery.

Reputation for Violence

Charles Starkweather hailed from Nebraska, and was one of seven children. His family was poor but seemingly settled. However, when he went to school he was teased and became oversensitive, often getting into fights with other boys in his class. The frenzied nature of his attacks was remarkable, and by the time he was a teenager, he had developed a reputation for violence. He and his close friend Bob Von Busch idolized the film star James Dean, imitating their hero down to the last detail, a pose that impressed Barbara Fugate, Bob's girlfriend, and her younger sister Caril.

Charles was not a very intelligent young man, but this did not bother the young, impressionable Caril, who was herself none too bright. The pair started going out together, despite the fact that Caril was only 13. Soon it became clear that Charles was besotted with his new girlfriend, boasting that he was going to marry her and that she was pregnant with his child – a claim that, even though untrue, did not endear him greatly to Caril's parents.

Fatal Robbery

Starkweather left school aged 16 and began work at a newspaper warehouse. However, he soon gave up the job, and took on work as a garbage man, mainly so that he could see more of Caril after she came out of school. He had moved out of his family home into a rooming house, but now found he could not pay the rent. He became increasingly frustrated by his life of poverty, and felt trapped in a situation that seemed to hold no future for him or his girlfriend. Finally, his patience snapped when he was refused credit to buy Caril a stuffed toy animal at a gas station, and he decided to take matters into his own hands.

At 3 am on a freezing cold night in December 1957, Starkweather returned to the gas station. There he robbed the attendant who had previously refused him credit, 21-year-old Robert Colville, took him out to a deserted area and shot him.

Caril Fugate and Charles Starkweather

His next crime was even more unbelievable. He drove to Caril's house and, after a violent altercation, shot her mother Velda Bartlett, her stepfather Marion Bartlett and stabbed her baby half-sister Betty Jean to death. Then he dragged Velma's body to the toilet outside, put Marion's in the chicken coop and stuffed the baby's into a garbage box. When Caril returned home from school, the pair cleaned up the blood and spent several days in the family home doing as they pleased. Visitors to the house were told to go away because everyone 'had the flu'. By the time the police investigated, the couple were on the run. The first victim they killed together was August Meyer, a bachelor of 72 who had been a family friend of the Starkweathers for many years. They shot him, hid his body in an outhouse and made off with his guns. They then hitched a ride with teenagers Robert Jensen and Carol King. They shot Jensen repeatedly in the head, while King was stabbed to death and left naked from the waist down.

Hostage or Accomplice?

The couple's next stop was a wealthy part of town where Starkweather had once collected garbage. They called on Clara Ward and her maid Lillian Fencl. Starkweather ordered Mrs Ward to make breakfast for them before stabbing her to death. When her husband came home, a fight ensued and he was killed. Finally, the maid was tied to a bed and stabbed to death. The pair then made off in the Wards' black Packard. On their journey, just for good measure, they shot a travelling shoe salesman, Merle Collison.

Finally, after a car chase, police arrested Starkweather and Fugate in Wyoming. To protect herself, Fugate alleged that she had been taken hostage by Starkweather. In response,

Starkweather claimed that some of the murders were her doing. No one believed their stories; both were tried for murder and both were found guilty.

Starkweather was sentenced to death and Fugate, because of her age, received a life sentence and was released on parole in 1976. Their extraordinary story, which seemed motivated not just by extreme violence but also by a curiously child-like lack of intelligence, inspired several successful Hollywood movies.

FRED AND ROSEMARY WEST

The crimes of Fred and Rosemary West utterly shocked the people of Britain when they emerged in 1994. It was not simply that nine bodies were found buried under the couple's house in Gloucester. It was not that one of the bodies belonged to their own daughter, Heather. It was not even the discovery of other bodies belonging to Fred West's first wife and child. What was almost unbearable for people to accept was that this bloody carnage had taken place in an apparently normal family home, a place full of children and visitors, presided over by a happily married couple.

Virtually Illiterate

To understand the crimes of the Wests one has, as so often in such cases, to go back to their early childhoods. Fred West was one of six children born to Walter and Daisy West in 1941, in Much Marcle on the edge of the Forest of Dean. At the time, the village was a very poor rural backwater. Fred was very close to his mother. He claimed that his father sexually abused his sisters, though whether this was actually the case is not known. He did badly at school and was virtually illiterate when he left, aged 15. He worked, like his father and grandfather before him, as a farmhand. At the age of 17 he had a serious motorbike accident in which he sustained a head injury – a common factor in the backgrounds of a large number of serial killers. Two years later, he was arrested for having sex with a 13-year-old girl. He managed to avoid going to prison after his lawyer told the judge that Fred suffered from epileptic fits, but his parents threw him out of the family home for a while.

A Different Story?

In 1962, Fred met Catherine 'Rena' Costello, a young woman with a record of delinquency and prostitution. They fell in love, moved to her native Scotland and got married, despite the fact that she was already pregnant by an Asian bus driver. The child, Charmaine, was born in 1963. The following year they had their own child, Anna Marie. They then moved back to Gloucester, where they split up. Fred took up with a friend of Rena, Anne McFall. By 1967 McFall was pregnant with Fred's child, and demanded that he divorce Rena and marry her. This provoked Fred's first murder: he killed McFall, dismembered her body and that of their unborn baby, and buried them near the trailer park in which they had been living. Curiously, he cut off the tops of McFall's finger and toes before burying her. This was to become a Fred West trademark.

Following McFall's murder, Rena moved back in with Fred. During this period, he is thought to have murdered 15-year-old Mary Bastholm, whom he abducted from a bus stop in Gloucester. Later the couple split up again, and it was then that Fred met a young girl who turned out to be as vicious and depraved as he was.

Rosemary Letts was born in November 1953 in Devon. Her mother, Daisy Letts, suffered from severe depression. Her father, Bill Letts, was a schizophrenic who had sexually abused her. A pretty, rather slow child, she became fat and sexually precocious as a teenager. When she met Fred West, 12 years her senior, he seemed to be the man of her dreams. Soon afterwards, however, Fred was sent to prison for non-payment of fines. By then Rose, not yet 16, was pregnant with his child.

When Fred came out of jail, Rose went to live with him, Charmaine and Anna Marie, and in 1970 gave birth to Heather. The following year, while Fred was once again in prison, Charmaine went missing. Rose told people that Charmaine's mother Rena had come to take her back. In fact Rose herself had murdered Charmaine while in the grip of one of the ferocious tempers her other children would become all too familiar with.

When Fred was released from prison, he buried the body of the child under the house. Not long after, Rena did indeed come looking for Charmaine. Fred killed her too, and buried her in the countryside.

In 1972, Fred and Rose married and had a second child, Mae. They moved to a house in Cromwell Street, Gloucester. There, they began to indulge in deviant sex, using the cellar of the house as a perverse sexual playpen. They even raped their own eight-year-old daughter Anna Marie there. Later that year, they employed 17-year-old Caroline Owens as a nanny. Owens rejected their sexual advances – Rose by now was having sex with both men and women – so they raped her. She escaped and told the police, but when the matter came to trial in January 1973 the magistrate, appallingly, believed Fred's word over that of Owens and let the Wests off with a fine.

At least Owens escaped with her life. Their next nanny, Lynda Gough, ended up dismembered and buried under the cellar. The following year, in which Rose gave birth to another child, Stephen, the couple murdered fifteen-year-old Carol Ann Cooper. In late December, they abducted university student Lucy Partington, tortured her for a week and then murdered, dismembered and buried her.

The Wests' perversions became ever more extreme. Over the next 18 months they killed three more women: Therese Siegenthaler, Shirley Hubbard and Juanita Mott. Hubbard and Mott had been subjected to almost unimaginable tortures: their bodies, when exhumed, were trussed in elaborate bondage

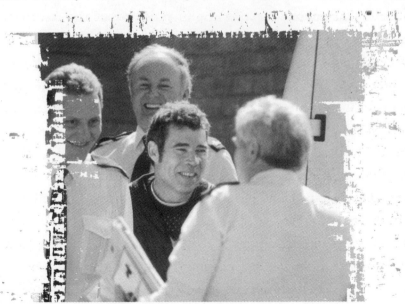

Fred West

costumes. Hubbard's head had been wrapped entirely with tape, with only a plastic tube inserted in her nose to allow her to breathe.

In 1977, Rose, who was also by now working as a prostitute, became pregnant by one of her clients. However, at around the same time, their latest lodger Shirley Robinson, an 18-year-old ex-prostitute, became pregnant with Fred's child. Rose was angry about this development, and decided the girl had to go. In December 1977, she was murdered and, as the cellar was now full, the Wests buried her in the back garden, along with her unborn baby.

In May 1979 the Wests killed once again. The victim this time was teenager Alison Chambers – another body for the back garden. Then, as far as is known, the Wests stopped killing for

Rosemary West

pleasure. It may be that they carried on killing and that their victims were never found; it may be that they found other sources of sexual excitement. Exactly what happened is still not known.

During the 1980s, Rose had three more children, two by another client, one more with Fred. She continued to work as a prostitute, specializing in ever more extreme bondage. Fred found a new interest in making videotapes of Rose having sex, and continued to abuse his daughters, until Heather told a friend about her home life. Her friend's parents told the Wests about Heather's allegation and Fred responded by killing her, the last of his known victims.

It was not until 1992 that a young girl whom the Wests had raped went to the police. On 6 August that year, police arrived at Cromwell Street with a search warrant to look for pornography and evidence of child abuse: they found plenty, and so arrested Rose for assisting in the rape of a minor. Fred was arrested for rape and sexual abuse of a minor. Anna Marie made a statement supporting the allegation, as did their oldest son Stephen, but following threats from the Wests they withdrew them and the case collapsed. Meanwhile, the younger children had been taken into care. While there, care assistants heard the children joke about their older sister Heather being buried under the patio. A day's digging revealed human bones – and not just Heather's. Eventually, a total of nine bodies were found in the garden. Other bodies buried elsewhere were later exhumed.

On 13 December 1994, Fred and Rosemary West were charged with murder. A week later, Fred hanged himself in prison with strips of bed sheet. Rose's defence tried to put the blame for the murders on Fred, but she was duly sentenced to life imprisonment.

Gold Diggers

Serial killers, typically, are individuals motivated by violent sexual drives that are difficult for most people to understand. Robbery may be an integral part of the killer's pattern of attacks, but it is seldom the only motivation for serial murder. Very few serial killers are motivated purely by financial gain. It seems that, although greed may cause individuals to kill once or twice, on the whole it does not provoke a series of brutal murders. However, there are exceptions to this rule. In some cases, there appears to be no sexual motivation whatsoever on the part of the killer; he or she kills, callously and brutally, to rob the victims of their possessions. These are the gold diggers, criminals who are prepared to murder over and over for no reason other than money – and often surprisingly small amounts of money at that.

Take Faye and Ray Copeland, an elderly couple of Nebraska farmers who murdered transient farm labourers for paltry profits. Likewise, Raymond Fernandez and Martha Beck, another couple who were prepared to kill as part of what were otherwise a series of low-level scams. Even Charles Sobhraj, a man often portrayed as a kind of evil genius among serial killers, mostly murdered backpackers for little more than a passport and a handful of travellers cheques.

The relatively insignificant gains that these killers make in terms of money and goods point to the fact that they are, in general, true psychopaths: criminals for whom the suffering of others is meaningless. For them, human life is cheap, so much so that they are able to kill again and again without any sign of conscience.

RAY AND FAYE COPELAND

Ray and Faye Copeland were perhaps the most unlikely team of serial killers in American history. An elderly married couple, they were old-fashioned farming people living an apparently simple life that revolved around the daily chores on their farm in Nebraska. As it turned out, however, their life was anything but simple; together they were hiring a series of young men to work as farmhands and then murdering them as part of a scam to make themselves rich. For a long time they went undetected, after all, they were both senior citizens, on the face of it living quietly in the countryside. But finally, the law caught up with them and revealed the horrifying truth about life – and death – on the Copeland farm.

Depression

Ray Copeland was born in Oklahoma in 1914. While Ray was growing up, his family moved around, struggling to survive during the Depression. As a young man, he began a life of petty crime, stealing livestock and forging cheques, until he was caught and served a year in jail. After his release, he met his future wife, Faye; a loyal accomplice to his crimes during their long marriage.

The couple quickly had several children and money became tight. Ray continued to steal livestock and to forge cheques; his increasingly bad reputation meant that the family had to keep moving around. During this time Ray served several jail sentences, until he finally came up with a new plan: not to go straight, but to improve his illegal money-making methods so that he would go undetected.

Fraudster

Since he was well known by now as a fraudster, Copeland could not buy and sell cattle himself. To circumvent this problem, he began to pick up drifters and hobos, employing them as farmhands. He would go to market with his employees, who would buy cattle for him and pay for them with bad cheques. After the transactions, Copeland would sell the cattle quickly, and the farmhands would disappear without trace. For a while the scam worked, but then police caught up with them. Once again, Ray Copeland went to jail.

On his release, Copeland resumed his criminal activities, but this time he made sure his farm hands operated more independently from him. This went on until a previous employee, Jack McCormick, phoned the Nebraska Crime Stoppers hotline in August 1989 to tell them about the Copelands. He had been employed on the farm, and claimed that he had seen human bones there. He also said that Ray Copeland had tried to kill him.

Police were initially sceptical of the claims, but once they checked Copeland's record, they decided to investigate them thoroughly. In October 1989, they visited the Copeland farm armed with a search warrant, dozens of officers and a team of bloodhounds. However, they initially failed to find any incriminating evidence. Then, just as they were beginning to give up hope, the remains of three bodies were found in a nearby barn. They were the bodies of three young men. All had died from a bullet shot to the head from behind. As the search went on more bodies were discovered, all killed by the same weapon, a .22 Marlin rifle that was later found in the Copeland home.

It was by now clear that Copeland was a cold-blooded murderer who had callously killed his employees in the pursuit of his money-scam. But what of his wife Faye? During the investigation, a piece of evidence came to light that was not only incriminating, but also deeply sinister: a quilt that Faye had fashioned out of the clothing of the dead men. When she came to trial, Faye's defence mounted a picture of her as a dutiful wife and mother who had endured beatings and general ill-treatment from her bully of a husband. However, the quilt remained a macabre reminder that whatever her involvement, Faye Copeland knew perfectly well that her husband was a serial murderer and did nothing to stop him.

Faye Copeland was sentenced to death by lethal injection. On hearing the news, Ray Copeland showed no emotion. Ray was also sentenced to death by lethal injection. Aged 69 and 76, Faye and Ray Copeland became the oldest couple in the United States ever to receive the death sentence. However, neither of the executions took place: Ray died while awaiting execution, and Faye's sentence was commuted to life imprisonment. She later died, aged 82, of natural causes.

MARTHA BECK AND RAYMOND FERNANDEZ

The story of Martha Beck and Raymond Fernandez, dubbed the 'lonely hearts killers', was one of the most sensational ever to hit the headlines. It was a sleazy tale of two lovers who met through a lonely hearts column, and went on to rob and murder a series of gullible single women. The couple's actions marked them out as an unusually sick, vicious pair, but there was another aspect to the case that the public readily identified with: obsessive love. Martha Beck was a lonely, overweight woman who had lived a relatively normal life as a single parent and a nurse, until she fell in love with Fernandez, a killer and conman. In the process, as she struggled to gain her lover's approval, she threw away any vestige of human decency that she might once have had. First she abandoned her own children and then helped to murder her lover's innocent victims, in one case a child of two. This sudden change in her personality fascinated commentators – at least until the full horror of her crimes was revealed – provoking a certain amount of sympathy from the American public.

As well as this central theme of crazed passion, there were other features of the story that mesmerized the public: in court, evidence of the couple's bizarre sexual practices, which included Voodoo rites, came to light; and the press also made constant reference to Beck's size, to such a degree that it sometimes seemed she was on trial for being overweight, rather than for being a vicious murderer.

Execution

The lurid details of the case emerged during a sizzling hot summer in 1949. During the trial, the court was packed with onlookers, mostly women, and police had to hold back the crowds. As the trial came to an end, both Beck and Fernandez were convicted of murder and sentenced to death. Even on death row, the dramas continued as the pair's constant feuds and reconciliations were reported in the press. On 8 March 1951, time finally ran out for both of them, and they were executed – first Beck and then Fernandez – by electric chair.

Raymond Fernandez was a Hawaiian-born Spaniard who had grown up in Connecticut and then, as a young man, had gone to Spain to work on a farm. There, he had married a local woman, Encarnacion Robles. During the Second World War he had worked for British intelligence, and then had gone back to the US to look for work, leaving his wife and baby in Spain. During the voyage, he had had an accident on board ship and had received a blow to the head. By the time he recovered from the injury, his manner had completely changed: instead of being friendly and outgoing, he had become aggressive and withdrawn.

Fernandez now began a career of theft and deception. He joined several lonely hearts clubs and corresponded with a number of women. After meeting them, he would steal their money, cheque books, jewellery and any other assets he could lay his hands on. Very few of the women he duped went to the police, ashamed as they were of their liaisons with a Latin lover. In one case, Fernandez went further than robbery: he left a woman, Jane Thomas, dead in a hotel after an altercation. He then went to her apartment with a forged will and cleaned out her belongings, even though her elderly mother lived on the premises.

Lonely Heart

One of Fernandez' many correspondents was Martha Beck, a single mother of two. Beck later attested that she had suffered a difficult childhood. She claimed to have been sexually molested by her brother and blamed for the incident by her mother. At a young age she had become obese and had been the butt of cruel jokes at school. Although she went on to do well at nursing school, her size prejudiced her employers against her, and she ended up working in a morgue. Then she had become pregnant by a soldier who refused to marry her, even trying to commit suicide to avoid it – a circumstance that she had naturally found very depressing. However, Beck had gone on to find herself a husband and had became pregnant again, but, sadly, the couple soon divorced. As a single parent, she had worked hard and had eventually done well in her career as a nurse – until her fateful encounter with Raymond Fernandez.

When Martha Beck met Fernandez, she immediately became obsessed by him to the point of madness. She followed him to New York with her two children, and when he complained about them, she promptly took them to a Salvation Army hostel and left them there. Fernandez then told her of the way he made his living, preying on lonely women, and she decided to aid him in his chosen career. She would accompany Fernandez on his missions, often posing as his sister or sister-in-law, and helping to gain the victim's confidence.

Initially, Beck and Fernandez merely robbed and swindled women; eventually, they began to kill. Their victims were always lonely single women who had advertised for a companion or husband, and who were unlucky enough to contact Fernandez and his 'sister' Beck. They met their deaths in horrifying ways: Myrtle Young died of a massive drug overdose administered by Fernandez; Janet Fay was beaten to death by Beck; and Delphine Downing was shot in the head by Fernandez, in front of her two-year-old daughter Rainelle. When Rainelle would not stop crying for her mother, Beck drowned the child in a tub of dirty water.

As the details of the case emerged, the American public became increasingly horrified by the placid-seeming Beck. By the time the trial was over, there were very few who continued to sympathize with the overweight single mother who claimed that she had committed her crimes 'in the name of love'.

GARY HEIDNIK

Ellen Heidnik drank during her pregnancies. She drank a lot. Even at a time when the sight of a pregnant woman holding a wine glass was not unusual, Ellen stood out from the crowd. By the time her first child, Gary, was born – on 22 November 1943 in Eastlake, Ohio – Ellen's alcoholism had already begun to affect her marriage. Two years and one more son later, her husband filed for divorce.

The effects of the split overshadowed Gary's early years, as well as his brother Terry's.

Initially, the two boys stayed with their unstable, unreliable mother, but when she remarried they were sent to live with their father, Michael Heidnik, and his new wife.

Misshapen head

They were very unhappy times for Gary. He disliked his stepmother and he was brutalized by his disciplinarian of a father. He was often punished for wetting his bed and suffered even further when his father deliberately hung the stained sheets out of the second-floor bedroom window for all the neighbours to see. Horrendous as this experience was for Gary, it was nothing compared to the terror he felt when Michael dangled him by his ankles in place of the sheets.

School was no better. Gary was not only taunted for the bed-wetting – he was also mocked because of his unusual appearance. As a young child he had fallen out of a tree, which had left him with a slightly misshapen head. Michael made his son's schooldays all the worse by painting bullseyes on the seat of his trousers, thereby creating a target for the bullies. In spite of all of these drawbacks, Gary excelled in the classroom. He was invariably at the top of his class and his IQ was once measured at 130.

His intelligence, combined with his status as an outcast, might have contributed to his unusual ambitions. While so many of his male classmates dreamed of becoming baseball players and stars of football, 12-year-old Gary's twin aspirations were the achievement of great wealth and a career in the military. He made an early start by entering Virginia's Staunton Military Academy at the age of 14. Once again Gary proved to be an excellent student. However, unlike Barry Goldwater and John Dean, two of the school's illustrious alumni, Gary never graduated from the prestigious school. After two years of study he left the academy, returning to his father's house. He attempted to resume his studies at a couple of different high schools, but he felt that he was learning nothing, so at the age of 18 he dropped out of school and joined the army.

Though he made few friends amongst his comrades, Gary shone in the military. After completing basic training, he was sent to San Antonio in Texas, where he was to become a medical orderly. Now that his military career seemed well and truly on its way, Gary began pursuing his other long-held dream – to become wealthy. He supplemented his pay by making loans with interest to his fellow soldiers. Though his modest business would have been frowned upon by his superiors, Gary was otherwise an exemplary and intelligent military man. In 1962, while at a field hospital in West Germany, he achieved a near-perfect score in his high school equivalency examination.

A few months later it was all over.

In August, Gary began to complain of nausea, dizziness and blurred vision. The doctors who attended him identified two causes – stomach flu and 'schizoid personality disorder'. Before the year was up, he had been shipped back home. He was granted an honourable discharge and a disability pension. With one of his two dreams dashed into smithereens, Gary enrolled at the University of Pennsylvania. His chosen courses – chemistry, history, anthropology and biology – were so diverse in nature that it appeared that he was looking for direction. If so, Gary was unsuccessful. Using his army medical training, he worked for a time at two Philadelphia hospitals, but he proved to be a poor worker.

Now without work and living on his pension his eccentricities grew, while his personal hygiene declined. Gary found a leather jacket, which he would wear regardless of the weather or the social situation. If he did not want to be disturbed, he would roll up one trouser leg as a signal to others. Then there were the suicide attempts – not just Gary's, but those of his brother and his mother, too. These were so frequent that they could be numbered in the dozens, but only Ellen was successful. In 1970, the four-times married alcoholic took her own life by drinking mercury.

Both Heidnik boys spent years moving in and out of mental institutions. Yet despite his many periods of confinement, Gary managed to begin amassing the wealth he had sought since he was a child. In 1971 he founded his own church, the United Church of the Ministers of God, and he ordained himself as its bishop. Although Gary had just four followers, they included two people who were close to him – his girlfriend, who suffered from learning disabilities, and his brother.

Out of control

As a self-anointed minister, Gary began investing in earnest. He bought property and played the stock market, making a great deal of money when Hugh Hefner's Playboy empire went public in 1971. But all of the time he was spinning increasingly out of control. Gary became one of those individuals who is often described as 'known to the police'. There were any number of reasons for his notoriety. In 1976, for example, he used an unlicensed gun to shoot one of his tenants in the face. Incredibly, it was not until 1978 that he first went to jail. But the three- to seven-year sentence had nothing to do with the earlier shooting. Instead, Gary had been found guilty of kidnapping, unlawful restraint, false imprisonment, rape, involuntary deviate sexual intercourse and interfering with the custody of a committed person.

All of this had come about because Gary had signed his girlfriend's sister out of a mental institution and had kept her confined to his basement. Not only had he raped the young woman but he had infected her with gonorrhoea. In the middle of what turned out to be four years of incarceration, he handed a prison guard a note explaining that he could no longer speak because Satan had shoved a cookie down his throat. Gary remained silent for over 27 months.

When he was finally released in April 1983, he returned to Philadelphia and resumed his role as a bishop with the United Church of the Ministers of God. Even though Gary's congregation had not grown much, from time to time it included women with learning disabilities, whom he would impregnate.

It is hardly surprising that Betty Disto, Gary's first bride, was not immediately aware of his odd behaviour and poor hygiene because the couple had become engaged before they had even laid eyes on one another. The couple had met through a matrimonial service. They had been corresponding for two years when, in September of 1985, Betty flew from her address in the Philippines to the United States. Their October marriage lasted for just three months. Betty could not stand to see her groom in bed with other women, but she had no choice because Gary made her watch. Beaten, raped and threatened, a pregnant Betty fled home with the help of the local Filipino community.

Betty made her escape in the first few days of 1986, but Gary's life really began to fall apart towards the end of that year. On the evening of 26 November 1986, Gary abducted a prostitute named Josefina Rivera. It all happened gradually.

She had been standing outside in the cold rain when Gary picked her up in his Cadillac Coupe De Ville. On the way, he stopped at McDonald's and bought her a coffee. She did not object when he took her to his home, a run-down house at 3520 North Marshall Street.

There was something surreal about it all. Gary's house had seen better days, as had the rest of the neighbourhood. Decades earlier, the area had housed working-class German immigrants. The streets had been spotless then, but now they were pockmarked and covered in litter. Drug dealers worked its streets selling crack cocaine and marijuana to passing motorists and poverty was everywhere, yet Gary had a Rolls-Royce in his garage.

The door to his home was like something from a children's movie. When it opened, Josefina noticed that Gary had glued thousands of pennies to the walls of his kitchen. As he led her upstairs to the bedroom, she realized that the hallway had been wallpapered with $5 bills. In many ways, the house was a reflection of its owner. Gary's gold jewellery and Rolex watch contrasted sharply with his worn and stained clothing.

Like the rest of the house, the bedroom was sparsely furnished. There was nothing more than a waterbed, two chairs and a dresser. Gary gave Josefina the money they had agreed upon – $20 – and then he got undressed. The energetic and emotionless sex act was over in a matter of minutes. Josefina had felt a little uneasy about Gary, but what happened next took her by surprise. He grabbed her by the throat and choked her until she blacked out. Brief as it was, her loss of consciousness provided Gary with enough time to handcuff her.

Josefina was ordered to her feet and then she was marched downstairs to the basement. The unfinished room was cold, clammy and filthy, much like the old mattress that he made her sit on, and the floor was concrete, though some of the surface had been removed. After attaching metal clamps and chains to Josefina's ankles, Gary got down to digging the exposed earth.

He talked as he worked, telling the shackled woman that he had fathered four children by four different women, but it had all gone wrong. He had no contact with any of his offspring and yet he really wanted and *deserved* a family.

'Society owes me a wife and a big family,' was how he put it. 'I want to get ten women and keep them here and get them all pregnant. Then, when they have babies, I want to raise those children here too. We'll be like one big happy family.'

And with that bit of information, he raped her.

Screaming blue murder

Once she was alone, Josefina tried to escape. After freeing one of her ankles, she managed to prise open one of the basement windows and squeeze through it. Then she was out in the open. She crawled as far as the chain around her other ankle allowed her to and then she screamed at the top of her voice. But in Gary's neighbourhood screams like Josefina's were an everyday thing. The only person who paid any attention to the sound was Gary.

He ran downstairs, grabbed the chain and pulled her back into the basement. The filthy mattress was too good for her now. Dragging her across the cement floor, he threw her into the shallow pit. She was covered over with a sheet of plywood, upon which Gary placed heavy weights.

On her third day of captivity she was joined by a young woman named Sandra Lindsay. The girl had learning difficulties and seemed to have a very limited understanding of what was happening, so it was easy for Gary to get her to write a short note home. *'Dear Mom, do not worry. I will call.'*

It was the last time Sandra's mother would ever hear from her daughter. Josefina and Sandra spent weeks together. Sometimes they were in the pit and sometimes they were chained to pipes in the basement. They endured repeated rapes, beatings and the ever-present cold.

On 22 December they were joined by 19-year-old Lisa Thomas, a third 'wife'. Gary lured the girl to 3520 North Marshall Street with offers of food and clothing and a trip to Atlantic City. In the end she only got the food and a spiked glass of wine. After she passed out, Gary raped her and then took her down to the basement.

On New Year's Day Gary abducted a fourth woman, but 23-year-old Deborah Dudley was totally unlike his other 'wives'. Ignoring the consequences, she fought back at nearly every opportunity. Her disobedience invariably led to the other three captives being beaten as well, which created disorder and tension within the group.

When Gary began to encourage the women to report on each other, Josefina saw an opportunity to gain Gary's trust. Though she continued to suffer at his hands, Gary came to believe that Josefina actually took pleasure in her circumstance.

Wife number five, 18-year-old Jacqueline Askins, arrived on 18 January. After raping and shackling the girl, Gary surprised his 'wives' with generous helpings of Chinese food and a bottle of champagne. After weeks of bread, water and stale hot dogs, it seemed like the most elaborate feast.

To what did they owe this unexpected treat? It was Josefina's birthday.

Wicked punishment

However, any hopes that Gary might be softening were soon dashed. If anything, his abuse escalated. When he caught Sandra Lindsay trying to remove the plywood covering from the pit, she was forced to hang by one of her wrists from a ceiling beam.

She responded by going on a hunger strike, but after a few days she appeared incapable of eating. When Gary tried to force food down her throat, she vomited.

By 7 February, Sandra had completely lost consciousness. At this point, Gary finally removed the handcuff that had kept her dangling and she fell into a heap on the concrete floor.

Kicking her into the pit, he assured his other wives that Sandra was faking. It was probably a matter of minutes later that Sandra died.

The women watched as Gary carried Sandra's body upstairs and then they heard the sound of a power saw. Later that day, one of his dogs entered the basement, tail wagging. In its mouth was a bone covered in fresh meat.

Within days, the house and the basement took on a foul odour. Gary was finding it hard to dispose of Sandra's remains. Using his food processor he ground up what he could, feeding the meat to his dogs and his wives – but some body parts were very difficult to deal with.

Sandra's severed head sat in a pot of boiling water for days, while her ribcage was broiled in the oven. The smell spread to some of the adjoining properties, which led to complaints from the neighbours. Although the police investigated they believed Gary's story that he had cooked some bad meat. Meanwhile, the torture endured by the women became even more intense. Gary began poking their ears with a screwdriver, in the belief that deaf wives would be easier to control. He also stripped the insulation from extension cords in order to shock his captives.

Josefina was not only spared these punishments, she became an administrator. On 18 March she helped with an elaborate method of torture. First of all the pit was flooded and then the other wives, still in chains, were forced into the water. After that the plywood covering was put in place and weighed down. Finally, the bare wire of the extension cord was pushed through a hole, thereby electrocuting the women.

The second of these shocks killed Deborah Dudley. Her death marked a significant change in Gary's relationship with Josefina.

In his eyes, her participation in the torture, combined with Deborah's death, meant she could be blackmailed. That made her trustworthy – or so he thought. For the first time in almost four months she was allowed to leave the basement. She shared Gary's bed, dined with him at restaurants and helped with his grocery shopping. Josefina even went so far as to accompany Gary to the country, where he disposed of Deborah's body.

On 24 March 1987, the day after she helped abduct a new woman, Agnes Adams, Josefina convinced Gary to let her visit her children. She promised him that she would return with yet another 'wife'. Gary dropped her off and waited in the car for her return. But Josefina did not visit her children – she had none. Instead, she sprinted to her boyfriend's apartment, where she poured out her bizarre and almost unbelievable story.

After the police arrived and noted the scarring that had been left by months of wearing heavy chains, they arrested Gary. His surviving 'wives' were rescued when the police converged on 3520 North Marshall Street on the following morning.

Gary's trial began on 20 June 1988. From the start, his defence lawyers attempted to prove that the one-time medical assistant was insane. They called a psychiatrist and a psychologist to the stand, but their efforts were in vain. Ten days later he was found guilty of two counts of first-degree murder, four counts of aggravated assault, five counts of rape, six counts of kidnapping and one count of involuntary deviate sexual intercourse. He was subsequently sentenced to death.

On the evening of 6 July 1999, 11 years after he had been sentenced, Gary Heidnik was executed by lethal injection. It is hardly surprising that his body was not claimed by the other members of his family.

Michael Heidnik, his father, had not seen him since the early 1960s. When he heard about the death sentence he made a brief statement to the press.

'I'm not interested. I don't care. It don't bother me a bit.'

CHARLES SOBHRAJ

It is a fact that, while most crimes are committed for financial gain, serial murder very rarely has money as its primary object. Serial murderers often rob their victims, but this is usually a secondary motivation, the main purpose being sexual gratification of some kind. Charles Sobhraj, nicknamed 'the serpent', is a definite exception to the serial killer rule. He stands accused of around 20 murders. All his victims were backpackers travelling around south-east Asia. In all cases, he murdered them for money. As he himself told a journalist at the time of his 1976 murder trial: 'If I have ever killed, or have ordered killings, then it was purely for reasons of business – just a job, like a general in the army.'

Charles Sobhraj was born in 1944 to an Indian tailor and his Vietnamese girlfriend, Song. His father refused to marry his mother or to take much responsibility for his son. Song later married a French soldier, Lieutenant Alphonse Darreau, and the family eventually moved to Marseilles, France. Charles was an unruly child, who did not feel part of his mother's new life; several times he stowed away on ships leaving Marseilles, in an effort to return to his natural father, but each time he was discovered. As

Charles Sobhraj

he got older, he acquired a reputation for dishonesty. A slight, small boy, he became adept at manipulating people, especially his half-brother Andre, into carrying out his plans for him.

Prison

In his late teens, Sobhraj left home and went to Paris, where he was arrested for burglary in 1963 and sentenced to three years in prison. This could have been a nightmare experience, but Sobhraj's talents for manipulating people – plus his martial arts skills – came into their own in the prison milieu. One of the people he charmed there was a rich young prison visitor called Felix d'Escogne.

On his release from prison, Charles went to live with Felix and was introduced into a world of glamour and money. Sobhraj felt in his element, and married an elegant young woman, Chantal. However, in order to keep up in this world he had to have money, and the only way he knew of getting money was to steal it. He began to burgle his wealthy friends' houses and write bad cheques. Finally, with his wife, he fled France. The couple spent the remainder of the 1960s scamming their way across eastern Europe and the Middle East before settling down in Bombay, India. Chantal gave birth to their son during this time.

Murder

In 1971, the family had to flee India following a botched jewel robbery. They went to Kabul, Afghanistan, for a while. Here Charles specialized in robbing hippies who were passing through. However, by now Chantal had had enough and she returned to Paris with their son. Charles went back to his wanderings, accompanied for a while by his brother Andre. Their partnership ended in a Greek jail from which Charles managed to escape, leaving his brother behind. Soon Charles found a new partner, Marie Leclerc, who fell madly in love with him. They moved to Thailand and set up home in the beach resort of Pattaya. Gradually Sobhraj built up an entourage around him, reminiscent of the 'Family' set up by Charles Manson.

It was at this time that Sobhraj started to add murder to robbery. His first victim was an American called Jennie Bollivar. She was found dead in a tide pool in the warm waters of the Gulf of Thailand, wearing a bikini. At first it looked like an accident, but the autopsy revealed that she must have died by being held under the water. The next victim was a young Sephardic Jew, Vitali Hakim, who was robbed, beaten and set on fire.

A pair of Dutch students, Henk Bintanja and his fiancée, Cornelia 'Cocky' Hemker, were next to go, both strangled and their bodies burned. At that point, a friend of Hakim's, Charmaine Carrou, came looking for him. Like Bollivar, she was drowned in her bikini, causing the unknown murderer to be branded the 'bikini killer'.

Discovery

After reports of the murders in the Thai press, Sobhraj decided to lie low for a while. He flew to Nepal, where he met and murdered another couple, Laddie Duparr and Annabella Tremont, then left the country using the dead man's passport.

Back in Bangkok, some of Sobhraj's erstwhile followers had found a stash of passports in his office and suspected him of murder. Sobhraj fled back to Nepal using Henk Bintanja's passport, then fled again to Calcutta, India, where he carried out another murder, that of an Israeli called Avoni Jacob. A bewildering series of moves followed, until he eventually returned to Thailand. By now the fuss had died down, and Sobhraj was able to bribe his way out of trouble. He soon went back to robbing and killing tourists, until the heat built up again and he returned to India in 1976, where he was finally arrested for the murder of a Frenchman.

When he was brought to trial, two of his associates testified against him. However, he was sentenced to only 12 years in prison. Once there, he began to live a life of luxury: special food, drugs and books were brought in to him, and he was free to spend his time more or less as he pleased. In 1986 he contrived a daring escape, but soon afterwards gave himself up to police in Goa. He realized that he needed to go back to prison in order to avoid being extradited to Thailand, where he would have faced the death penalty.

Finally, after 21 years in captivity (by which time, under Thai law, he could no longer be charged for his crimes), he was released from prison and deported to France. There he sold the rights to his story and enjoyed living off his notoriety. For a while, it looked as though he had actually managed to get away with murder.

However, in 2003, for reasons that remain inexplicable, Sobhraj returned to Nepal, where he was arrested. He was charged with the murders of Duparr and Tremont, and sentenced to life imprisonment. In 2004 he was convicted of the murder of Connie Jo Bronzich, an American tourist, and in 2014, he was convicted of the murder of her Canadian friend Laurent Carrière in Kathmandu in 1975.

Highway Hunters

Serial killers are essentially a product of the modern world. They flourish amid the anonymity of our cities in a way they could never have done when people lived within small, stable communities. However, from Jack the Ripper in Victorian London to Fritz Haarmann in interwar Düsseldorf and Jeffrey Dahmer in contemporary Milwaukee, the anonymous streets of the city have long been the serial killer's habitat. And with the growth of the automobile in the postwar period, a new killing ground emerged: the highway.

The anonymity of the highway made it possible for killers like Henry Lee Lucas and G.J. Schaefer to hunt down their prey for many years without being detected. They looked for hitchhikers and truck-stop hookers, the flotsam and jetsam of life, because no one knew or cared where they were in the first place. Ironically, it was precisely one of these lost souls, Aileen Wuornos, the kind of truck-stop hooker who could easily have ended up as a murder victim herself, who became one of the very few female serial killers in modern history. She turned the tables by killing the men who picked her up, rather than vice versa.

The highway hunters have a particular power to disturb us because they remind us of a truth we would rather not face: that on every freeway in the world there are many thousands of unidentified people travelling from one place to another, at any one time – people who no one is waiting up for, people whose whereabouts are unknown to their families and friends, people whose disappearance will never be noticed.

HENRY LEE LUCAS

The case of Henry Lee Lucas is one of the oddest in the annals of serial killers. He was either one of the most prolific killers ever to walk the face of the earth, or was responsible for just three murders. According to the stories he told the police during the mid-1980s, he committed between 70 and 600 murders, all over the United States. However, the only murders he can conclusively

Henry Lee Lucas

be linked to are the killing of his mother, for which he served time in the 1960s, and the murders of his 15-year-old girlfriend and an 82 year old woman who had helped the pair. These were the crimes that led to his final arrest.

Desperately Poor

Henry Lee Lucas' background was tailor-made to produce a serial killer. He was born in 1936 in the town of Blacksburg, Virginia, in the desperately poor Appalachian Mountains. He was the youngest of Viola and Anderson Lucas' nine children. Both parents were alcoholics. Viola dominated the home and provided most of the family's income by prostitution; Anderson was known as 'No Legs', having lost his lower limbs in a drunken accident.

Viola Lucas seems to have loathed her youngest child from birth. She sent him to school shoeless and, initially, wearing a dress. When the school gave him some shoes she beat him for accepting them. Later in his childhood he cut his eye with a knife while playing around; Viola let the wound fester until he had to have the eye removed and replaced by a glass one. She would also force her children to watch her having sex with her clients and her lover 'Uncle Bernie'. Lucas' father finally died of pneumonia after spending a night outside the house lying in the snow. His main contribution to his son's upbringing was to introduce him to moonshine whiskey. By the time he was ten, Henry was virtually an alcoholic.

Not long after that, Uncle Bernie and Henry's older half-brother introduced him to bestiality, which involved sexually assaulting animals and then killing them. This was an activity Henry later claimed to have taken to with relish. By his own unreliable account, his first sexual experience with a woman resulted in his first murder; aged 14, he raped and strangled an unknown girl.

Almost inevitably, Lucas drifted into crime and in June 1954 he was sentenced to six years for burglary. He twice managed to escape custody but was recaptured both times, and finally released on 2 September 1959. On release, he went to live with his sister in Tecumseh, Michigan. Soon afterwards his mother arrived and tried to persuade Henry to return with her to Blacksburg. This led to a drunken argument that culminated in Henry stabbing Viola Lucas, resulting in her death two days later. Henry was convicted of second-degree murder and served ten years in prison.

Attempted Kidnap

He was released in June 1970 but was soon rearrested for attempting to kidnap two teenage girls. Released again in 1975, he was briefly married to Betty Crawford, who divorced him, claiming he had molested her daughters. At around this time, according to his later confessions, he began his epic orgy of killing, travelling the highways of the United States in search of women to rape and murder.

In late 1976, he met Ottis Toole in a soup kitchen in Jacksonville, Florida. Toole, like Lucas, was a sexual deviant and murderer, and also prone to exaggeration. The pair became friends and, by 1978, Lucas was living in Toole's house in Jacksonville, along with Toole's young niece and nephew. Lucas fell in love with the niece, a girl with learning difficulties called Becky Powell, despite the fact she was just ten years old when they met.

From 1979 to 1981 Lucas and Toole worked together for a roofing company. If their stories are to be believed, they frequently took time off to rape and slaughter. In 1981, Becky and her brother were taken into care. Lucas and Toole snatched them back and headed out on the road. In May 1982 Lucas and Becky, now 15 and claiming to be married to Lucas, went to Texas to work for an old lady named Kate Rich. Rich's neighbours kicked the couple out of the house when they discovered that they were cashing cheques in the old lady's name.

Lucas and Powell spent some time in a religious commune nearby, before Becky decided that she wanted to go home. Lucas appeared to agree and the two left the commune. The next day, he returned alone. Three weeks later the old lady, Kate Rich, disappeared. Lucas left town the following day. He was eventually arrested on 11 June, when he returned to the commune and was found in possession of an illegal handgun.

Confession

After four days in jail Lucas began to confess, first to the murders of Becky Powell and Kate Rich, and then to a string of other crimes. He was convicted of the murders of Powell and Rich and sentenced to 75 years in prison. However, this did not halt his stream of confessions. For 18 months he kept on confessing, his body count spiralling into the hundreds. He implicated Toole in many of these murders.

By this time, detectives from all over the country were queuing up to see if Lucas would help solve any of their murder cases. More often than not Lucas was happy to oblige, particularly if they took him out of prison to tour the murder sites, put him up in hotels and bought him steaks and milk shakes. By March 1985, police across the States had cleared 198 murders as having been committed by Lucas either alone or in tandem with Toole. Alarm bells started to go off in the minds of some prosecutors when Lucas, who had never left the country, started to claim that he had committed murders in Spain and Japan, not to mention having supplied the poison used in the Jonestown Massacre.

A Fraud?

A series of newspaper articles appeared claiming that Lucas was a fraud who was using – and being used by – unscrupulous police departments looking to clear their backlogs of unsolved murders. At this point, Lucas himself began to recant his confessions. Now he claimed that, apart from his mother, he had only killed Powell and Rich.

Nevertheless, while the claim of 600-plus victims seems obviously exaggerated, there are many who still believed the Lucas and Toole may have killed as many as a hundred people. Lucas was tried again for just one murder, that of an unknown female known as 'Orange Socks'. He was found guilty and sentenced to death. However, subsequent investigation proved that this was one murder Lucas could not have committed, as he was working in Florida at the time. Lucas died of heart failure on 13 March 2001.

GERARD JOHN SCHAEFER

Gerard John Schaefer was a vicious serial killer convicted for the murders of two teenage girls but probably responsible for the slaughter of many more. While serving life imprisonment, he wrote disturbing fiction about rape, murder and his experience of living on death row. Whether his work was autobiographical or merely described the violent sexual fantasies of a demented imagination remains unclear; Schaefer himself oscillated between boasting about the body count of girls he had murdered and denying that he was a serial killer. Today, we will never know the exact truth about how many young women he murdered, for he was stabbed to death in his cell by a fellow prison inmate in 1995. At the time, the mother of one of Schaefer's victims commented: 'I'd like to send a present to the guy who killed him... I just wish it would have been sooner rather than later.'

G.J. Schaefer, as he was known, was born in 1946 in Wisconsin. Family life for the three Schaefer children, of which G.J. was the eldest, was by all accounts a misery. His father was an alcoholic and a womanizer. His parents later divorced. The young Schaefer felt that his parents, especially his father, preferred his sister to

Gerard John Schaefer

him, and showed early signs of mental disturbance, tying himself to trees to gain sexual thrills, wearing women's underclothes and fantasizing about dying.

As a young man, Schaefer had tried various vocational jobs, but was unable to find work. He attempted to join the Roman Catholic Church as a priest, and then tried to become a teacher, but was unsuccessful in both fields because of his unbalanced personality.

Divorced Due to Cruelty

Schaefer married in 1968, but two years later his wife divorced him, citing cruelty as the reason. He resolved to become a policeman and managed to find a job, even though he had failed a psychological test when he applied. He started well, but was then fired for obtaining personal information on women traffic offenders, and asking them out for dates. He relocated and found police work in Martin County, Florida, where he was soon in much more serious trouble again.

Schaefer picked up two teenage hitchhikers, Pamela Wells and Nancy Trotter, and told them that it was illegal to hitchhike in the county, which it was not. He then drove them home and said that he would drive them to the beach the next day. The following day, he drove the girls out to a swamp, drew a gun on them and bound them to tree roots with nooses around their necks. They managed to escape and contacted the police. This time, he was sentenced to a year in prison.

While awaiting trial, he picked up two more teenage hitchhikers, Georgia Jessup and Susan Place. He took them to the swamp, tied them to trees and savagely attacked them. By the time their mutilated bodies were found, Schaefer was already in jail. When police searched his mother's home, they found items belonging to several more young women and girls who had disappeared from the area: teenage hitchhikers Barbara Wilcox and Collette Goodenough; waitress Carmen Hallock; neighbour Leigh Bonadies; and schoolgirls Elsie Farmer and Mary Briscolina.

Despite the mounting evidence that Schaefer was a maniacal serial killer, he was only charged with two murders: those of Susan Place and Georgia Jessup. He was convicted in 1973, and ordered to serve two life sentences, which was more than enough to make sure that he would no longer be a threat to the public. For this reason, no other charges were brought.

Cult Fiction

For almost two decades, Schaefer languished in jail, more or less forgotten by the rest of the world. It was only when a collection of his stories was published under the title Killer Fiction that his heinous crimes were remembered. Schaefer described the stories as 'art'; however, many saw them as fictionalized descriptions of actual crimes he had committed. In addition to his tales of rape and murder, there were stories that were evidently products of his demented imagination, including one about copulating with dead bodies recently killed in the electric chair.

Not surprisingly, G.J. Schaefer was not a popular man among his fellow inmates. In 1995, prisoner Vincent Rivera, who was serving a life sentence for murder, rushed into Schaefer's cell and stabbed him in the throat and the eyes, killing him. Very few mourned his passing. However, his fiction continues to have a cult following to this day.

AILEEN WUORNOS

Aileen Wuornos has become one of the most famous of all serial killers, not because she killed a huge number of victims, nor because she killed them in an exceptionally brutal way, but because of the simple fact that she was a woman. Before her arrest, the received wisdom was that there was no such thing as a female serial killer.

This was not true. There had been many female serial killers before Wuornos, but they had mostly committed domestic murders, such as poisoning husbands or killing elderly invalids. In addition, there were a few female serial killers who had acted as accomplices to men. Wuornos, however, did not fit either pattern; she conformed more closely to the image of the reckless male gunslinger, robbing and killing victims in cold blood. It was no wonder that she sold the movie rights to her story within two days of being arrested.

Severe Burns

Of course, Hollywood would never have come calling if Wuornos had remained a petty thief instead of a murderer. Hers was the kind of life that the movies prefer to ignore. She was born Aileen Pittman in Rochester, Michigan, on 29 February 1956. Her teenage parents had split up before she was born. Her father, Leo, later became a convicted child molester. Her mother, Diane, proved unable to cope alone and, in 1960, Aileen and her brother Keith were legally adopted by Diane's parents, Lauri and Britta Wuornos. This failed to improve matters. Aged six, Aileen suffered severe burns to her face after she and her brother had been setting fires. Aged 15, she gave birth to a child, who was adopted. Her grandmother died that same year, apparently of liver failure, though Diane suspected her grandfather, Lauri, of murder.

School Drop-Out

Aileen dropped out of school early, left home and hit the streets. It was not long before she started to work as a prostitute. She had regular run-ins with the law, mostly for drink-related offences. A brief marriage was annulled after her elderly husband took out a restraining order. She then served a year in prison following a farcical attempt at armed robbery conducted while wearing a bikini. In 1986, she met lesbian Tyria Moore, who became the love of her life. Aileen and Tyria set up home together, living off Aileen's prostitution. Aileen became a notoriously belligerent individual, often in fights and always carrying a gun in her purse. In her efforts to keep Tyria happy, she supplemented her income with theft, mainly from her clients. Some time in November 1989, Aileen Wuornos went one giant step further – into murder.

Her first victim was Richard Mallory, a 51-year-old electrician whose main interests were commercial sex and drinking. Wuornos would later claim that she killed Mallory to defend herself against rape. While she went on to make this claim in regard to all her murders, in this case there may have been some truth to it, as it later emerged that Mallory had a conviction for rape.

Mallory's body was found in the woods near Daytona Beach on 13 December, shot with a .22. In June 1990, another body was found in Florida woodlands, once again shot with a .22 and this time naked. The corpse was identified a week later as David Spears. By then another victim had been found, Charles

Carskaddon. Once again he had been shot with a .22 and, like Spears, had last been seen travelling down the main Florida freeway, I-75.

The next victim was Peter Siems, who had last been seen on 7 June, heading off to visit relatives. His car was found a month later, dumped by two women whose descriptions approximately matched those of Wuornos and Moore.

Aileen Wuornos

Victims five, six and seven followed in August, September and November of 1990. All of them were shot with a .22. The police were reluctant to admit that a serial killer was at large but they finally agreed to release the sketches of the women who had dumped Peter Siems' car.

Very soon reports came in that the two women might be Aileen Wuornos and Tyria Moore. The police arrested Wuornos in a biker bar in Florida on 9 January 1991. They then found Moore at her sister's house in Philadelphia. In the interests of saving her own skin, Moore helped the police to extract a confession from Wuornos. The ploy worked. Rather than see Moore charged with murder, Wuornos confessed to six of the murders; however, she did not confess to the killing of Peter Siems, whose body has never been found to this day.

Media Circus

At that point, the media furore began. Film-makers and journalists vied for the rights to tell Wuornos' story. Some portrayed her as a monster, others presented her as a victim. The truth of the matter seems to be that Wuornos was a woman brutalized by a miserable life, but that the murders she committed were motivated by rage rather than, as she argued, by the need to defend herself.

Certainly that was the verdict of the jury that sentenced her to death on 27 January 1992. Wuornos spent the next ten years on death row while campaigners attempted to have the death penalty rescinded. However, in the end, Wuornos herself demanded that the death penalty be carried out. She was executed by lethal injection on 9 October 2002.

Maniacal Murderers

Serial killers often appear to be driven by forces beyond their control, compelled to commit crimes in a way that they themselves do not understand. However, their methods vary enormously. Some serial killers are fanatically precise and fastidious in their attempts to remain undetected. These are sometimes referred to as organized killers, and what makes them so terrifying is that, for many years, they continue to get away with murder, quite literally. Others killers, however, are the polar opposite. These are the disorganized killers: their killing lust is so frenzied that they take enormous risks, and are entirely careless about evidence. These are the maniacal murderers, berserk with bloodlust, and what makes them terrifying is the pure animal savagery of their actions, the sense that with them, humanity has been reduced to the level of the bestial.

The very nature of disorganized killers, with their propensity for leaving clues behind, means that they are often caught relatively quickly. The most extreme examples tend to come from poverty stricken countries that lack the law enforcement resources to track down a killer, particularly if, like the South American Pedro Lopez, the murderer specializes in choosing victims from the most marginalized sections of society.

However, there is no cause for complacency in richer countries. In Los Angeles and San Francisco, Richard Ramirez managed to kill dozens of people, despite being completely chaotic in his attacks. It is a sobering thought that sometimes it is a killer's disorganization that makes his or her movements so hard to predict, and that makes a killer, however crazed, so difficult to catch.

ADOLFO CONSTANZO

One of the most horrifying cult murderers of modern times was Adolfo Constanzo. Constanzo's speciality was ritually torturing and killing his victims: he ripped out their hearts and brains, boiled them and then ate the result. According to Constanzo's perverted logic, this ritual slaughter – which was derived from the Santeria and Voodoo religious practices his mother had taught him as a child – was intended to ensure him success in his career as a drug dealer. As it happened, he did prosper for some years and became a rich man, but in the end he met his fate as violently as had his unfortunate victims.

Sorcerer's Apprentice

Adolfo de Jesus Constanzo was born in 1962 to a teenage Cuban mother, and grew up in Puerto Rico and Miami. As a child, he served as an altar boy in the Roman Catholic religion, and also accompanied his mother on trips to Haiti to learn about Voodoo. As a teenager, he became apprenticed to a local sorcerer, and he began to practise the occult African religion of Palo Mayombe, which involves animal sacrifice. Later, as an adult, he moved to Mexico City and met the men who were to become his first followers: Martin Quintana, Jorge Montes and Omar Orea. He set up a homosexual ménage a trois with Quintana and Orea (calling one his 'man' and the other his 'woman') and began to run a profitable business casting spells to bring good luck, which involved expensive ritual sacrifices of chickens, goats, snakes, zebras and even lion cubs. Many of his clients were rich drug dealers and hitmen who enjoyed the violence of Constanzo's 'magical' displays. He also attracted other rich members of Mexican society, including several high-ranking, corrupt policemen, who introduced him to the city's powerful narcotics cartels.

At this time, Constanzo started to raid graveyards for human bones to put in his nganga or cauldron, but he did not stop at that: before long, live human beings were being sacrificed. Over 20 victims, whose mutilated bodies were found in and around Mexico City, are thought to have met their end in this way. Constanzo began to believe that his magic spells were responsible for the success of the cartels, and demanded to become a full business partner with one of the most powerful families he knew, the Calzadas. When his demand was rejected, seven family members disappeared; their bodies were later found with fingers, toes, ears, brains and even – in one case – the spine missing.

Not surprisingly, relations soon cooled with the Calzadas, so Constanzo made friends with a new cartel, the Hernandez brothers. He also took up with a young woman named Sara Aldrete, who became the high priestess of the cult. In 1988, he moved to Rancho Santa Elena, a house in the desert, where he carried out ever more sadistic ritual murders, sometimes of strangers, and sometimes – killing two birds with one stone, as it were – of rival drug dealers. He also used the ranch to store huge shipments of cocaine and marijuana.

However, on 13 March 1989, he made a fatal mistake. Looking for fresh meat to put in the pot, his henchmen abducted a student, Mark Kilroy, from outside a Mexican bar and took him back to the ranch. There Constanzo brutally murdered him. This time, however, the victim was no drug runner, petty crook or local peasant; he was a young man from a respectable Texan family that was determined to bring their son's killer to justice.

Under pressure from Texan politicians, police initially picked up four of Constanzo's followers, including two of the Hernandez brothers. They interrogated the men, eliciting horrifying tales of occult magic and ritual human sacrifice. Officers then raided the ranch, discovering Constanzo's cauldron, which contained various items such as a dead black cat and a human brain. Fifteen mutilated corpses were then dug up at the ranch, one of them Mark Kilroy's.

Death Pact

Constanzo meanwhile had fled to Mexico City. He was only discovered when police were called to his apartment because of a dispute taking place there. As the officers approached, Constanzo opened fire with a machine gun, but he soon realized that he was surrounded. He handed the gun to a follower, Alvaro de Leon, who was a professional hitman, and ordered Leon to open fire on him and his lover, Martin Quintana. By the time police reached the apartment, Constanzo and Quintana were dead, locked in a ghoulish embrace. De Leon, known as 'El Duby', and Sara Aldrete, Constanzo's female companion, were immediately arrested.

A total of 14 cult members were charged with a range of crimes, from murder and drug running to obstructing the course of justice. Sara Aldrete, Elio Hernandez and Serafin Hernandez were convicted of multiple murders and were ordered to serve prison sentences of over 60 years each; El Duby was given a 30-year term. The reign of Adolfo de Jesus Constanzo, high-society sorcerer and maniacal murderer, was over.

LEONARD LAKE AND CHARLES NG

As individuals, Leonard Lake and Charles Ng were both unsavoury characters. Together, they were a deadly combination. In the space of little over a year, they killed, tortured and raped at least 12 and perhaps as many as 25 people, including men, women and two baby boys. The men were mostly killed for money; the women, for sexual thrills; and the babies simply for being in the way.

Interest in Guns

Leonard Lake was a fat old hippie obsessed with survivalism. Charles Ng was a young ex-marine from Hong Kong, with an addiction to stealing. What brought the two of them together initially was an interest in guns.

The sexual enslavement of women had long been a fantasy of the older of the two men, Leonard Lake. Lake was born in San Francisco on 20 July 1946. His parents by all accounts had a dreadful relationship and, when Lake was six, his mother walked out, leaving him with his grandmother.

As a child, Lake collected mice and enjoyed killing them by dissolving them in chemicals (a technique he would later use to help dispose of his human victims). In his teens, he sexually abused his sisters.

At 18, Lake joined the US Marines and made the rank of sergeant. He served two tours in Vietnam as a radar operator. Following a spell in Da Nang, he suffered a delusional breakdown and was sent home before being discharged in 1971. He was already married by this time, but his wife left him because he was violent and sexually perverted.

Lake became part of the hippie lifestyle centred around San Francisco. He also became increasingly obsessed with the idea of an impending nuclear holocaust, and for eight years lived in a hippie commune near Ukiah, in northern California. There he met Claralyn Balazs, or 'Cricket', as he nicknamed her. A 25-year-old teacher's aide when he met her, Balazs became deeply involved in Lake's fantasies. She starred in the pornographic videos he began to make, the latest manifestation of his sexual obsession. His other obsession was with guns – part

Leonard Lake   *Charles Ng*

of his survivalist paranoia – and through a magazine advert he placed in 1981, he met Charles Ng.

Arsonist

Born in Hong Kong, Ng, or 'Charlie' as Lake called him, was a disruptive child, obsessed with martial arts and setting fires. His parents sent him to an English private school in an effort to straighten him out, but he was expelled for stealing. Next, he went to California where he attended college for a single semester before dropping out. Soon after that he was involved in a hit-and-run car crash and to avoid the consequences he signed up for the US Marines, fraudulently claiming to be a US national. It was at this time that he met Lake. They came up with a plan to sell guns that Ng would steal from a marine arsenal. However, Ng was caught stealing the guns and was sentenced to three years in prison.

When he was released in 1985, he immediately contacted Lake, who invited him to his new place, a remote cabin near Wilseyville, California, that he was renting from Balazs. He had custom-built a dungeon next to the cabin ready for his friend Charlie to come up and have fun. It is thought that by then Lake had already murdered his brother Donald and his friend and best man Charles Gunnar, in order to steal their money and, in Gunnar's case, his identity.

Over the next year Lake and Ng indulged themselves in an orgy of killing, rape and torture. Their victims included their rural neighbours, Lonnie Bond, his girlfriend Brenda O'Connor plus their baby son Lonnie Jr, and another young family, Harvey and Deborah Dubs and their young son Sean. In both cases the men and babies were killed quickly, while the women were kept alive for Ng and Lake's perverse sport. They would rape and torture the women – Lake filming the whole awful business – before putting them to death. Other victims included workmates of Ng's; relatives and friends who came looking for Bond and O'Connor; and two gay men.

Their career of evil might have gone on a lot longer if it had not been for Ng's addiction to stealing. On 2 June 1985, Ng was spotted shoplifting a vice from a San Francisco hardware store, probably for use as a torture implement. Ng ran away from the scene. Lake then appeared and tried to pay for the vice. By then, however, the police had arrived. Officer Daniel Wright discovered that Lake's car's number plates were registered to another vehicle, and that Lake's ID, in the name of Scott Stapley, was suspicious. When Wright found a gun with a silencer in the trunk of the car, he arrested Lake. Once in custody, Lake asked for a pen, paper and a glass of water. He then wrote a note to Balazs, and quickly swallowed the cyanide pills he had sewn in to his clothes. After revealing his true identity and that of Ng, he went into convulsions from cyanide poisoning and died four days later.

Kilos of Bone

Further investigation soon led the police to the Wilseyville ranch. Ng was nowhere to be seen. However, they found Scott Stapley's truck and Lonnie Bond's Honda there and, behind the cabin, they found the dungeon. Officers noticed a human foot poking through the earth, and proceeded to unearth 18 kilograms of burned and smashed human bone fragments, relating to at least a dozen bodies. (A month or so later, less than a mile away, they were to find the bodies of Scott Stapley and Lonnie Bond, stuffed into sleeping bags and buried.) They also came across a hand-drawn 'treasure' map that led them to two five-gallon pails buried in the earth. One contained envelopes with names and victim IDs suggesting that the full body count might be as high as 25. In the other pail, police found Lake's handwritten journals for 1983 and 1984, and two videotapes that showed the horrific torture of two of their victims. If there was any doubt that the missing Ng was as heavily involved as Lake, it was dispelled by these tapes, that showed Ng right there with Lake, even telling one of the victims, Brenda O'Connor: 'You can cry and stuff, like the rest of them, but it won't do any good. We are pretty – ha, ha – cold-hearted, so to speak.'

Ng, meanwhile, was on the run. He had flown to Detroit and crossed the border into Canada where he was eventually arrested. In a Canadian prison, he began an epic legal battle against extradition back to the United States on the grounds that Canada did not have the death penalty, and thus to send him back to the US would be in breach of his human rights. It was not until 1991 that he finally lost this battle and was shipped back to the States. Even that was not the end of the story. Ng managed to stretch out pretrial proceedings for another seven years at the astronomical cost to the state of $10 million. Finally, in May 1999, some 15 years after his crimes, Ng was convicted of murder and sentenced to death. To no one's surprise, Ng appealed against the verdict.

PEDRO LOPEZ

Pedro Lopez, the 'Monster of the Andes', has a claim to being the most prolific serial killer of modern times. If his own unverified estimate of 300 victims is to be taken seriously, then only Harold Shipman can rival him for the sheer number of lives brought to an untimely end.

Street Life

Pedro Lopez was born in Tolina, Colombia, in 1949, the seventh of 13 children born to a prostitute mother. At any time this would have been a hard start in life, but in 1949 Colombia was going through what became known as 'La Violencia', a time of brutal lawlessness and civil war. Pedro's mother was a tyrannical figure, but he realized from a young age that home life was preferable to being out on the streets. When Pedro was eight years old, however, that is exactly where he found himself. His mother found him making sexual advances to a younger sister and threw him out.

The first person to take him in posed as a Good Samaritan, but turned out to be a paedophile who raped Pedro repeatedly, before casting him back out on to the streets. Utterly traumatized, the boy became a feral, nocturnal being, hiding in buildings and emerging at night to scavenge for food.

He endured this existence for a year, finally ending up in the town of Bogota, where an American couple saw him begging on the streets, took pity on him and took him in. They gave him room and board and sent him to a local school for orphans. This good fortune did not last, however. Aged 12, Pedro ran away from school after breaking into the school office and stealing money. He later claimed that this was in response to a teacher at the school making sexual advances to him.

Prison Rape

Whatever the reason, Pedro Lopez was soon back on the streets again. La Violencia was over and times were a little easier. He was able to survive by a mixture of begging and petty theft, building up, in his mid-teens, to a specialization in car theft. Aged 18, he was finally arrested and sentenced to seven years in prison. After only two days there he was gang-raped by four of his fellow inmates. Lopez, however, was tired of being a victim; he constructed a homemade knife and in the following weeks succeeded in killing three of his attackers. The prison authorities, little interested in the well-being of the inmates, added on a mere two years to his sentence.

By the time of his release in 1978, Lopez was a very angry and dangerous individual, with a major grudge against society in general and women in particular – he blamed his mother for everything that had gone wrong in his life. On release, he started to take a perverse form of revenge and embarked on a two-year killing rampage. His targets were invariably young girls, mostly from Indian tribes, as he knew the authorities would be particularly uninterested in their fate. Nor did he confine himself to Colombia; his murderous spree saw him following the Andes south to Peru and Ecuador. In Peru alone he reckoned to have killed as many as a hundred girls before he was captured by Ayachuco Indians while attempting to abduct a nine-year-old girl. They were about to bury him alive when an American missionary intervened and persuaded them to hand Lopez over to the authorities. The authorities simply deported him over the border to Ecuador and let him go.

Caught

For the next year or so, Pedro Lopez moved back and forth between Ecuador and Colombia, killing with apparent impunity. The authorities did notice an increase in missing girls but generally put this down to slave traders. Then, in April 1980, there was a flash flood in the Ecuadorian town of Ambato and the bodies of four missing children were washed up. A few days later, still in Ambato, a woman named Carvina Poveda spotted Lopez in the act of trying to abduct her 12-year-old daughter. She called for help. Lopez was overpowered and handed in to the police.

Lopez started to confide in the prison priest. After a day of grisly confession, the priest had to ask to be released, as he could not stand to listen any more. The priest told the interrogators what he had learned; they put the new evidence to Lopez and he began to confess.

Daylight Murder

He told them that he had murdered a hundred girls in Colombia, at least a hundred and ten in Ecuador, and many more than that in Peru. He expressed a particular enthusiasm for Ecuadorian girls, who he said were much more innocent and trusting than Colombians and stated a preference for murdering by daylight so he could see the life leave his victims' eyes as he strangled them.

At first the police were not sure whether all this was anything more than the ravings of a madman. Preferring to be branded a monster rather than a liar, Lopez said he would show them his burial sites. He was placed in leg irons, then allowed to lead the police to a site outside Ambato, where they found the remains of 53 girls. The police had now seen more than enough to convince them that Pedro Lopez was indeed the monster he claimed to be.

Further detailed confessions allowed prosecutors to charge Lopez with having committed a hundred and ten murders in Ecuador. He was duly sentenced to life imprisonment. On his eventual release he was rearrested and deported to Colombia where he was certified insane and confined to a hospital in Bogotá. There have been media reports that he subsequently absconded and his whereabouts is uncertain. Lopez has never appeared remorseful; rather, he seems proud of his crimes: 'I am the man of the century,' he said in an interview given from his prison cell.

ALEXANDER PICHUSHKIN

In June 2006, Moscow police found a chess board with dates written on 61 of its 64 squares. Alexander Pichushkin was only too willing to explain its significance. He was trying to break the record set by the prolific Russian serial killer and cannibal, Andrei Chikatilo, who had murdered a minimum of 52 women and children and eaten their body parts. Each covered square on the board represented a victim. He was caught with just three to go before completing his horrific game. In 2007, he was convicted of 48 murders although he claimed to have been responsible for over 60 murders. His crimes were so terrible they led to a serious consideration of reinstating the death penalty.

A Childhood Accident

Alexander Pichushkin was born in 1974 in Mytishchi, a small city on the outskirts of Moscow. A year after his birth his father left.

He said himself that he had a 'difficult life' because he had never known his father. He spent much of his childhood in Bitsevsky Park (or Bitsa Park), a sprawling and densely wooded area where locals would hang out, smoke and drink alcohol.

As a young child he was known to be friendly and sociable, but early on in his young life an accident would change this. When he was four years old he fell off a swing and was struck in the forehead by the seat. The injury damaged the frontal cortex in his brain – an area that is used to regulate impulses and limit aggression. Soon after the accident he became hostile and aggressive and he was transferred to a school for those with learning disabilities. He was soon beset by bullying from children from his old school who referred to him as 'that retard'.

Encouragement from his grandfather led him to the game of chess. Pichushkin was fascinated by chess and soon became an outstanding player. He began to participate in regular exhibition games, usually against older men in Bitsa Park, with great success. He was also an animal lover – his neighbour, Svetlana Mortyakova, once found him in tears over the death of his cat. Towards the end of his school days, Pichushkin's grandfather died which came as a great blow to him and he began to drink heavily to dull the pain. Psychologists would later suggest that Pichushkin's murders were prompted by anger at his grandfather for "abandoning" him.

Around this time, he also developed a disturbing passion for filming young children and watching the footage, which allegedly gave him a feeling of superiority. Pichushkin began to take a camera with him if he knew he would come into contact with children. On one occasion, he held a child upside down by one leg and spoke into the camera: 'You are in my power now ... I am going to drop you from the window … and you will fall 15 metres to your death.'

Pichushkin was obsessed by Andrei Chikatilo. He committed his first murder while he was still a teenager during the serial killer's trial in 1992. Pichushkin pushed a boy out of a window and remembered the experience fondly. When questioned by the police, he said, 'This first murder, it's like love, it's unforgettable.'

He treated murder as a game: the 64 squares on his chessboard functioned as his motivation to achieve a set target. His life, otherwise, was very dull. He worked as a supermarket shelf-stacker and lived in an apartment with his mother near Bitsa Park. The setting was important to Pichushkin because the size of the park, spanning some ten kilometres and covered in forests, provided the ideal location for a determined serial killer to practise his art.

For Pichushkin, murder was the only change to his dull routine. He targeted elderly homeless men – similar to those he had spent his teenage years playing chess against – and lured them to his house with the offer of free vodka. He often talked to his victims about his dog as a way to befriend them. Usually they were elderly men, but when the opportunity arose, he had no qualms killing women and children. Not all of his victims were killed in this cold, calculating manner. He was motived to kill his neighbour, Valery Kulyazhov, because the man had told him 'to take away his enormous, mongrel mutt.' Pichushkin could not tolerate an insult to the one thing he loved most in the world – his dog.

Shortly after his arrest he stated that, 'In all cases I killed for only one reason. I killed in order to live … For me, life without murder is like life without food for you.'

He always attacked his victims from behind. He did not like to get blood on his clothes. Psychoanalyst Tatyana Drusinova said he was 'detached from human beings ... Human beings were no more than wooden dolls, like chess pieces, to him.'

In 2001 people began vanishing from Bitsa Park. Maria Viricheva was a shop clerk from Tatarstan. In 2001, she entered a secluded part of the forest with Pichushkin, lured by the promise of black market goods. Pichushkin grabbed her by the hair and threw her down a nine-metre deep well. Unbeknown to Pichushkin she survived the ordeal, but, unbelievably, police refused to investigate. Pichushkin was allowed to roam free and become more brazen in his attacks. Viricheva finally came forward to identify her attacker years later after his arrest for his other crimes.

In October 2005, one of Pichushkin's victims was found along one of the park's footpaths. The skull had been smashed and a vodka bottle driven into the brain. By June 2006, police had found 13 more bodies, all killed in the same way. They dubbed the killer the "Bitsa Park Maniac".

Pichushkin's last victim was Marina Moskalyova. Moskalyova had told her son of her plans to go on a date with a co-worker, and even left the man's phone number – this man's name was Alexander Pichushkin. This was the police's first major lead. Next, when they discovered the dead body of Moskalyova they also discovered her metro ticket in the pocket of her jacket. They were able to identify Pichushkin from the security cameras at the metro station walking alongside Moskalyova. Pichushkin was arrested on 15 June 2006 for Moskalyova's murder. He told police: 'I kept thinking whether to kill her or take caution. But finally I decided to take a risk. I was in that mood already.'

Soon Pichushkin was confessing to a bewildering array of crimes. Detectives checked his confessions against missing persons reports. They quizzed him on the locations of the murders and he recalled them with astounding accuracy. His victims included old men, young women and even a nine-year-old boy. Forty-three of the bodies he had disposed of by throwing them in the sewer pits of the park. He showed no hint of remorse.

His trial lasted six weeks. Like his old hero, Chikatilo, he was kept inside a glass cage for his own protection during the trial. Moscow prosecutor Yury Syomin stated, 'This is the first such case in Moscow. We are charging him with 52 murders. He insists that he killed 63, but there are no bodies, no murder weapons, no testimony, and not even records of people gone missing.'

The jury only needed three hours to make their decision. Pichushkin was found guilty of 48 counts of murder and of three counts of attempted murder. He was sentenced to life imprisonment and during his first 15 years he was to be kept in solitary confinement.

Tamara Klimova, the wife of one of Pichushkin's alleged victims, told Russian media, 'He should be handed over to the public for punishment rather than allowed to live in prison at our expense.'

Pichushkin had one last thing to say. If he had reached his goal of 64 murders, it would not have been enough.

'I never would have stopped, never. They saved a lot of lives by catching me.'

RICHARD RAMIREZ

Richard Ramirez, the 'Night Stalker', was a nightmare made flesh: the bogeyman who slips in through the windows in the middle of the night to rob, rape and murder. Throughout the summer of 1985 he had the people of Los Angeles living in terror, as he killed more than a dozen times, before a mixture of good police work and luck finally saw him captured.

Family Values

Ramirez was born on 28 February 1960 in El Paso, the city that sits right on the Mexican border of west Texas. He was the youngest of seven children of Mexican immigrants Julian and Mercedes Ramirez. It was a strict Catholic household and Julian Ramirez was a bad-tempered, physically abusive father. Richard became an increasingly disaffected loner at school, and in his teens started to spend time with his uncle Mike (Miguel).

Mike had served in Vietnam and he loved to tell his nephew about his exploits – in particular about all the women he had raped there.

He allegedly showed Richard photos of his war crimes, including ones that pictured him first raping a Vietnamese girl and then displaying her decapitated head.

Worse still, 15-year-old Richard was present when Mike shot his wife in the face, killing her.

This clearly had a pivotal influence on Ramirez' life. He dropped out of school aged 17 and devoted himself to smoking huge quantities of marijuana and listening to heavy metal music. He hung around El Paso, sometimes living with his sister Ruth, and getting involved in petty crime. He lived on junk food and carbonated drinks to such an extent that his teeth rotted and his breath was foul.

First Murder

Around the turn of the decade he moved from Texas, first to San Francisco and then to Los Angeles. There he switched his drug of choice from marijuana to cocaine, began to listen obsessively to the music of AC/DC – particularly a song called 'The Night Prowler' – and took to stealing cars to make a living. Over the next year he served two brief sentences for car theft. After he came out of prison the second time, he committed his first murder.

The victim was a 79-year-old woman named Jennie Vicow. On 28 June 1984, she was sleeping in her suburban Los Angeles apartment when Ramirez broke in. He sexually assaulted her, stabbed her to death and stole her jewellery.

It was nine months before he killed again. This time, he attacked a young woman named Maria Hernandez as she was entering her apartment. He had come armed with a gun and used it to shoot Hernandez but, miraculously, the bullet was deflected by her keys and she was simply knocked down. She then played dead as he kicked her prone body. Clearly not yet satisfied, Ramirez then went into the apartment where he found her roommate, Dayle Okazaki, and shot her dead.

Frenzy

Even this murder failed to satisfy his perverse craving and that same evening Ramirez found another victim, Tsa Lian Yu, whom he dragged from her car in the Monterey Park area and shot several times. She died in hospital the following day.

Just three days later Ramirez struck again – this time sexually abusing, but not killing, an eight-year-old girl. A week later, he attacked a couple, Vincent and Maxine Zazzara. He murdered both of them and cut out Maxine's eyes as a trophy. This double murder clearly had a particular thrill for Ramirez as, from then on, most of his assaults were on couples.

Richard Ramirez

Six weeks later, on 14 May 1985, Ramirez attacked another couple. He began by shooting 65-year-old William Doi in the head, then beat and raped his wife. However, Doi was strong enough to make it to the phone and dial the emergency number before he died, an action that may well have saved his wife's life, as Ramirez promptly fled the building.

Two weeks later, Ramirez varied his routine a little. His next victim was 42-year-old Carol Kyle, whom he raped after gagging her 11-year-old son and shutting him in a cupboard. Both of them were allowed to live, however, and Carol Kyle was able to give the police a good description of her attacker.

Ramirez' blood lust was now reaching fever pitch. He struck again the next day, attacking two sisters in their eighties, Mabel Bell and Florence Lang. He beat them with a hammer, then drew pentagrams on Bell's body and elsewhere in their apartment. They were found the following day: Mabel was dead; Florence had survived her injuries.

His next victim, three weeks later, was 29-year-old Patty Higgins, whose throat he cut. Another ten days brought another four attacks: two older victims died, while two younger women survived.

Then the final rampage began. In the course of one terrible night he killed three times and left two more victims traumatized. The first two victims were a couple in their sixties, Max and Lela Kneiding, both of whom he shot dead. That same evening he broke into a house in the Sun Valley area, where he shot dead Chainarong Khovanath as he slept, before raping and beating his wife Somkind, and then tying her up while he raped her eight-year-old son.

Night Stalker

At this stage police were still loath to admit that a serial killer was on the loose. However, when, on 6 August, Ramirez shot a couple in their home, non-fatally, then followed up two days later by attacking another couple, this time killing the husband and raping the wife, it was clear that they had to act. A Night Stalker task force was set up, and the press was told about this new menace to the community. Ramirez responded by leaving town briefly, heading back to San Francisco, where he attacked his next victims, the improbably named Peter Pan and his wife, once again killing the man and raping his wife, and once again leaving satanic symbols there.

He then went to Los Angeles and, in the last week of August, struck for the last time. Once again he attacked a couple. Fortunately, the man, 29-year-old William Carns, survived, despite being shot three times. His partner Renata Gunther, who had been raped and forced to repeat after Ramirez the words 'I Love Satan', was still alert enough to spot the car he drove away in, a Toyota station wagon. Another local resident had also noticed the car and had taken down the registration number.

Soon afterwards, the police found the car abandoned; luck was on their side and they managed to find a fingerprint left on the vehicle. It just so happened that the fingerprint database in Sacramento had been updated and put on to computer only a few days before. There was an instant match: the fingerprint identified petty criminal Richard Ramirez.

The next day Ramirez's photo was on the front page of every newspaper in Los Angeles. Ramirez only discovered this himself when he walked into a drugstore in east LA and saw the customers staring at him. He ran from the store, then attempted to steal a car. He was swiftly apprehended by angry locals, and the police arrived only just in time to save him from being lynched.

At trial Ramirez was reportedly ready to confess all, but was persuaded by his defence team to plead not guilty. Despite this, he adopted an aggressive pose throughout the trial, flashing a pentagram drawn on his hand at photographers, and addressing the court with remarks such as 'You maggots make me sick. I am beyond good and evil.' Unsurprisingly, he was found guilty of 13 counts of murder and sentenced to death. On being told of the verdict, he said: 'Big deal. Death always went with the territory. See you in Disneyland.'

Ramirez became the focus of a cult following. Women literally fought each other outside the courtroom for his favours. One of them, Doreen Lioy, married him in October 1996 in San Quentin Prison. Ramirez appealed against his sentence, an appeal that was still pending when he died of lymphoma in 2013.

DAVID PARKER RAY

Truth or Consequences, New Mexico was once a place of relaxation. The first people to enjoy its hospitality arrived over one hundred years ago. They were there to soak in the Geronimo Springs at John Cross Ranch. It would be the first of several dozen spas to be built around the heated groundwater that continues to bubble up in this city of less than 8,000 souls. The entire community was built around this natural phenomenon. Anyone who wonders how important it once was to the local economy need look no further than the city's original name: Hot Springs.

The city became Truth or Consequences in 1950, when the popular radio quiz show of that name offered to broadcast from the first community to rename itself after the show. It was all good fun.

The first indication of David Parker Ray's crimes came on 26 July 1996, when the sheriff's office in Truth or Consequences received a call from a young Marine. On the previous day he had argued with his wife Kelly Van Cleave and he had not seen or heard from her since. The anxious husband received only advice.

His wife had been gone such a short time that she could not be considered as a missing person. Based on past experience, the office had every reason to believe that Kelly would turn up.

Sure enough, the young man's wife returned home on the very next day. She had been brought back by an employee of nearby Elephant Butte State Park, where she had been found wandering in a dazed and incoherent state.

Kelly could account for only a few of the many hours she had been missing. After the fight with her husband, she remembered going to a friend's house. This was followed by trips to a number of bars, the last of which was the Blue Waters Saloon. It was there that Kelly ordered a beer, her first drink of the evening.

She soon began to feel dizzy. The sensation was not dissimilar to being drunk, but something was not quite right. Kelly could recall little else from this point onwards, though she was certain that an old friend, Jesse Ray, had offered to help. Those missing hours brought an end to Kelly's marriage. Her husband could never accept her disappearance, or her claim that she could not remember what had happened.

Nightmares

Jesse Ray might have been able to help... but she could not be found. Kelly soon left Truth or Consequences, never to return. She would never see Jesse again.

Now separated, Kelly began to suffer from nightmares. The horrifying images were remarkably consistent – she saw herself being tied to a table, being gagged with duct tape and having a knife held to her throat. Nothing quite made sense so Kelly never did report her strange experience to the authorities. All the sheriff's office at Truth or Consequences had on file was a seemingly trivial phone call from a distrusting husband. They could not have known that the woman who walked through their door on 7 July 1997 was bringing information that was related to Kelly's disappearance.

The woman had come to report that she had not heard from her 22-year-old daughter, Marie Parker, for several days. This time, there would be an investigation. In such a small city, it was not difficult to track the young woman's movements. Marie had last been seen on 5 July at the Blue Waters Saloon. She had been drinking with Jesse Ray. Jesse told the authorities that Marie had been drinking heavily so she had driven her home, but she had not seen her since.

But Jesse was not the only person that Marie had been drinking with on the night of her disappearance. Roy Yancy, an old boyfriend, had also been raising a glass at the Blue Waters Saloon. A Truth or Consequences boy born and raised, there was nothing in Roy's past to make the community proud.

As a child he had been part of a gang that had roamed Truth or Consequences strangling cats, poisoning dogs and tipping over gravestones, acts that led the city to cancel that year's Hallowe'en festivities. He had also received a dishonourable discharge from the navy.

Marie might well have been in the company of an unsavoury character, but the Truth or Consequences sheriff's office saw nothing unusual about her disappearance. After all, the city was known for its transient population. They were all too ready to accept someone's hazy recollection of a girl accepting a ride out of the city. It was a typical story.

At around this time a new woman arrived in the small city. Cindy Hendy's history was anything but enviable. A victim of sexual abuse, she had been molested by her stepfather before being turned out on the street at the age of 11. Cindy had been a teenage mother, but only in the sense that she had given birth – other people had taken on the job of raising her daughter. When she arrived in Truth or Consequences, Cindy was on the run from a drugs charge. Several months earlier, she had supplied cocaine to an undercover agent. She was a violent woman with a short fuse, so it was not long before she found herself in the local jail. Days later she was sent out to Elephant Butte Lake on a work-release programme. It was there that she first met David Parker Ray, the father of her friend Jesse.

He was a quiet, though approachable and friendly man. Ray had been a neglected child. Unloved by his mother, his only real contact with his drifter father came in the form of periodic drunken visits. These invariably ended with the old man leaving behind a bag of pornographic magazines that portrayed sadomasochistic acts. His adult life was one of many marriages and many jobs. He had lived a transient life before 1984, when he settled down with his fourth wife in Elephant Butte. After acquiring a run-down bungalow on a little piece of property, Ray supported them by working as an aircraft engine repairman.

By 1995, his wife had left him. The fourth Mrs Ray would be the final Mrs Ray, but she was not his last companion. In January 1999, Cindy Hendy moved into Ray's bungalow. It mattered little that he was two decades older because the 38-year-old had met her soulmate – someone who, like herself, was obsessed with sadomasochistic sex.

Lonely newcomer

Cindy had been living with Ray for just one month when, on 16 February, she invited Angie Montano over for a visit. Angie, a single mother, was new to Truth or Consequences, and was eager to make friends. She had come to the wrong place, because she was blindfolded, strapped to a bed and sexually assaulted. Ray and Cindy's sadistic tastes went beyond rape. Angie was stunned by cattle prods and various other devices that Ray had made himself. After five days, Angie managed to get Ray to agree to her release. He drove her to the nearest highway and let her out. As luck would have it, she was picked up by a passing off-duty police officer. Angie shared her story with him, but she would not agree to making an official report. Just as Kelly Van Cleave had done four years earlier, Angie left Truth or Consequences, never to return.

Even as the assaults on Angie Montano were taking place, Cindy's mind was sometimes elsewhere. Though her 39th birthday had only just passed, she was about to become a grandmother. She made plans to attend the birth in her old home town of

Monroe, Washington, but before she could go she needed to find a sex slave for Ray, someone who would meet his needs in her absence.

On 18 March, they drove through the streets of Albuquerque in Ray's motorhome, where they came upon Cynthia Vigil. She was a prostitute, so it was not difficult to get her into the vehicle, nor was it hard to overpower the 22-year-old. After being bound, Cynthia was taken back to the Elephant Butte bungalow, where she was collared, chained, blindfolded and gagged. A tape was then played to her. The voice was Ray's.

'Hello, bitch. Well, this tape's gettin' played again. Must mean I picked up another hooker. And I'll bet you wonder what the hell's goin' on here.'

Those were just the first few sentences in a recording that lasted over five minutes. Ray went on to describe how he and his 'lady friend' were going to rape and torture the listener.

'The gag is necessary,' he explained, 'because after a while you're goin' to be doin' a lot of screaming.'

True to the words of the tape, Ray and Cindy tortured and raped the prostitute over the course of the next three days. The assaults had no effect on Ray's work habits. As the fourth day began, he donned his state park uniform and drove off. Cindy was charged with keeping their victim under control. But his lady friend wasn't quite up to the task. In fact, she was downright sloppy.

When Cindy left the room to prepare a lunch of tuna sandwiches, the young prostitute noticed that her abductor had left behind the keys to her chains. After releasing herself, she grabbed the phone and called the Sierra County Sheriff's Office. Before she could say a word, Cindy was back in the room, bottle in hand. She took a violent swing at the prostitute, cutting her with the breaking glass. Cynthia noticed an ice pick while she was lying on the floor. She quickly grabbed it and stabbed her abductor in the back of the neck.

It was not a lethal blow, but it was enough to give Cynthia time to get out of the house. Naked except for a dog collar and chain, she ran out of the door and down the dusty, unpaved street. She was spotted by the drivers of two cars, but they just swerved to avoid the distressed, bleeding woman.

After about a mile, she came upon a trailer home. She burst through the door and fell at the feet of a woman watching television.

Scene of the crime

Just minutes after the first interrupted call, the Sierra County Sheriff's Office received a second one. When the authorities arrived at the mobile home they heard a horrific tale of torture and assault. As Cynthia Vigil was being transported to the local hospital, the sheriff's department decided to call in the state police.

Over a dozen officers converged on Ray's bungalow, only to find that Cindy had fled.

The house was a mess, with garbage littering the floor. If there was any order, it was found in Ray's instruments of torture, which were arranged on hooks hanging from the walls of several rooms. His library included books on Satanism, torture and violent pornography. There were also a number of medical books, which presumably enabled him to carry out many of his fantasies.

The hunt was now on for Ray and Cindy. The chase was as short as it was easy. The couple had not fled – instead, they were driving along the nearby roads, looking for their captive. Ray and Cindy were spotted within 15 minutes, a mere two blocks from their home. They quickly admitted that they had been looking for Cynthia Vigil, but they also came up with an implausible explanation for their actions. The abduction of the prostitute had been a humanitarian act, claimed Ray and Cindy. Her confinement had been nothing more than an effort to help the young woman kick her addiction to heroin.

The story fooled no one. Ray and Cindy were arrested and taken into custody. As the investigation of Ray's property began, the state law enforcement officials realized that they did not have the resources to deal with their discoveries. Lieutenant Richard Libicer of the New Mexico State Police explained the situation:

> *I think it's safe to say that nothing that was inside that house was anything any of us had experienced before – or come across before – except maybe in a movie somewhere. It was just completely out of the realm of our experience.*

The assortment of shackles and pulleys and other instruments of torture inside the bungalow appeared almost mundane compared to what was discovered inside a padlocked semi-trailer that was parked outside.

What Ray described as the 'Toy Box' contained hundreds of torture devices. Many of them, such as a machine that was used to electrocute women's breasts, had been designed and built by the former mechanic. At the centre of this horror was a gynaecology table. Cameras were installed, so that the women could see what was happening to them. Ray had also videotaped his assaults, including the one involving Kelly Van Cleave. She had supposedly been found wandering by a state park official – but the state park official was David Parker Ray.

The videotapes were a revelation. For a start, they linked Jesse Ray to her father's crimes. Kelly's evidence also proved useful, but the most damning testimony came from Cindy Hendy.

Within days of her arrest, the 39-year-old turned on her boyfriend. She told the investigators that Ray had been abducting and torturing women for many years. What is more, she said, Ray had told Cindy that his fantasies had often ended in murder, the bodies dismembered and dumped in Elephant Butte Lake.

Subsequent searches of the lake and the surrounding countryside revealed nothing, but the police remain convinced that Ray has killed at least one person. Cindy also confirmed that Jesse had participated in at least some of the abductions. She added that she often worked in tandem with Roy Yancy.

Soft centre

Despite his tough demeanour, Roy caved in when he was arrested. He told the police that he and Jesse had drugged Marie Parker, the young woman who had gone missing three years earlier. They had taken her to Elephant Butte, where she was tortured. When Ray tired of her, he instructed Roy to kill the woman who had once been his girlfriend.

The body was never found.

Roy Yancy pleaded guilty to second-degree murder and was sentenced to 20 years in prison.

After pleading guilty to kidnapping Kelly Van Cleave and Marie Parker, Jesse Ray received a nine-year sentence.

Facing the possibility of 197 years in prison, Cindy Hendy made a deal with the prosecutors. After pleading guilty to her crimes against Cynthia Vigil she received a 36-year sentence, with a further 18 years on probation.

Even Ray appeared to co-operate with the authorities, but only to the extent of describing his fantasies. He denied that he had abducted or murdered anyone. Any sadomasochistic activities had been between consenting adults. 'I got pleasure out of the woman getting pleasure,' he told one investigator. 'I did what they wanted me to do.'

Ray faced three trials for his crimes against Kelly Van Cleave, Cynthia Vigil and Angie Montano. He was found guilty in the first trial, but part of the way through the second he too made a deal. Ray agreed to plead guilty in exchange for Jesse's release. The case concerning Angie Montano was never heard because she had died of cancer.

On 30 September 2001, David Parker Ray received a 224-year sentence for his crimes against Kelly Van Cleave and Cynthia Vigil. In the end, Ray did not serve so much as a year. On 28 May 2002 he slumped over in a holding cell, killed by a massive heart attack.

'Satan has a place for you. I hope you burn in hell forever,' Cynthia Vigil's grandmother had once yelled at him.

One wonders whether the words meant anything to Ray. The one sign he had put up in his 'Toy Box' read: 'SATAN'S DEN'.

SERHIY TKACH

Short in stature, a quiet man who shied away from eye contact, Serhiy Tkach didn't much look like a murderer, yet for a quarter of a century he took one life after another. It's possible that he was the most prolific serial killer in Ukrainian history. After he was caught, Tkach would happily tell anyone who would listen that his victims numbered over one hundred. This was no confession, but a boast. Tkach was, and remains, proud of the murders he committed.

Serhiy Tkach was born on 12 September 1952 in Kiselyovsk, a Russian city that was then a part of the Soviet Union. By all accounts he did well academically, though he wasn't much interested in higher learning. After fulfilling his compulsory military service, Tkach continued his studies briefly in order to become a police officer. Upon graduation, he became a criminal investigator in Kemerovo, an industrial city in the central Soviet Union. However, what looked to be a long, successful career in law enforcement ended abruptly when Tkach was caught committing fraud. He was only able to avoid prison by writing a letter of resignation.

According to Tkach, he killed for the first time in 1980, not long after his exit in disgrace from the police department. A pleasant, pastoral afternoon, fuelled by numerous bottles of wine, turned horrific when the then 27-year-old grabbed a young woman, dragged her into the bushes and strangled her. Rape, he told one reporter, was his intent; the murder had taken place only because he was fearful that his victim might somehow escape before he'd completed the assault.

Into the cold

Tkach never identified the woman by name, saying only that she was a former schoolmate whom he had dated on and off for nine years. He added that, in all that time, the two had not had sexual relations. Tkach claimed that on the day of her death, the unnamed woman had slapped his face at the mere suggestion.

'Do you want to know why I killed?' he asked one journalist. 'My main motive was revenge!'

After he returned home, Tkach called the police to report his crime, but was irritated when the officer on the other end of the line refused to identify himself.

'I was going to tell him where to find the corpse,' Tkach told investigators pursuing the case. 'I was going to help my former colleagues, but changed my mind.'

With the loss of his respected position in law enforcement, Tkach became a man adrift. The former criminal investigator worked in mines, on farms and as a low-paid factory worker. He moved from one city to another, leaving a trail of cold bodies in his wake.

Tkach was as meticulous as he was calculating. He was always careful to strip his victims of their jewellery and clothing, some of which he would keep as a trophy. Tkach used his police training in making certain that no fingerprints or traces of semen would be left behind. So as to lend the impression that his murders had occurred far away, he left the bodies close to roads and railways.

It's likely that the most of the murders took place in Ukraine. He killed in the cities of Zaporizhia, Kharkov and, finally, in Dnipropetrovsk, where he lived his final years as a free man.

The vast majority of Tkach's known victims were between 9

and 17 years of age, a fact that has led to doubts about the story of his first killing. His final victim, a nine-year-old identified in the media only as 'Kate', was the daughter of one of Tkach's friends. The girl had been playing with four other children one August 2005 day when she was grabbed. Tkach drowned the girl and, as he had with so very many others, left the body to be found.

Zeroing in on a child whom he had known and carrying out the abduction in front of her friends was uncharacteristically sloppy. Tkach pushed his luck even further by attending the little girl's funeral. He was recognized immediately by her playmates. The former criminal investigator would later express regret that he hadn't bothered to kill them as well.

Tkach was soon dubbed 'The Pologovsky Maniac' after the area of Dnipropetrovsk he had called home. News of his crimes came as a shock to neighbours. Known as a former criminal investigator, the killer had a certain stature within the immediate community. While he was a bit of a loner, and a man of few words, these qualities only added to Tkach's reputation as someone who was highly intelligent. True, Tkach had two failed marriages in his past, but he appeared for all the world to be a devoted husband to wife number three. Unlike so many men in his neighbourhood, he never said a negative word about women. As far as anyone knew, he'd never so much as raised a hand against his wife and four children.

No remorse

More than two years passed before Tkach was put on trial. Much of the delay had to do with the significant challenges that faced investigators.

It wasn't that they had no experience of investigating serial killers – the previous decade, Anatoly Onoprienko, 'The Beast of Ukraine', had been convicted of 52 murders – but with Tkach, the number of victims looked to be much higher. What's more, the Pologovsky Maniac's killing spree had lasted five times longer and stretched to hundreds of miles.

There were also legal issues that needed attention. Over the decades, nine innocent men were tried and sentenced for murders that Tkach committed. One of the convicted had committed suicide in prison.

Finally, there were the questions about Tkach's sanity. It beggared belief that anyone in his right mind could commit such horrible acts. Psychiatrists, however, were unanimous in their opinion that Tkach was a sane man. Though he routinely consumed a litre of vodka before each rape and murder, all were convinced that he'd been fully aware of the crimes he had been committing.

Even before the lengthy investigation truly got under way, Tkach began taunting the police. At his arrest, he told officers that he had been expecting them for years, adding that they should have figured things out much sooner.

In interviews with the press Tkach painted those investigating his case as lazy. 'The police couldn't be bothered exhuming bodies,' he said, 'they'd rather I write a letter of confession. I've long laughed at them!'

When it finally began, the trial lasted almost all of 2008.

Speaking from a cage within the courtroom, Tkach demonstrated that the memories of his victims remained fresh in his mind. Twenty-eight years after his first murders, he was able to recall in detail each victim, and the manner in which he'd hunted them down.

Tkach expressed no remorse – not for his victims, not for the wrongly accused. He defended his actions with the claim that the killings had been committed for no other reason than to expose the police as a group of bumbling incompetents. Yet, he would also describe himself frequently as a beast, a creature who not only deserved, but desired the death penalty.

Ultimately, Tkach would be disappointed in his wish for a quick end to his life. Ukraine having abolished capital punishment, Tkach was sentenced to life in prison for the murders of 36 of the more than one hundred girls and women that he claimed to have deprived of life. 'No one has been able to determine the motives for his actions,' declared Judge Serhiy Voloshko after delivering his verdict.

Christmas Day 2008 marked the first full day of his sentence, but to Tkach the date meant nothing.

'I do not believe in God or the Devil,' he'd declared. Perhaps not, but to many his actions were clear evidence of the existence of the latter.

Paedophile Killers

For many years paedophilia was a subject too terrible even to be mentioned. It was the crime whose name we dared not speak. Now, in our more open times, we acknowledge its existence, but one of the effects of this has been to terrify us. The paedophile has become the bogeyman of modern times: he is somewhere out there, ready to steal our children, to rape and murder them. Our terror is such that sometimes we imagine we are experiencing an epidemic of paedophilia; thankfully, this is not the case. The number of abductions and murders of children has remained at a stable level for decades.

That said, paedophile killers are the ones, out of all the different types of serial murderers, who perhaps strike most fear. There is something particularly inhuman about murderers who rape, torture and kill innocent young children, something that as adults we find especially unbearable. Their crimes are difficult to forget, and their names live on in infamy: John Wayne Gacy, the killer clown from Chicago; Andrei Chikatilo, the cannibal of the Ukraine; Marc Dutroux, the Belgian fulcrum of a paedophile ring, who starved little girls to death.

Gacy was a popular figure in his neighbourhood. He was a building contractor who employed teenage boys and performed part-time as a children's entertainer. As such, he found it easy to lure teenage boys into his world and, once behind closed doors, turned into a monster, delighting in the torture, rape and murder of his victims. Chikatilo and Dutroux forcibly abducted young girls, but were every bit as ruthless as their American counterpart. Whatever their methods, it is impossible to contemplate the actions of these men without seeing them, in the hierarchy of serial killers, as the lowest of the low.

ANDREI CHIKATILO

Andrei Chikatilo, the 'Rostov Ripper', killer of over 50 women, girls and boys, came to the attention of the world following his arrest in 1990, just as the Soviet Union was starting to break up. Indeed, had he been caught earlier it is more than likely that his name would have remained obscure. Soviet Russia liked to pretend that such crimes as serial murder were purely a product of the decadent West; we still do not know the full extent of criminality during the years of the communist regime.

Hannibal Lecter

Chikatilo was born in Yablochnoye, a village deep in the heart of rural Ukraine, on 19 October 1936. The baby was found to have water on the brain, which gave him a misshapen head and, it was later revealed, a degree of brain damage. He was also unlucky enough to be born during the period of forced collectivization imposed by Stalin, a time of terrible famine and untold suffering. According to Chikatilo's mother, Andrei had an older brother named Stepan who was kidnapped and eaten by starving neighbours during this time. It is unclear if this was actually true – there is no record of a Stepan Chikatilo ever existing – but it was certainly a tale that succeeded in traumatizing the young Chikatilo. (Thomas Harris later borrowed this awful story to explain the pathology of his fictional serial killer Hannibal Lecter.) To make matters worse, the boy's early childhood was spent during the Second World War, when the region's misery grew even worse. His father was taken prisoner during the war, then sent to a Russian prison camp on his return.

On leaving school, Chikatilo joined the army. He also joined the Communist Party, which was essential for any ambitious young person who wanted to succeed in Soviet Russia. On leaving the army, he worked as a telephone engineer and studied in his spare time to gain a university degree, which eventually allowed him to became a schoolteacher near his home in Rostov-on-Don. At the same time he married a woman named Fayina, found for him by his sister. As it emerged later, Chikatilo had lifelong problems with impotence, but he did manage to father two children.

False Alibi

Chikatilo appeared to be living a regular life. By the time his darker urges began to express themselves, he was 42, much older than most serial killers. In 1979 he chose his first victim, a nine-year-old girl called Lenochka Zakotnova. He took her to a vacant house in the town of Shakhty, attempted to rape her, failed, and then using a knife, stabbed her to death and dumped her body into the Grushovka River. She was found there on Christmas Eve. Luckily for Chikatilo – who was questioned as a suspect in the case but was given a false alibi by his wife – a known local rapist

Alexander Kravchenko was beaten into confessing to the crime and put to death.

Nevertheless, evidence of Chikatilo's true nature was starting to leak out and he was fired from his teaching job for molesting boys in the school dormitory. His party membership stood him in good stead, however, and he was soon given a new job as a travelling procurement officer for a factory in Shakhty. The job involved plenty of moving around the area and thus plenty of opportunity to kill. His preferred method was to approach

Andrei Chikatilo

Topfoto

his victims at a train or bus station and lure them into nearby woodland to kill them.

He started in earnest in 1982 with the murder of 17-year-old Larisa Tkachenko, a girl known locally for exchanging sexual favours for food and drink. Chikatilo strangled her and piled dirt into her mouth to muffle her screams. He later claimed that his first killing had upset him, but that this second one thrilled him. In June 1982 he killed his next victim, 13-year-old Lyuba Biryuk, cutting out her eyes, an act that became his trademark.

Increasing Savagery

Over the next year he killed six more times, two of the victims young men. What the killings had in common was their increasing savagery and the removal of body parts, particularly the genitals. It is believed that Chikatilo ate the parts he removed in a hideous echo of his brother's fate, however, he himself only confessed to 'nibbling on them'.

The murders attracted much police concern, but the Soviet media was not permitted to publicize the existence of a maniacal killer on the loose. In the single month of August 1984, eight victims were found. The only clue the police had was that, judging by the semen found on the bodies of some of the more recent victims, the killer's blood group was AB.

Soon afterwards, in late 1984, Chikatilo was arrested at a railway station where he was importuning young girls. He was found to have a knife and a length of rope in his bag but, because his blood group was A, not AB, he was released. This discrepancy has never been explained.

Released by the police, Chikatilo simply carried on killing. Dozens more innocents lost their lives over the next five years. In 1988, he claimed eight lives and in his last year of freedom, 1990, he killed nine more people. By then a new detective, Issa Kostoyev, had taken over the case.

Kostoyev hit on a strategy of flooding the train and bus stations with detectives, and eventually the plan paid off. Immediately after murdering his final victim, 20-year-old Svetlana Korostik, Chikatilo was spotted, perspiring heavily and apparently bloodstained, at a station. A detective took his name and, when it was realized that he had previously been a suspect, he was arrested. After ten days in custody he finally confessed to 52 murders, more than the police had been aware of. He was arrested and brought to trial in April 1992.

Locked inside a cage to protect him from victims' relatives, Chikatilo was a shaven-headed madman who ranted and raved in the courtroom. Found guilty, on 15 February 1994, he was executed by a single bullet to the back of the head.

MARC DUTROUX

Every serial killer leaves a trail of destruction, not only of victims whose lives are destroyed, but also of whole networks of families, friends and loved ones. In the case of the Belgian serial killer Marc Dutroux, however, the havoc he wrought had even wider repercussions. His crimes traumatized the entire nation, provoked the biggest demonstrations ever seen in the country and caused the resignations of several government ministers. For not only was Dutroux a paedophile and a murderer, but he was linked

Paedophile Killers

to a paedophile ring that included many people in positions of authority.

Homosexual Prostitute

Marc Dutroux was born in Brussels, Belgium's capital city, on 6 November 1956. He was the eldest of six children born to Victor and Jeanine Dutroux. Both parents were teachers; Marc later claimed that they frequently beat him. However, Dutroux's statements on this or any other matter must be regarded with extreme caution. What we do know is that the couple split in 1971, when Dutroux was 15. Soon afterwards he left home, drifted into petty crime and, according to some press accounts, became a homosexual prostitute.

By the time he was 20, Dutroux had found a trade as an electrician. He had married his first wife and had two children with her, before she divorced him on the grounds of infidelity and violence. One of the women with whom he had had extra-marital affairs was Michele Martin, who later became his second wife. She evidently shared his darker sexual predilections.

In 1989, the pair were both convicted of child abuse, jointly abducting five girls for Dutroux to rape. Dutroux was sentenced to 13 years in prison but was released for good behaviour after serving only three years inside. This was despite Dutroux's mother writing to the prison authorities at the time to say that, during supervised outings from prison to visit his grandmother, Dutroux had terrified the old lady by making an inventory of her possessions. The prison authorities had never replied to Madame Dutroux's letters.

Prior to going to prison, Dutroux had become involved in various criminal enterprises ranging from mugging to drug dealing. On his release, he made no effort to find work; instead, the first thing he did was to build a dungeon underneath a house in the town of Charleroi, one of several houses he had bought with his criminal gains. The dungeon was to be used not only for the abuse of children but also to film that abuse; the videos would be sold to a network of paedophiles who would pay vast sums of money for this sort of material.

As with so many serial killers, it is quite possible that Dutroux is guilty of more crimes than we are aware of. It seems unlikely that his dungeon was unused for three years. However, the first atrocity we know of took place on 24 June 1995 when two eight-year-old girls, Julie Lejeune and Melissa Russo, were abducted from near their homes in Liege, Belgium. They were taken to Dutroux's dungeon, where they were kept as sexual playthings and almost certainly abused by the members of a paedophile ring.

Two months later, Dutroux and an accomplice Bernard Weinstein abducted two teenage girls, An Marchal and Eefje Lambreks, from the seaside town of Ostend. They were taken to Weinstein's house and raped by both men. At some point both girls were killed, and then for unknown reasons Dutroux also killed Weinstein. He buried all three bodies under a shed in the garden.

Starved to Death

Meanwhile the two children were still alive in the Charleroi dungeon. The police received a tip-off about Dutroux, and called at the house; however, during their search they failed to notice the dungeon, even though they had been specifically told of its existence. Then, in December 1995, Dutroux was sentenced to four months in prison for car theft. When he left for prison he told Michele Martin to feed the two girls. Almost unbelievably, she failed to do this. Even though she visited the house regularly to feed Dutroux's dogs, she claimed to have been too scared to go down into the cellar to feed the girls. They starved to death.

When Dutroux came out of prison he found their dead bodies, put them in a freezer for a while, and then buried them in the

Marc Dutroux

garden of another of his houses, in Sars-la-Buissiere. On 28 May, he kidnapped Sabine Dardenne, aged 14, and took her to the dungeon. He told her that he was rescuing her from a paedophile gang that was responsible for kidnapping her and was awaiting a ransom from her family. As she recorded in her diary, he then raped her around 20 times. After 72 days in the dungeon, on 9 August, she was joined by Dutroux's latest victim, Laetitia Delhez, aged 12.

This time, however, a witness noticed a suspicious car close to where Delhez was abducted. The car belonged to Dutroux and, on 13 August the police arrested Dutroux and Martin at the house in Sars-la-Buissiere. Two days later, they raided the Charleroi house and found the dungeon. They brought out Dardenne and Delhez alive. Over the next few weeks, Dutroux insisted that he was merely a pawn in a much wider conspiracy. As the nation looked on in horror, he led the police to the bodies of his five victims.

That horror turned to anger as the prosecution of the case dragged on endlessly, fuelling speculation that it was being deliberately sabotaged by paedophiles in the higher echelons of Belgian society. The lead prosecutor in the case was then suddenly removed from his job. The Belgian people responded by mounting a huge demonstration, complaining at the authorities' corruption.

Two years later, Dutroux briefly escaped custody, further angering the public. This episode forced the resignation of two government ministers. Even so, it was another six years before the case at last came to trial, in March 2004. Dutroux tried to blame his accomplices for everything, but the testimony of the surviving victims, particularly Sabine Dardenne, incriminated him utterly. In June 2004 Dutroux was found guilty of murder and sentenced to life in prison without the possibility of parole. Michele Martin was sentenced to 30 years for her unspeakable cruelty in abetting Dutroux and letting the two girls starve to death.

JOHN WAYNE GACY

Even by comparison with his fellow serial killers, John Wayne Gacy, 'the killer clown' has become something of an icon of pure evil. This is partly to do with the way he dressed up as a clown to entertain children at parties near his suburban Chicago home – what more sinister notion could there be than that beneath the clown's make-up lies a sex killer? And partly it is because of the sheer enormity of his crime: 33 young men raped and murdered, almost all of them buried beneath his suburban house.

John Wayne Gacy was born on 17 March 1942, St Patrick's Day, the second of three children born to Elaine Robinson Gacy and John Wayne Gacy Sr.

He grew up in a middle-class district of northern Chicago, and was raised as a Catholic. His childhood was largely uneventful. Look a little closer, though, and there were troubles. John Gacy Sr was a misanthropic man who frequently took out his anger on his son through physical beatings and verbal abuse. John Gacy Jr in turn became very close to his mother. Aged 11, he sustained a nasty accident when he was struck on the head by a swing. It caused him to have regular blackouts during his teens. During his teenage years he also complained of heart problems, though this seems likely to be just a symptom of a lifelong tendency to hypochondria – whenever he was under pressure he would claim to be on the brink of a heart attack.

Gacy did poorly in high school, left without graduating and headed for Las Vegas in a bid to make his fortune. Instead, he ended up working in a mortuary, where he showed an unhealthy interest in the corpses. He then returned to Chicago and began attending business college. While there, he discovered his considerable ability as a salesman; he was able to talk people into anything.

Model Citizen

In 1964, Gacy married Marlyn Myers, a woman he had met through work and whose father had a string of Kentucky Fried Chicken franchises. Gacy decided to join the family business and became a restaurant manager. The couple had a child and Gacy became extremely active on the local charity and community group circuit around their new home in Waterloo, Iowa.

All this came to an end in May 1968, when Gacy was charged with raping a young employee named Mark Miller. Gacy was sentenced to ten years for sodomy and his wife promptly divorced him.

Good Behaviour

He was released from prison after just 18 months, thanks to his good behaviour while inside. His father had died while he was in prison, but now his mother – to whom he had always been close – stood by him and helped him to set up in business again. He bought a new house in the Chicago suburbs and established himself as a building contractor. In June 1972 he remarried, this time to divorcee Carole Hoff. Carole and her two daughters moved into Gacy's house and the family soon became popular in their neighbourhood. Gacy would give parties with Western or Hawaiian themes and was active in local Democratic politics.

Court Case

Carole Hoff was aware of Gacy's past but under the impression that he had put it all behind him. This was far from true. In fact, just before they married, Gacy had been charged with sexually assaulting a minor, but the case had collapsed when his accuser failed to come to court. However, rumours soon began to circulate about Gacy's conduct with the teenage boys he liked to employ in his business. By 1975, his marriage was definitely deteriorating. Carole was disturbed to find homosexual pornography around the house. Gacy refused to apologize and even told her he preferred

John Wayne Gacy

men to women. The couple divorced in 1976. It emerged that throughout their marriage Gacy had been picking up strangers in Chicago's gay bars and had carried out several murders, burying the bodies under the house. Neighbours had even complained about the terrible smell.

Now that his marriage was over, Gacy gave full vent to his lust for killing. He developed a modus operandi. Victims, either picked up on the streets or chosen from his work force, would be lured back to the house and given alcohol and marijuana. Gacy would then offer to show them a magic trick. The victim would be asked to put on a pair of handcuffs, and would then find out that this was no trick: the handcuffs were all too real and they were now in Gacy's power. Gacy would proceed to torture his victims before finally killing them by strangling them to death while raping them.

Clown Visits

Time and again, Gacy got away with it. His neighbours suspected nothing, although they persistently complained about the smells coming from his house. He carried on giving parties and started dressing up as 'Pogo the Clown' to visit sick children in hospitals. He became such a valued member of the local Democratic Party that he had his photograph taken shaking hands with the then First Lady, Roslyn Carter.

Finally, in 1978, his secret life began to catch up with him. In February of that year he abducted a young man called Jeffrey Rignall, chloroformed him, raped and tortured him and then, oddly, dumped him in a park rather than killing him. Rignall went to the police who showed little interest, but, acting alone, he managed to track down his abductor and made an official complaint that was just starting to be investigated late that summer.

House Search

Gacy had still not been charged with anything when, on 16 October, a 15-year-old boy called Robert Piest went missing. His parents discovered that he had been going to meet John Wayne Gacy about a job. Gacy pleaded ignorance but the investigating officer decided to press ahead with a search of Gacy's house. They discovered an array of suspicious objects: handcuffs, pornography, drugs and so forth. They also noted the terrible smell. Gacy was confronted with this evidence and eventually confessed to having carried out a single murder. The police returned to the house and began to dig. Soon they realized there was not one victim but dozens. In all, 28 bodies were found around the house; the five most recent victims had been dumped in nearby rivers, as Gacy had run out of burial space.

Charged with 33 counts of murder, Gacy entered a plea of insanity. However, the jury found it hard to believe that a man who dug graves for his victims in advance was the victim of uncontrollable violent impulses, so he was duly sentenced to death. While in prison he became a grotesque celebrity: credulous admirers were able to call a premium-rate number to hear his refutation of the charges against him. He gave frequent interviews and showed admirers his paintings. Towards the end of his time on death row, he began to claim that he had not killed after all, but had been the victim of a mysterious conspiracy. All to no avail, however. On 10 May 1994 he was put to death by lethal injection.

Psycho Snipers

Most serial killers like to get close to their victims, their motivation often a sexual lust. However, there are a few who have a very different modus operandi, one that keeps them well away from their victims. These are the psycho snipers, the men (and they are always men) who take lives without their victims ever even knowing who shot them. For that reason, although they do not rape and torture their victims, they are in some ways the most terrifying of all killers, for what could be more frightening than knowing that as you go about your daily business, shopping or pumping gas into you car, a killer might have you in his sights, ready to blow you away in an instant, on a random whim?

Such is the menace of a psycho sniper, and so difficult are they to catch, that they can virtually bring a city to a total halt. Certainly that is what the most famous snipers did: David Berkowitz had parts of New York City under a virtual curfew during the long, hot summer of 1977. A quarter century later, in October 2002, John Muhammad and his sidekick John Malvo brought the same terror to the suburbs of Washington DC, all the more traumatic as it came just months after the events of 9/11.

These are the hardest serial killers to understand. The motivation of sex killers, while repugnant, is at least clear; what brings a man to shoot down strangers from a distance seems unfathomable. Both Berkowitz and Muhammad may have been found legally sane, but theirs, surely, are acts of the purest madness.

DAVID BERKOWITZ

For just over a year the killer known as the 'Son of Sam' terrorized New York City. He was a lone gunman who killed without warning or apparent reason; his victims were young women and couples, shot dead as they sat in their cars or walked down the street. The terror intensified when the killer began to leave notes for the police and to write to the newspapers – strange, rambling letters in which he referred to himself as the 'Son of Sam'. For a while this killer achieved demonic status in the popular imagination, but when he was finally caught he turned out to be a seemingly ordinary individual named David Berkowitz, a 23-year old native New Yorker.

For the first 20 or so years of his life, David Berkowitz was not someone people took a lot of notice of. He was born on 1 June 1953 and was immediately given up for adoption by his birth mother, Betty Falco. His adoptive parents, Nathan and Pearl Berkowitz, were quiet people who kept to themselves. David grew into a big, awkward boy who found it hard to make friends. His adoptive mother tragically died of pancreatic cancer when David was 14.

Mother's Death

His mother's death deeply affected him and his previously good grades in school started to slip. Then his father married again, to a woman who did not take to David. In 1971, his father and stepmother moved to a retirement community in Florida, leaving David in New York. He responded by joining the army, where he remained for three years, learning to become an expert marksman along the way. It was also during this time that David, who was extremely awkward with women, had his only sexual experience, with a Korean prostitute who left him with a venereal disease.

Violent Fantasies

Berkowitz left the army in 1974, returned to New York and got a job as a security guard. Meanwhile, he was starting to nurse increasingly violent fantasies about women and his overall mental state was declining rapidly. He evidently had some awareness of this, as he wrote to his father in November 1975 that: 'The world is getting dark now. I can feel it more and more. The people, they are developing a hatred for me. You would not believe how much some people hate me. Many of them want to kill me. I do not even know these people, but still they hate me. Most of them are young. I walk down the street and they spit and kick at me. The girls call me ugly and they bother me the most. The guys just laugh. Anyhow, things will soon change for the better.'

With hindsight this was part cry for help and part warning. Berkowitz believed he was surrounded by demons urging him to kill, and he felt increasingly powerless to resist them. Finally, he snapped. At Christmas he went out armed with a knife and stabbed two young women. Both survived. Next time the demons spoke to him he was armed with a gun. In July 1976, two young women, Jody Valenti and Donna Lauria, were sitting in a car in Queens, New York when an unseen assailant approached and shot them both through the windscreen. Lauria was killed, Valenti survived.

There was not a huge reaction immediately: it was just another New York horror story. Then, three months later, in October, Berkowitz struck again. Carl Denaro and Rosemary Keenan were also sitting in a parked car when a shot rang out, hitting Denaro. The pair survived. The bullet matched the one that had killed Lauria.

A month later, Berkowitz shot his next victims, Donna DeMasi and Joanna Lomino, outside a house in Queens. Both survived, though DeMasi was left paralysed as the bullet had struck her spine. By now, police and public alike were aware that a deranged gunman was on the loose.

Berkowitz waited until the New Year before killing again. In January 1977 he shot Christine Freund dead as she sat in a car with her boyfriend John Diel. Next, in March, he shot Virginia Voskerichian dead as she walked home. A month later, he went

David Berkowitz

for a couple again. This time, both Valentina Suriani and her boyfriend Alexander Esau were killed instantly. A note was found at the scene, addressed to the policeman leading the investigation:

'Dear Captain Joseph Borrelli, I am deeply hurt by your calling me a wemon (sic) hater. I am not. But I am a monster. I am the "Son of Sam". I am a little brat. When father Sam gets drunk he gets mean. He beats his family. Sometimes he ties me up to the back of the house. Other times he locks me in the garage. Sam loves to drink blood. "Go out and kill," commands father Sam.'

The note was leaked to the press in early June and public anxiety mounted. Then, in June, Berkowitz struck again, shooting Salvatore Lupo and Judy Placido as they sat in their car. Fortunately, both survived.

More letters from the 'Son of Sam' followed, both to the police and to the press. It was a boiling hot summer but New Yorkers, especially those living in Queens, were afraid to go out. The police investigation was drowning in too much information, too little of it concrete. Among the leads they did not have time to follow up was a tip from Yonkers resident Sam Carr, who had been receiving anonymous letters about his dog, followed by his dog being shot. Carr had come up with a suspect, a neighbour called David Berkowitz.

The police did not act in time to prevent Berkowitz from striking again. In July, Robert Violante and Stacy Moskowitz parked their car, feeling safe because they were in Brooklyn, not Queens. Berkowitz shot them both, killing Moskowitz and blinding Violante.

Following this murderous assault, the police received a tip-off that a man had been seen fleeing the scene in a car that had recently received a parking ticket. A check on parking tickets given that night produced the name of David Berkowitz, among others. Cross-referencing this with the tip from Sam Carr, the police were confident they had found their man.

They staked out Berkowitz's house and found his car parked outside with a rifle lying on the front seat. When Berkowitz emerged they arrested him and he immediately confessed. Though evidently a paranoid schizophrenic, he was found sane and guilty and sentenced to 365 years in prison, a sentence he is still serving. While in prison he has become an evangelical Christian and his church maintains a website on which Berkowitz publishes his, mostly religious, thoughts. In recent years, the Spike Lee film *Summer of Sam* has reminded New York of the time when one paranoid loner held the entire city to ransom.

ANDERS BREIVIK

On the afternoon of 22 July 2011, a curious compendium titled *2083 – A European Declaration of Independence* was emailed to over a thousand recipients around the globe. Its author was a complete unknown, but by the end of the day he would be famous – not for his writing, but as the worst spree killer in world history.

Anders Behring Breivik was born on 13 February 1979 in Oslo, but lived most of his earliest days in London, where his father, an economist, worked as a diplomat for the Royal Norwegian Embassy. At the age of 1, his parents divorced, setting off a custody battle that his father lost. Still an infant, Breivik returned with his mother, a nurse, to Oslo. Although she was soon remarried, to a Norwegian Army officer, Breivik would later criticize what he perceived as an absence of the masculine in his childhood home. In his writings, he disparages his mother for his 'matriarchal upbringing', adding 'it completely lacked discipline and has contributed to feminizing me to a certain degree.'

Anecdotal evidence shows Breivik to have been an intelligent, caring boy, one who was quick to defend others against bullying. However, his behaviour changed markedly in adolescence. Over a two-year period, so Breivik claims, he engaged in a one-man 'war' against Oslo's public transit company, causing £700,000 ($956,000) in property damage. His evenings were spent running around the city with friends, committing acts of vandalism. At the age of 16, Breivik was caught spray-painting graffiti on the exterior wall of a building, an act that brought an end to his relationship with his father. The two have had no contact since.

Though the stepson of an army officer, Breivik was declared 'unfit for service' in Norway's mandatory conscription assessment. The reason for this surprising judgement has yet to be disclosed; Breivik told friends a story that he'd received an exemption to care for his sickly mother. However, a possible explanation is his use of anabolic steroids, a drug that he'd been taking since his teenage years in an effort to bulk up. Breivik was a man obsessed with his appearance.

In 2000, at the age of 21, he flew off to the United States to have cosmetic surgery on his forehead, nose and chin. Unmarried at 32, Breivik considered himself a most desirable bachelor, and boasted frequently of his conquests, yet not one of his acquaintances can remember him ever having had a girlfriend.

'When it comes to girls,' Breivik wrote in his journal, 'I'm tempted – especially these days, after training and I'm feeling fantastic. But I try to avoid entanglements, because they may complicate my plans and put the whole operation in jeopardy.'

The operation he referred to was part of a nine-year plan that culminated on that horrible day in July 2011. According to Breivik, work began in 2002 with the establishment of a computer programming business that was intended to raise funds. Instead, the company went bankrupt, forcing him to move back to his mother's house. This humiliating setback seems to have brought on a period of relative inactivity. By 2009, however, Breivik was back in business. He set up a company, Breivik Geofarm, which was nothing more than a cover so that he might buy large quantities of fertilizer and other chemicals used in bomb-making without raising suspicions. The next year, after a failed attempt at buying illegal weapons in Prague, he purchased a semi-automatic Glock pistol and a Ruger Mini-14 semi-automatic carbine through legal channels.

Breivik murdered with these guns, but his first victims on 22 July 2011 were killed with a car bomb planted in his Volkswagen Crafter. That afternoon, he drove the automobile into the government quarter of Oslo, taking care to park it in front of the building housing the Office of the Prime Minister, the Minister of Justice and Police and several other high-ranking government ministers. At 3:22 pm, the car bomb exploded, shattering windows, and setting the ground floor of the building on fire. Though Labour Prime Minister Jens Stoltenberg, thought to have been a chief target of the attack, survived without a scratch, the explosion killed eight people and left 11 more with critical injuries.

Things could have been much worse. It's curious that through all Breivik's years of planning, he'd never taken into account the fact that July is the month Norwegians go on holiday. What's more, he'd chosen to carry out his attack late on a Friday afternoon, a time when most government employees had already left for the weekend.

During the mayhem in downtown Oslo, Breivik changed into a fake police uniform, made his way some 25 miles to the shores of Lake Tyrifjorden, and caught a ferry to the island of Utoya. His destination was a summer camp that was held annually by the youth wing of the Norwegian Labour Party. By the time he arrived – 4:45, one hour and 23 minutes after the Oslo blast – news of the tragedy had already been announced to the camp staff and roughly 600 teenagers on the island. Breivik appeared as he presented himself: a police officer who had come to ensure that the 26-acre island was secure. After first asking people to gather around so that he could speak with them, Breivik opened fire. He shot indiscriminately, apparently intent on killing as many people as possible. Breivik's bullets struck people as they took to the lake, hoping to swim to safety.

It wasn't until 32 minutes after the shooting began that police on the mainland were aware of something taking place on Utoya Island, and the delayed response became one of the subjects of the subsequent Gjørv Commission report. They waited until the Beredskapstropen, a special counter-terrorism unit, arrived from Oslo, before making the crossing. The boat that they sailed on was so overloaded that it nearly sank before reaching the island. Before they left shore, Breivik placed a phone call to surrender, only to change his mind. The killing continued until 6:26 pm – one hour and 24 minutes after it had begun – when the gunman made a second call. He was apprehended by the Beredskapstropen eight minutes later.

In all, Breivik killed 69 people on Utoya Island and its surrounding waters. Many of the survivors escaped with their lives by swimming to areas that were only accessible from the lake, while others hid in a schoolhouse, which the gunman chose not to enter. Some survivors played dead, even after being shot for a second time. Still others were rescued by vacationers and others with boats, who risked coming under fire from the shore.

Breivik claimed a total of 77 lives with his two attacks; a further 153 people were injured. The dead ranged in age from 14 to 61, with a median age of just 18 years. He'd killed 55 teenagers.

Anders Breivik has acknowledged that he committed the bombing in Oslo and the shootings on Utoya, but has denied guilt. In his words, both events involved 'atrocious but necessary actions'. These four words came from his lawyer. Much of the gunman's motivation can be gleaned through *2083 – A European Declaration of Independence*, the 1,513-page document that he released to the world just 90 minutes before setting off the Oslo bomb. In this collection of writings, much of it plagiarized from others, Breivik argues against feminism and for a return to a patriarchy that he felt was lacking in his own upbringing. The murderer rails against multiculturalism and what he sees as opening the door to the Islamization of Europe. Portraying himself as a knight, Breivik calls on other white Europeans to wage a religious war against Muslims and Marxists. His ultimate goal, as reflected in the title of the document, was the deportation of all followers of Islam from Europe by 2083.

'A majority of the people I know support my views,' he writes, 'they are just apathetic. They know that there will be a confrontation one day, but they don't care because it will most likely not happen within the next two decades.'

Breivik appeared in Oslo District Court three days after the attack. Facing charges of terrorism, the accused entered a not guilty plea, adding that he did not recognize the system under which he would be tried. The arraignment was held in camera, due to fears that he might somehow use the venue to communicate with compatriots. He was convicted in August 2012 and sentenced to a period of containment of around 21 years.

JOSEPH PAUL FRANKLIN

In 1978, the publisher of *Hustler*, the American adult magazine, Larry Flynt was returning to the courthouse in Lawrenceville, Georgia. A bullet came out of nowhere. He was left with permanent spinal cord damage and paralysed from the waist down. He would never walk again. The shooter was the racist serial killer Joseph Paul Franklin. He had been outraged by an interracial photoshoot in the magazine and sought to extact his revenge. His killing spree lasted three years and by its end he had taken the lives of more than 20 men, women and children across 11 states.

A Nazi sympathiser and racist

Joseph Paul Franklin was born in 1950 in Mobile, Alabama under the name James Clayton Vaughn Jr. His family was a poor one. His father was an alcoholic drifter. He would disappear for months and when he returned, he celebrated by beating his children. James Jr took the brunt of the beatings. His mother was not much better. "She could really hit hard with her hands", said Franklin in an interview.

At high school he developed an interest in Nazism. As a teenager he read one book that would change his life – *Mein Kampf* by Adolf Hitler. He quickly became involved in neo-Nazi movements around the United States. He joined both the Ku Klux Klan and the National Socialist White People's Party. After an accident left him with impaired eyesight he dropped out of school.

His personality seemed to change soon after he married his wife. He began beating her and acting like the father he hated. The neighbourhood he lived in was beginning to be racially integrated, much to Franklin's disgust. His mother, the last restraining influence on him, died in 1972. Soon afterwards he joined the National States Rights Party and began insulting interracial couples in public.

Franklin was determined to move beyond mere words. On Labor Day 1976, he attacked a mixed-race couple in Atlanta with Chemical Mace. At this time, he legally changed his name to Joseph Paul Franklin – a name he took to show his admiration for American founding father Benjamin Franklin and Nazi propaganda minister Joseph Goebbels. On his right forearm was a tattoo of the grim reaper. He was ready to begin his war.

Killing Spree

In July 1977, he allegedly bombed a synagogue in Chattanooga, Tennessee. It marked the beginning of a killing spree that would last three years. Just a few days later he was at work in Madison, Wisconsin. There he killed a mixed-race couple, 23-year-olds Alphonse Manning Jr and Toni Schwenn, in a parking lot. From 1977 to 1980 he roamed across the country, employing as many as 18 different pseudonyms, preaching hate and fighting his one-man war against those he regarded as his racial enemies – Jews and blacks particularly. He said "I felt like I was at war. The survival of the white race was at stake". He hoped, by his example, he would encourage other hate groups to take action. To fund his war, he needed money. He took the only approach he knew – he began robbing banks. In total, he robbed a total of 16 banks.

His weapon of choice was the sniper rifle. On 8 October 1977, he set his sights on a Jewish man he had selected from a listing in the phone book, Gerald Gordon, in St. Louis, Missouri. He took ten-inch nails and hammered them into a telephone pole to create a makeshift gun-rest for his rifle. There were at least 200 guests at the bar mitzvah that day and when Gordon left the Brith Sholom Kneseth Israel synagogue, Franklin opened fire. He killed Gordon while his wife and three children watched.

In 1978, he turned to higher profile targets. On March 6, he took his Ruger .44 semi-automatic rifle to ambush the publisher of *Hustler*, Larry Flynt, and his lawyer, Gene Reeves, as they returned to the courthouse in Lawrenceville, Georgia. He targeted Flynt because one of his editions of *Hustler* had depicted interracial sex. "It made me sick", Franklin said. "I threw the magazine down and thought, I'm gonna kill that guy." On 29 July 1978, he returned to the scene of his first attack in Chattanooga. Hiding by a Pizza Hut he took a shotgun and fired at another interracial couple: Bryant Tatum, a black man, and his white girlfriend, Nancy Hilton. Tatum was killed, but Hilton survived the attack.

On 22 July 1979, Harold McIver, a 27-year-old black man and manager of a fast-food restaurant was on the night-shift in Doraville, Georgia. An unseen sniper took his life. Franklin's methods were simple, his attacks deadly. The year 1980 saw

Franklin continue his campaign. He shot the civil rights activist Vernon Jordan, Jr in May after seeing him with a white woman; in June he killed the black teenagers, cousins Darrell Lane (14) and Dante Evans Brown (13) in Cincinatti, Ohio, while they were jogging with friends; by 25 June he had made his way to West Virginia to kill two young hitchhikers, Nancy Santomero and Vicki Durian – white girls – after one of them said she had a black boyfriend; and in August he killed two more black men, Ted Fields and David Martin, near Liberty Park in Salt Lake City, Utah.

Capture, Conviction and Execution

Franklin could not evade the law for ever. Nancy Hilton had been left alive and Franklin was a distinctive character. Racist tattoos covered his body and he had a habit of visiting blood banks. After murdering Ted Fields and David Martin in Utah, Franklin was travelling through Kentucky when he was detained and questioned about a firearm in his car. He escaped from the interrogation but the car had provided more than sufficient evidence to link him to the murders. In October 1980, Franklin turned up at a blood bank in Florida. The FBI was alerted and Franklin was finally arrested.

At his trial in Missouri, he was sentenced to death. Franklin was unrepentant.

'The only thing I'm not sorry about is that it's not legal.'

'What's not legal?'

'Killing Jews.'

Around this time, the state of Missouri was struggling to source the required drugs to perform the execution as many manufacturers objected to supply these drugs on moral grounds

– in response, the state found an experimental barbiturate called pentobarbital. On Tuesday 19 November 2013, Franklin's lawyers thought they had managed a stay of execution when they argued that the use of pentobarbital constituted cruel and unusual punishment. Franklin had also seemed to overcome his racist views saying of the black inmates, 'I saw they were people just like us.' He recanted his earlier ideas of racial war, but many believe this was just a ploy to avoid execution. It had seemed there might be a longer reprieve for him, but his final appeal was quickly overturned by a federal court.

On 20 November 2013, Franklin was executed. Missouri had not executed a prisoner in three years and Franklin was the first ever inmate to be injected with pentobarbital – it took him ten minutes to die.

DALE HAUSNER AND SAMUEL DIETEMAN

Dale Hausner was born in Nebraska in 1973. To those who knew him, the idea of him as a serial killer was unthinkable. He was polite, timid and shy. He worked as a custodian at Sky Harbor International Airport in Phoenix, Arizona and spent his spare time working as a boxing photographer. Mary Ann Owen, a Las Vegas photographer who had known him since 1999, said 'He doesn't even look like he would know which end of the barrel the bullet would come out of.'

In 1994, Hausner suffered an immense personal tragedy. His two sons, aged two and three, drowned in a creek during a car accident when his wife, Karen, fell asleep at the wheel.

He became severely depressed. When his wife threatened to leave him, he drove her to the desert and pulled out a gun. She obtained a restraining order against him and left Hausner to live alone. He threatened to shoot her, but in the end thought better of it. Hausner turned to joy-riding with his brother Jeff. It was his brother who introduced him to Samuel Dieteman in early 2006.

Dieteman was born in 1976. He had two daughters. His wife left him in 2001 and, as his family claim, he developed a drug addiction. When his apartment was repossessed he moved in with his mother and stepfather, but they eventually threw him out because of his alcoholism. Hausner offered him a place to stay. The two men, sharing the history of their broken lives, soon became friends. They set up a small-scale shoplifting and fencing business: Dieteman would steal alcohol, CDs and other small items, and Hausner would sell them to his coworkers. Eventually, Hausner stopped showing up to boxing fights. Clement Vierra, who met Hausner in 2004, said 'It was really pretty strange because he was really involved with boxing.' But the truth was that by mid-2005, Hausner had another hobby.

The two men began to see crime as a form of entertainment. Dieteman described his relationship with Hausner as 'just random, senseless destruction.' They started shooting dogs and horses for recreation and set trash cans on fire as well as engaging in other various acts of violence such as breaking car windows and puncturing tires with their BB guns. On one occasion, they pulled up to a woman on the street, armed with the BB gun. Hausner said to her 'Are you working? Do you need a ride?' When she said no, he shot her in the chest with the BB gun. Soon they would progress to murdering people for their thrills. In January

2006, the Phoenix police linked the killing of several animals to the murders of three people in the area. It seemed that the serial killers did not discriminate between species.

Drive-By Shootings and Recreational Violence

The first body turned up in May 2005. It was 56-year-old Reginald Remillard who had been shot in the neck while he slept at a bus stop. One year later, in July 2006, the 'Serial Shooters' would take their last victim – 22-year-old Robin Blasnek. Over this short period, the two killers were responsible for eight murders and at least 29 other shootings in the Phoenix area.

They described their killings as 'RV', short for 'random recreational violence.' Murder was a game for the two partners. During the nights they would drive around the streets of Phoenix in Hausner's Toyota Camry looking for victims walking or cycling alone. Their method was the drive-by shooting. Once they had found an innocent pedestrian they would open fire from behind with a .22 rifle or a .410-gauge shotgun. Hausner and Dieteman would take turns at the wheel and on the trigger. When they were arrested, a video of *America's Most Wanted* was found in their apartment. Hausner and Dieteman kept track of their killings with a map marked by red and blue dots.

At his trial, Dieteman said: 'My favourite thing is, you know, when somebody is walking away ... it gives me, you know, a couple of extra seconds to aim. I don't have to worry about them looking.'

Even the killings were not enough to keep the pair entertained. On 8 June 2006, they set fire to two Walmart stores. Sometimes they decided just to beat their victims rather than shoot them. Hausner was not just in it for the entertainment. He believed that he was helping with social cleansing. Hausner had a deep hatred for illegal immigrants, homeless people and prostitutes, while Dieteman had no ideological purpose behind his participation.

They gloated over their killings and closely followed the news on their own killings and the progress of other serial killers in the country. A police wire-tap captured their conversation:

Dieteman: 'On the 5 am news, it was when they first said "Phoenix and Mesa Police have now officially linked the ... death of a young Mesa woman to the serial killer, which now brings their total to six."'

Hausner: 'It's higher than that! What about the guy I fucking shot on 27th Avenue in the yard.'

They were keeping score. The 'Serial Shooters' wanted the police and the public to know just how many they had killed. They seemed proud of their notoriety. A wire-tap in their apartment before their arrest recorded the two men's conversation. Upon hearing that police were looking to link similar shootings in neighbouring states, Hausner said: 'So we're being copycatted, Sam? We're pioneers, Sam? We're leading to a better life for everybody, Sam?'

Investigation and imprisonment

Their joy in the murders would be their downfall. In July, Dieteman began bragging about the shootings to a drinking partner of his, Ron Horton. His friend duly reported him to the police. They began trailing the pair. They tapped their phone lines. 'We were on him 24/7, because if this turned out to be our suspect, we were not going to let another incident happen.' Soon they had accumulated enough evidence to pursue a trial.

The two were arrested on 3 August 2006. Hausner's two-year-old, terminally ill daughter was in the apartment at the time.

As they went to trial, their partnership quickly broke up. Dieteman pleaded guilty to two murders and was sentenced to life imprisonment without parole. Dieteman's statements labelled Hausner as the ringleader. Consequently, Hausner was found guilty of six of the eight murders and a total of 80 criminal charges including aggravated assaults, cruelty to animals and arson. Hausner's comment on Dieteman was: 'I don't see Sam as a cold-blooded killer but if they've got evidence saying he is, there's not much I can do to refute that.'

Hausner was sentenced to death: one death sentence for each of his six murders. However, he was not prepared to wait out his time on death row. On 19 June 2013, he was found dead in his cell. He had committed suicide by overdosing on antidepressants that he had been secretly hoarding.

JOHN MUHAMMAD

For three weeks in October 2002, John Allen Muhammad, a black ex-US army sergeant, and John Malvo, a Jamaican teenager Muhammad had adopted as his son, brought terror to the area surrounding Washington DC. Known to the media as the 'Beltway Sniper', Muhammad and Malvo killed at least 14 people and wounded at least five more before they were finally captured. Muhammad was definitely the dominant partner in the killings but his motivation remains obscure. Some believe that, as a convert to Islam, Muhammad may have been carrying out a deliberate terror attack on Washington. By contrast, his ex-wife,

Mildred, believes it was part of an elaborate, if crazy, plot to kill her and gain custody of his three children.

Expert Marksman

John Muhammad was born John Allen Williams in Louisiana on 30 December 1960. His mother died when he was young and his father was absent, so his grandfather and aunt raised him. Muhammad became a excellent football player, marrying his high-school sweetheart Carol Williams in 1982. He enlisted in the army in 1985, training as a mechanic and combat engineer. He was transferred to Germany in 1990, fought in the Gulf War in 1991, returned to the United States the following year, and was given an honourable discharge from the army, as a sergeant, in 1994. Unconfirmed reports suggest that his discharge was connected with a grenade attack that Muhammad was accused of carrying out on his fellow soldiers. He did not receive specific sniper training while in the army, but qualified as an expert with the M-16 rifle, a civilian version of which – the Bushmaster .223 – would be the weapon he was finally arrested with.

Conversion to Islam

After leaving the army, Muhammad settled in Tacoma, in Washington state. By now he was living with his third wife, Mildred, and their three children. Muhammad worked as a car mechanic and started a martial arts school. He converted to the Nation of Islam, changing his name to Muhammad.

At his stage, Muhammad appears to have been a well-respected member of the community. Then things started to go wrong.

Soon, he was locked in a bitter custody battle with Mildred. He took the children and fled to Antigua in the Caribbean. There he tried to establish himself as a businessman but ended up helping people to obtain false papers for entry into the US. One of those he helped was a teenage boy called Lee Malvo, originally from Jamaica. When things failed to work out in Antigua, Muhammad returned to Washington state with his three children plus Malvo, whom he claimed was his stepson. Muhammad moved to the town of Bellingham, close to the Canadian border, and attempted to register his children in school there. At this point investigators tracked him down and returned his three children to their mother, who promptly left the state and went into hiding in Maryland. Muhammad and Malvo, now calling himself John as well, stayed in Bellingham for a while. They lived in a homeless shelter but Muhammad seemed to have enough money to take regular flights around the States. During this period, the pair carried out their first murder: they intended to kill a friend of Mildred's in Tacoma, but accidentally shot the woman's niece instead.

In the late summer of 2001, Muhammad and Malvo took a trip down to Louisiana, where Muhammad visited his relatives. He claimed to be doing well, to have a family and business in the Virgin Islands, but his big talk was belied by the fact he had not washed or cut his hair. His relatives were worried about him, as well they might have been. After leaving Louisiana, Muhammad and Malvo bought a car, a blue 1990 Chevrolet Caprice. As they roamed around the States they are suspected of having committed a whole series of robberies and shootings: three in Maryland, one in Alabama and one in Louisiana. Another murder, in Atlanta, is suspected to be their work as well.

By the end of September, the duo may have killed as many as nine times. At first, the murders seemed to be part and parcel of robberies. However, they increasingly seemed to have been carried out for their own sake.

Then came the events of October 2002. On the evening of 2 October, a 55-year-old man was shot and killed in the parking lot of a grocery store in Wheaton, Maryland. The next day, five more people were shot and killed as they went about their business; one mowing a lawn, one mailing a package, one crossing a street, two filling their cars with gas – none of them with any inkling that their next breath would be their last.

Random Victims

Panic was immediate. What could be more terrifying than a sniper – few people imagined there were two of them – hiding out and taking pot shots at passers-by, deciding on a whim whose life to take, and whose to spare.

The next shooting was of a woman in Spotsylvania, Virginia. She survived, but it was now becoming clear that the sniper was circling the Washington suburbs, keeping close to the Beltway, the ring road that surrounds the city. Three more days passed without a shooting, then the duo shot a 13-year-old boy outside his school in Bowie, Maryland, leaving a Tarot card at the scene.

The following day, Baltimore police stopped a vehicle driving erratically. The driver identified himself as John Muhammad; John Malvo was also in the car. However, a background check indicated that Muhammad had no outstanding warrants, and – tragically, as it turned out – he was allowed to carry on. Over the next ten days the pair killed three more times.

State of Emergency

The whole area was now in a state of emergency; people were afraid to go shopping or to fill their cars with gas.

The day after the last killing – a bus driver in Aspen Hill on 22 October – the authorities, acting on a phone tip, searched a house in Tacoma, where Malvo and Muhammad had once lived. Neighbours had complained in January that Muhammad routinely used his backyard for target practice. The authorities issued a nationwide alert for the blue Chevrolet Caprice, and it was announced that an arrest warrant had been issued for Muhammad.

Finally, on 24 October, the vehicle was spotted by a motorist at a rest stop. Washington police soon surrounded the car and found Muhammad and Malvo sleeping inside. They arrested both of them and found that the car had been modified for use as a sniper's hideout. They also found a .223-calibre Bushmaster XM15 rifle in the car.

At trial both Muhammad and Malvo were found guilty of murder. On 9 March 2004, Muhammad was sentenced to death, while Malvo received a sentence of life imprisonment. Muhammad was executed in 2009.

ANATOLY ONOPRIENKO

Anatoly Onoprienko was the second major serial killer to emerge in the former USSR after the collapse of communism, following the Rostov Ripper, Andrei Chikatilo. Onoprienko was a brutal killer with a particularly unusual pathology. Quite simply, Onoprienko liked to kill families – children and all – acting with a ruthlessness that led the newspapers to dub him 'the Terminator'.

Onoprienko was born in the town of Laski in the Ukraine. His mother died when he was just four years old and his father placed him in an orphanage, though he kept his older son at home. This appears to have been the foundation of Onoprienko's rage at humanity and families in particular. He never forgave his father for discarding him, and he took a terrible revenge.

Jack of All Trades

After he left the orphanage, Onoprienko worked as a forester and as a sailor, and was known to the mental health authorities in the Ukrainian capital of Kiev. The first spate of killings with which

Anatoly Onoprienko

he is associated happened in 1989. With an accomplice, Sergei Rogozin, Onoprienko carried out a series of burglaries. During one of these robberies the pair were interrupted by the house owners. Onoprienko promptly killed them. He followed this up by killing the occupants of a parked car.

Afterwards, Onoprienko split with Rogozin. His movements over the next six years, as communism collapsed and the Ukraine became an independent state, remain mysterious. He is known to have roamed around central Europe for a while and was expelled from both Germany and Austria, but whether he was responsible for any further murders during that time remains unclear.

Bloodiest Spree in History

What is certain is that he was back in the Ukraine at the end of 1995, for it was then that he began one of the bloodiest murder sprees in history, killing 43 victims in little more than three months. As before, Onoprienko targeted houses on the edge of small towns and villages across the Ukraine; this time, however, he was not interested in burglary, only in killing.

He began on Christmas Eve 1995 by breaking into the home of the Zaichenko family. He murdered the couple and their two children with a double-barrelled shotgun, took a few souvenirs, then set the house on fire. Six days later in the town of Bratkovichi, a place that was to become a regular hunting ground, he broke into another house and killed the couple who lived there and the wife's twin sisters. Before his next family killing, almost as a side show, he spent 6 January killing motorists, four in all, along the Berdyansk-Dnieprovskaya highway. He later explained: 'To me it was like hunting. Hunting people down.'

Next, on 17 January, he headed back to Bratkovichi. There he broke into the house of the Pilat family, killing the five people who lived there and then setting the house on fire, As he left, two people saw him, so he shot both of them as well.

Later that same month he headed east to the town of Fastova, where he killed four more people, a nurse and her family. He then went west to Olevsk, where, on 19 February, he broke into the home of the Dubchak family. He shot the father and son, and battered the mother and daughter to death with a hammer. He later told investigators that the daughter had seen him murder her parents and was praying when he came up to her. 'Seconds before I smashed her head, I ordered her to show me where they kept their money,' he said. 'She looked at me with an angry, defiant stare and said, "No, I won't." That strength was incredible. But I felt nothing.'

Just over a week later, Onoprienko drove to Malina, where he murdered all four of the Bodnarchuk family, shooting the husband and wife and using an axe to despatch two daughters, aged seven and eight. Once again a passer-by who was unfortunate enough to witness the killer leaving the house was added to the death list.

Just over three weeks passed before Onoprienko struck again on 22 March 1996. He travelled to the small village of Busk, just outside the beleaguered town of Bratkovichi, to slaughter all four members of the Novosad family, shooting them and then burning their house. At this stage, the terrified villagers demanded help from the government, who responded by sending a full National Guard Unit, complete with rocket launchers, to ward off this unknown menace. Meanwhile, 2000 officers became part of a gigantic manhunt.

Cache of Weapons

In the end, however, it was a relative of Onoprienko who brought about his capture. Onoprienko was staying with a cousin who, on finding a cache of weapons in his room, told him to leave the house and phoned the police. The police tracked Onoprienko to his girlfriend's house, where he was arrested on Easter Sunday, 16 April 1996. They found him listening to music on a tape deck stolen from the Novosad family. Further investigation revealed weapons used in the murders, plus a collection of souvenirs taken from his victims.

Once in custody Onoprienko demanded to speak to 'a general', and as soon as one was provided he confessed to 52 murders. He claimed to have been hearing voices that told him to commit the crimes. He also said that he had been treated for schizophrenia in a Kiev mental hospital. Disturbingly, Kiev's Interior Ministry initially disclosed that Onoprienko was an outpatient whose therapists knew him to be a killer, but they then refused to say any more about the matter.

In 1999, Onoprienko was convicted on 52 counts of murder and sentenced to life imprisonment. He died of heart failure in prison in 2013.

Rape Slayers

There are some crimes that, thankfully, tend to be one-offs: the domestic killing of a family member, for instance. There are others that become habitual, such as burglary. Then there are the crimes that take hold of the perpetrator and become compulsive. Rape, particularly the rape of a stranger, is such a crime, and so too is serial murder.

It is little surprise that the two crimes are, more often than not, linked. Rape is a way of taking another person's will from them; murder is that impulse taken to its logical, terrible extreme. Some serial killers begin as rapists and then move on to murder. For many, however, the two acts are inseparable; for these killers, sexual satisfaction is intricately bound up in the killing of another human being.

Rape slayers come from many different walks of life. Their sexual pathology crosses all class boundaries. Those such as Pee Wee Gaskins are from an appalling background of poverty, neglect and abuse. In his case, it is not altogether surprising that he should have grown into a twisted killer. However, there are other cases that are not so easy to understand. Ted Bundy was from a troubled but reasonably settled family and grew up to study law, yet this apparently ordinary background produced a man who delighted in rape and murder, killing at least 30 young women and probably many more, with ever-increasing savagery.

Nor, interestingly enough, are rape slayers always crippled by ugliness or deformity. Killers like Bundy and Paul Knowles were young, good-looking men who had no difficulty in attracting women. Their deformity, it seems, was all on the inside.

TED BUNDY

Ted Bundy is one of the most terrifying of all serial killers. Why? It is not simply because he was a sadist and necrophile who confessed to the murders of more than 30 women, and may conceivably have murdered as many as a hundred. It is also because, unlike most such monsters, he could actually pass for a regular guy – the good-looking young lawyer who lives down the street. Bundy was not a skid-row slasher who operated a safe distance away from respectable folk. He was a killer who spent time in ordinary places: the university campus, the mall, the park over the holiday weekend.

Apparent Normality

Perhaps the most deadly aspect of Bundy's modus operandi was that he played ruthlessly on his apparent normality. Typically, a victim – always a young woman with long dark hair in a centre parting – would be walking back to her student dorm, or out in the park. She would be approached by a personable, tousle-haired young man with his arm in a cast. He would explain that he needed help lifting something into his car. The nice young woman would offer to help the nice young man and she would follow him to his car. She would then disappear forever, or would be found in the woods, her body raped and sodomized, her head staved in by a furious assault with a blunt instrument.

Ted Bundy was born Theodore Robert Cowell in November 1946 in Vermont. However, he enjoyed little of the privilege typically credited to his generation. His mother, Louise Cowell, had become pregnant by a serviceman who had disappeared before Ted was born. She and her baby lived with her strict parents in Philadelphia, and in an effort to avoid scandal the family pretended that Ted was actually his grandparents' child, and that his mother was in fact his sister. When Ted was four his mother moved to Tacoma, Washington, and married a man called John Bundy; a year later, in 1951, Ted took his stepfather's name.

Bundy was a bright child who consistently achieved good grades in school. However, he was not an easy mixer. He was bullied when he was young and later, while becoming more apparently gregarious, he also acquired a reputation for petty theft and lying.

After high school he attended the University of Puget Sound in Washington. Around this time he met a young, pretty woman called Stephanie Brooks, who had long dark hair worn in a centre parting. Stephanie was from a moneyed California family and she and Bundy went out together for a time. However, while Bundy became obsessed with her, she found him lacking in ambition and, when she left college, she broke off with him. Bundy was devastated.

Murderous Rage

He left college and moped for a while. Then he turned his disappointment into motivation to succeed. He re-enrolled in college, studied psychology and became active in the Republican Party. He worked for a suicide hot line, and received a commendation from the Seattle Police Department for catching a mugger. He found a new girlfriend, divorcee Meg Anders. He could scarcely have looked more like a model citizen.

Underneath, however, a murderous rage was building. First, he got back in touch with Stephanie Brooks, meeting up with her in California while on a business trip in 1973. She was impressed by the new go-ahead Ted, and – unbeknown to Anders – Stephanie and Ted began to talk of marriage.

In February 1974, Bundy broke off all contact with Brooks. Just as suddenly as she had dumped him, he did the same to her. What she did not know was that, just beforehand, Bundy had committed his first murder. The victim was a young woman called Lynda Healy who he had abducted from her basement flat in Seattle. Over the next few months, five more young

Ted Bundy

women would vanish in the surrounding area. Each one was last seen out walking, and each one had long dark hair with a centre parting.

It was clear that there was a serial killer on the loose, but at this stage the police had no bodies and no clues. Then came the events of 14 July. On that hot summer's day crowds had flocked to the shores of Lake Sammammish, but two of them – 23-year-old Janice Ott and 19-year-old Denise Naslund – had failed to make the journey back. Both had wandered off from their friends and vanished. When police investigated, several passers-by reported seeing Ott in conversation with a man whose arm was in a sling and was heard to say his name was Ted. Then another witness came forward and said that this Ted had asked her to help secure a sailboat to his car, a tan Volkswagen Beetle. She had gone with him as far as his car but, when he told her the boat was somewhere up the road and they would have to drive there, she had become suspicious and declined.

The police put out a description of the man called Ted and various calls came in. One of these was an anonymous call from Meg Anders, saying she thought the man might be her boyfriend Ted Bundy, who was starting to alarm her with his interest in violent sex and bondage. The police checked out Bundy, but the young Republican law student seemed too innocuous to worry about, and the lead was dropped.

Over the next three months bodies started to be discovered. Ott and Naslund were found buried in the woods, along with the skeleton of a third woman who could not be identified. Two more bodies were found the following month. Then Bundy moved his operations out of the state.

His next three victims were all abducted in Utah during the month of October. At this point, Bundy made his first mistake. On 8 November he attempted to abduct Carol DaRonch from a shopping mall in Salt Lake City. He pretended to be a police officer and lured her into his car, a VW Beetle, but she became suspicious and managed to escape, following a struggle. Later that night, 17-year-old Debbie Kent was not so lucky; Bundy abducted and murdered her.

Arrested

In the New Year, Bundy moved his hunting ground again, this time to Colorado. He abducted four more women there in the first half of 1975. Just before the fourth body was discovered, however, he was finally arrested. A policeman had stopped Bundy in Salt Lake City and looked inside the car, finding handcuffs and a stocking mask. Carol DaRonch was called in and picked Bundy out of a line-up as the man who had tried to abduct her. Her evidence was enough to have him convicted and sentenced to jail for attempted kidnapping.

Meanwhile other evidence linked Bundy to the killings in Colorado, and in January 1977 he was taken to Aspen to be tried for the murder of Caryn Campbell. The game was clearly up for Bundy. However respectable his exterior, it was all too plain that underneath was an appalling sexual sadist and murderer.

This should have been the end of the story but, waiting for trial, Bundy demonstrated new levels of resourcefulness. He escaped from custody during a court appearance and spent eight days hiding out in Aspen before being recaptured. Incredibly, he then managed to escape again, cutting a hole in the roof of his cell, crawling along and cutting another hole down into a janitor's room, then walking unchallenged out of prison. This escape would last longer, and have far worse consequences.

At Large

Bundy fled to Tallahassee, Florida, where he rented a room under an assumed name, close to the university. Two weeks after his escape, on 15 January 1978, he murdered again, giving up all subtlety in his approach. He broke into a sorority house and brutally raped and murdered two young women, leaving a third badly injured.

The following month, he failed in his attempt to abduct a schoolgirl. Three days later, he succeeded in abducting and murdering his final victim, 12-year-old Kimberley Leach. After another three days, he was finally recaptured and this time he was convicted of first-degree murder: the evidence against him was the match of his teeth with the bite marks left on his victims. In July 1979 he was sentenced to death by electric chair.

Law student Ted Bundy launched several increasingly tenuous appeals and became a celebrity. While in prison, he confessed to more than 30 murders. Women proposed marriage to him; one even succeeded in exchanging marriage vows with him when she appeared as a defence witness during an appeal court appearance. The courts were not impressed however, and finally, on 24 January 1989, Ted Bundy was put to death.

PEE WEE GASKINS

Five foot two inches of vicious cruelty, Pee Wee Gaskins has a claim to being the United State's most prolific serial killer – that is, if his own account, which has him killing well over a hundred victims, is to be believed. What is certain is that Pee Wee Gaskins was as cold-hearted a killer as there has ever been as, unusually among serial killers, he was capable of committing two distinct kinds of murder. On the one hand, he was a career criminal who murdered for purely business reasons. On the other, he was a sex killer, preying on both men and women. Street smart and utterly amoral, Gaskins became a virtual killing machine.

Regular Beatings

Gaskins was born in South Carolina on 31 March 1933, in the middle of the Depression. His mother's name was Parrott, and Pee Wee was the last in a string of illegitimate children. His early life was characterized by neglect and regular beatings from assorted 'stepfathers'. Small for his age, he was immediately nicknamed Pee Wee; his mother took so little interest in him that the first time he ever learned his given name – Donald – was when it was read out on the occasion of his first court appearance, in his mid-teens.

The court appearance followed a brief crime spree indulged in by Pee Wee and a couple of fellow school dropouts. They gang-raped the sister of one of their number and committed a string of robberies. They were arrested after a witness was able to identify them to the police after surviving a savage hatchet assault carried out during a botched burglary. Pee Wee was sent to reform school.

There, the diminutive boy was regularly raped by his fellow inmates. He was released when he was 18, in 1951, and briefly worked on a tobacco plantation, but was soon arrested again, this time for arson and assaulting a woman with a hammer. In prison he was raped again. This time, though, he fought back, cutting his rapist's throat. He received an extra three years in prison for this, but from that time on, Pee Wee Gaskins became the aggressor rather than the victim.

He escaped briefly from prison in 1955 but was recaptured and sentenced once again. Finally released in 1961, he was back in prison a year later for statutory rape. In fact, it was not until his release in 1968 that Gaskins finally spent a significant time outside prison. Unfortunately for the rest of the world, he was by now 35 years old and absolutely lethal.

He killed for the first time in September 1969, torturing and murdering a hitchhiker he picked up, before drowning her body in a swamp. 'All I could think about is how I could do anything I wanted to her,' he later wrote in his memoirs. She was to be the first of many hitchhikers he picked up and killed on the back roads between Sumter and Charleston. Unbelievably, he used to drive around in a purple hearse with a plastic skeleton hanging from the rearview mirror. When asked why he chose such a vehicle, he used to reply: 'Because I kill so many people.' Unfortunately, everyone thought he was joking. Further evidence of his maniacal inclinations was the fact that he stored dynamite in his fridge and vats of sulphuric acid in his backyard.

Killing closer to home

Gaskins' appetite for murder soon led him to kill closer to home. In November 1970 he raped and murdered his own 15-year-old niece Janice Kirby and a friend of hers. The following month he is thought to have tortured and murdered the 13-year-old daughter of a local politician; a crime Gaskins later confessed to. In 1973, in the most horrifying of all his murders, he raped and murdered two of his neighbours: Doreen Dempsey, aged 23 and eight months pregnant, and her one-year-old daughter.

No one yet suspected that Pee Wee was a serial sex killer, but some of his acquaintances knew that he was prepared to commit murder for a reasonable reward. In February 1975 a woman named Suzanne Kipper Owens hired Gaskins to kill her boyfriend, Silas Barnwell Yates. The pair briefly considered marriage, but events conspired against them: in order to cover up the murder, Gaskins ended up killing four more times. One of the victims was a woman called Diane Bellamy Neely, who had helped set up Yates for his murder. Her brother Walter Neely, who was involved in Gaskins' main business, a stolen car racket, initially helped Gaskins to cover up the killings.

It was the stolen car business that led to Gaskins' arrest at the end of the year. At this point, Walter Neely lost his nerve and confessed to his involvement in the cover-up murders and testified that Gaskins was responsible for the murders.

From now on, Gaskins' main priority was to avoid the death penalty. He made endless deals with the police, if they guaranteed that he would not be put to death. In May 1976, he was convicted of one murder, and then received nine more life sentences in 1978. In return for his confession, the sentence was indeed kept down to life imprisonment.

That should have be the end of the Pee Wee Gaskins story. Instead, his lust to kill was such that, while serving his sentence, he accepted a contract to kill Randolph Tyner, a prisoner on death row. Gaskins managed to rig up a bomb in the radio belonging to Tyner, and it did indeed kill him. This time, however, Gaskins had no bargaining power. He was sentenced to death, a punishment that was finally carried out in the electric chair in 1991.

PAUL KNOWLES

Journalists usually only meet serial killers once they are safely locked behind bars. British journalist Sandy Fawkes had a rather different experience when she met a good-looking young man named Paul Knowles in an Atlanta bar, and ended up spending several days with him. Ten days later, she was to see her lover's mugshot on the cover of the newspaper – arrested for the latest in a string of at least 18 murders.

A native of Florida, Paul Knowles was a serial killer who lacked the usual patterns of behaviour common to murderers of this type. He roamed from place to place, killing young and old, men and women. Sometimes he raped his victims, both men and women; sometimes he did not. Sometimes his crimes were financially motivated, sometimes sexually. The only common thread in his actions was an utter lack of moral scruple.

Born in 1946, from his teenage years Knowles was consistently in trouble with the law. He served his first prison sentence when he was 19 and from then on was constantly in and out of jail, mostly for burglary or car theft.

His first verified murder came shortly after being arrested following a bar fight in Jacksonville, Florida, on 26 July 1974. He escaped from prison using his lock-picking expertise and broke into the house of 65-year-old Alice Curtis. He stole her money and possessions, including her car, and left her bound and gagged. Later, she choked to death on the gag and, when news of her death hit the local media, Knowles decided to dump the car. As he did so, he saw two young girls, aged seven and 11, whom he thought had recognized him. He abducted them both, strangled them and dumped their bodies in a swamp.

On the Road

Next, he headed south to Atlantic Beach, Florida, where he broke into another house and strangled the occupant. From there he went north, picking up a hitchhiker and raping and strangling her along the way, before stopping off in Musell, Georgia, to break into yet another house where he strangled Kathie Pierce as her three-year-old son watched. He did, however, leave the boy unharmed.

Knowles spent the next two months driving aimlessly around the country, killing, raping and stealing as he went. On 3 September 1974, he robbed and killed a businessman named William Bates in Lima, Ohio. On 18 September, he murdered two campers in Ely, Nevada. On 21 September, in Texas, he saw a stranded motorist looking for help. He stopped to rape and kill her. Two days after that, heading back towards his home territory, he met

Paul Knowles

a beautician named Ann Dawson in Birmingham, Alabama. They spent six days together as lovers, Dawson paying the bills, until, on 29 September, he killed her.

Three more weeks of drifting elapsed before Knowles found his next victim, Doris Hovey, whom he shot dead a little way north of Woodford, Virginia. Back south in Macon,

Georgia, on 6 November, a man named Carswell Carr made the mistake of inviting Knowles back to his house for drinks. Knowles stabbed Carr to death and then strangled his 15-year-old daughter Mandy, attempting to have sex with her corpse.

Road Block

Two days later, Knowles was in Atlanta, where he met Sandy Fawkes. She was immediately attracted to what she called his 'gaunt good looks'. Knowles was unable to perform sexually, however, and failed repeatedly over the next few days. When they parted, Fawkes had no idea how lucky she was to be alive; she found out when, on the following day, Knowles picked up one of her friends, Susan Mackenzie, and pulled a gun on her before demanding sex. Mackenzie managed to escape and alert the police, who were soon on Knowles' trail.

The chase lasted several days. Finally apprehended by a police officer, Knowles managed to draw his gun first and kidnap the officer, stealing his car. He then used the police car to stop another motorist, whose car he stole in turn. Now he had two hostages, the policeman and the motorist, James Meyer. He soon tired of them, and tied the two men to a tree in Pulaski County, Georgia, before shooting them both in the head.

Time was running out for Knowles, however. He ran into a police roadblock, and tried to escape on foot before finally running into an armed civilian who took him prisoner.

Knowles did not live long enough to provide the police with a very detailed confession. The day after his arrest, he was taken by police officers to the site of one of his murders. As they drove along Knowles managed to unlock his handcuffs using a paperclip. He then made a grab for the gun in the holster of the driver, Sheriff Earl Lee. As they struggled, the FBI agent who was also in the car, Ron Angel, drew his own gun and shot Knowles dead.

CARL PANZRAM

Carl Panzram was a true misanthrope – a man who positively loathed his fellow human beings. His 39 years on earth saw him drift from an abusive childhood to a nomadic adulthood spent in and out of a hellish prison system. In between, he took his revenge by killing at least 21 victims, and robbing and raping many more. When he was put to death in 1930, his last action was to spit in the hangman's face and say: 'Hurry it up, you Hoosier bastard, I could hang a dozen men while you're fooling around.'

Panzram was born on a farm in Warren, Minnesota, on 28 June 1891, one of seven children in a dirt-poor German immigrant family. Theirs was a desperately hard life that became even harder when Carl was seven years old: his father walked out one day and never came back. His mother and brothers struggled to keep the farm going, working from dawn till dusk in the fields. During this time, his brothers used to beat him unmercifully for no reason at all. At the age of 11 he gave them a good reason: he broke into a neighbour's house and stole whatever he could find, including a handgun. His brothers beat him unconscious when they found out.

Brutal Correctional Institution

Panzram was arrested for the crime and sent to the Minnesota State Training School in 1903, aged 12. This was a brutal institution in which he was regularly beaten and raped by the staff. Here he acquired a taste for forced gay sex and an abiding hatred of authority. In 1905 he expressed this hatred by burning part of the school down. He was not identified as the culprit, however, and was able to persuade a parole panel that year that he was a reformed character. The opposite was closer to the truth: the Carl Panzram who emerged from the school was in reality a deformed character.

Panzram returned home for a while, went to school briefly, then left after an altercation with a teacher. He worked on his mother's farm until, at 14, he jumped on a freight train and headed westwards. For the next few years he lived the life of a teenage hobo. He committed crimes and was the victim of them; he was sent to reform schools and broke out of them. When he was 16, in 1907, he joined the army but refused to accept the discipline and was then caught trying to desert with a bundle of stolen clothing. He was dishonourably discharged and sent to the fearsome Leavenworth Prison, where he spent two hard years, breaking rocks and becoming a very strong, dangerous man. On his release, he returned to his roaming. He was arrested at various times and under various names for vagrancy, burglary, arson and robbery. The one crime he was not arrested for, but took particular pleasure in carrying out, was homosexual rape. Once he even raped a policeman who was trying to arrest him. His crimes escalated in savagery and so did his prison sentences; he served time in both Montana and Oregon.

In 1918, Panzram escaped from Oregon State Prison, where he had been serving a sentence under the name Jefferson Baldwin. He decided to leave the north-east, where he had become very well known to the police. He changed his name to John O'Leary and headed for the east coast, where he would make the transition from robber and rapist to cold-blooded killer.

Bait

He began by carrying out a string of burglaries that made him enough money to buy a yacht. He would lure sailors on to the yacht, get them drunk, rape them, kill them and then dump their bodies in the sea. This went on until his boat crashed and sank, by which time he reckoned he had killed ten men. Broke once more, Panzram stowed away on a ship and ended up in Angola, Africa. He signed on with an oil company who were drilling off the coast of the Congo. While he was there, he raped and killed a 12-year-old boy. Then he went on a crocodile hunting expedition that ended when he killed the six local guides he had hired, raped their corpses and fed them to the crocodiles.

Captured

Panzram retuned to the States soon after, as witnesses had seen him engage the guides. He went on to rape and murder an 11-year-old boy, George McMahon, in the town of Salem, Massachusetts. Over the next months, he carried out two more murders and numerous robberies. Finally, he was captured while in the act of burgling a railway station. This was to be his toughest sentence yet: he began it in Sing Sing, but proved so unruly that he was sent on to Dannemora, an infamous establishment where he was beaten and tortured by the guards. His legs were broken and left untreated, leaving him semi-crippled and in constant pain for the rest of his life.

On release in July 1928, Panzram immediately carried out a string of burglaries and at least one murder before being rearrested. By now he was evidently tired of life. On arrest he gave his real name for the first time and, while in prison in Washington DC, confessed to several murders of young boys. Encouraged by a prison guard with whom he struck up an unlikely friendship, he went on to write a 20,000-word account of his terrible life and crimes. This remains a remarkable document, a horrifying but unusually even-handed account of a serial killer's inner life. Following the confessions, and amid a flurry of media interest, Panzram was tried for the most recent of his murders: the strangling of Alexander Uszacke. He was found guilty and sentenced to serve 25 years at the federal prison in Leavenworth, Kansas.

Following the sentence, Panzram warned the world that he would kill the first man who crossed him when he was inside. He was as good as his word. He was given work in the laundry and one day murdered his supervisor, Robert Warnke, by staving in his head with an iron bar.

This time, Panzram was sentenced to hang. He positively welcomed the court's verdict and claimed that now his only ambition was to die. When anti-death penalty campaigners tried to have his sentence commuted, he ungraciously wrote to them to say: 'I wish you all had one neck and I had my hands on it.' Shortly afterwards, on 3 September 1930, his wish to die was granted, and he was duly hanged.

Ruthless Rippers

Our modern-day notion of the serial killer has its roots in the crimes of Jack the Ripper, committed over a century ago in Victorian London. Here was a killer who struck without warning in the dead of the night. His victims were prostitutes, whose bodies he literally ripped apart with his knife. He even made up his nickname, signing 'Jack the Ripper' on the taunting letters he wrote to the newspapers. However, it was not simply the fact that he had murdered these women that so captured and horrified the public imagination; it was the callous and fetishistic way in which he ripped apart their bodies, and carved out the ghastly souvenirs that he festooned around the scene of the crime or took away with him.

This combination of brutality and aberrant sexual fetishism is at the heart of the serial killer's psyche, and has provided a terrible model for other sick souls to follow. When someone started killing prostitutes in the northern English city of Leeds in the 1970s, it was not long before the press branded him the 'Yorkshire Ripper'. Likewise, when a group of satanically inclined young Chicagoans started picking up prostitutes, savagely mutilating them and cutting off their breasts, it was inevitable that they should become known as the 'Chicago Rippers'.

The unknown man who called himself Jack the Ripper picked an apposite word, for the serial killer not only rips apart the bodies of his victims, but he also rips apart our sense of humanity as something raised above the merely bestial.

JACK THE RIPPER

Jack the Ripper is the definitive serial killer. His brief and monstrous career established the serial killer in the public mind as the most terrifying of all criminals. So why does this killer, whose crimes were committed over a century ago, still haunt us? Partly, it is the sheer ferocity of his crimes: the disembowelling, the removal of body organs. Partly, it is the setting: Victorian Whitechapel is fixed in our minds as a seedy location for murder. Mostly, however, what has made the Ripper an immortal among murderers is the simple fact that he was never caught.

Who Was He?

For that reason, his crimes provide endless scope for speculation. Scarcely a year passes without another book being published that promises to name the real killer – a trend that reached its zenith when the crime novelist Patricia Cornwell spent a reputed $8 million of her own money in an effort to prove that the Victorian painter Walter Sickert was the murderer, a claim that remains tenuous at best.

The killer we know as Jack the Ripper announced himself to the world on 31 August 1888 with the murder of a prostitute named Mary 'Polly' Nichols. This was the third prostitute murder of the year in London's East End and did not initially attract too much attention, even though it was an unusually brutal killing: her throat and torso had been cut, and there were stab wounds to the genitals. At this stage, of course, there was nothing to suggest a serial killer at large.

It was little more than a week, however, before the murderer struck again. The victim was another prostitute, Annie Chapman, known as 'Dark Annie'. Like Polly Nichols, she had been killed by a knife slash to the throat, but this time the killer had disembowelled her, pulled out her entrails and draped them over a shoulder, and then cut out her vagina and ovaries. What struck investigators, apart from the sheer horror of the scene, was the precision of the cuts; it seemed possible that the killer had medical training and was familiar with dissecting bodies in the post-mortem room.

Twice in One Night

This gruesome crime already had the public in an uproar, but it was as nothing compared to the reaction that followed the murderer's next atrocity on 30 September. This time, he killed not once but twice on the same night. The first victim was Elizabeth Stride, 'Long Liz', a seamstress and occasional prostitute. She had been killed by a knife wound to the throat, but there was no other mutilation. One can only presume that the killer was interrupted in his work, and thus dissatisfied, because, before the night was over, he also killed prostitute Catherine Eddowes – and this time the attack had all his characteristic savagery. In addition, someone had written on the wall the strange message: 'The Juwes are not the men that will be blamed for nothing.' The police were not sure if the killer had written it, or what it meant, so the investigating officer ordered it to be removed to avoid anti-Jewish hysteria developing.

Letters

Just before the double murder, the Central News Agency had received a letter that purported to be from the killer. There had already been many such letters, most of them obvious hoaxes, but when a second letter came from the same writer within hours of the double murder, the agency passed them on to the police. The writer signed himself 'Jack the Ripper', which caused a sensation in the press. Now, the murderer had a name.

Two weeks later another letter arrived, sent to George Lusk, head of the Whitechapel Vigilance Committee. It appeared to have a different author from the previous ones – this correspondent was far less literate – but was even more chilling. In place of a return address it simply said 'From Hell'. Enclosed in it was a piece of human kidney, which the writer claimed belonged to Eddowes. Eddowes had indeed had a kidney removed by her killer.

Unimaginable carnage

Three more weeks went by, and then the Ripper struck again. Once again, the victim was a prostitute, Mary Kelly. In a change from previous behaviour she was killed indoors, in a room in Miller's Court. Mary Kelly's body was utterly destroyed; she was partially skinned, disembowelled, grotesquely arranged and numerous trophies were taken, including her uterus and a foetus taken from it (Kelly had been pregnant at the time). It was a scene of unimaginable carnage and one that left Whitechapel – and the world – bracing itself for the Ripper's next atrocity.

However, the next killing never came. There was a knife murder of a prostitute two years later, and another two years after that, but neither had any of the hallmarks of a Ripper killing. As mysteriously as he had appeared, the Ripper had vanished.

Since that time, detectives – both amateur and professional – have speculated about who he (or even she in some far-fetched accounts) was. To date, suspects have included Queen Victoria's grandson Prince Eddy, in a rage against the prostitute who supposedly gave him syphilis; Sir William Gull, the Queen's surgeon, as part of a conspiracy to cover up the fact that Prince Eddy had conceived an illegitimate child with a Whitechapel girl (another theory sadly lacking in evidence); and Liverpool businessman James Maybrick, supposed author of The Ripper Diaries, published in 1994 and generally deemed to be fake.

The truth is that we shall probably never know who he was, or why he killed so brutally. However, there is a likely explanation for the sudden end to his reign of terror, put forward at the time by Sir Melville Macnaghten, the Chief Commissioner of the Metropolitan Police. He speculated that 'the murderer's brain gave way altogether after his awful glut in Miller's Court, and that he immediately committed suicide, or, as a possible alternative, was found to be so hopelessly mad by his relations that they confined him to an asylum'.

THE CHICAGO RIPPERS

That one lone killer might abduct, rape, torture and kill a string of young women is horrifying enough. That four men should get together to carry out such crimes as a team almost beggars belief. That, however, is exactly what Robin Gecht, Edward Spreitzer and the Kokoraleis brothers, Andrew and Thomas, did. Known as the 'Chicago Rippers', they were responsible for at least seven and conceivably as many as 18 murders of women, all of them carried out with dreadful savagery and without any apparent motive, beyond the basest of sadistic urges.

The first murder to be carried out by the gang was that of 28-year-old Linda Sutton. On 23 May 1981, she was abducted. Ten days later her body was found in a field, in the Villa Park area of the city, not far from an establishment called the Rip Van Winkle motel. Sutton's body had been mutilated and her left breast amputated. This was evidently the work of a sexual sadist but, as yet, the police had no clues to go on.

It was almost a year before the Rippers struck again. On 15 May 1982 they abducted another young woman, Lorraine Borowski, as she was about to open up the realtor's office in which she worked. This time, however, it was five months before the body was discovered in a cemetery in Villa Park.

By this time, the Rippers had struck several more times. On 29 May, they abducted Shui Mak from Hanover Park, a little way to the north of Villa Park. Her body was not found for four months. Two weeks after the abduction of Shui Mak, a prostitute known as Angel York was picked up by a man in a van, who handcuffed her and slashed her breast before throwing her out, still alive.

More Breast Amputations

York's description of her attacker failed to produce any leads, and two months passed before the Rippers struck again. On 28 August 1982 the body of Sandra Delaware, a prostitute, was discovered by the Chicago River. She had been stabbed and strangled and her left breast amputated. On 8 September 30-year-old Rose Davis was found in an alley, having suffered almost identical injuries to Delaware. On 11 September, Carole Pappas, whose husband was a pitcher for the Chicago Cubs, vanished, never to be seen again.

A month later, the killers committed their last crime, one that was to prove to be their downfall. Their victim, a prostitute named Beverley Washington, was found by a railway track on 6 December. In addition to other injuries, her left breast had been cut off and her right breast severely slashed. Amazingly, she was still alive and was able to offer a description of her attacker and the van he had used to abduct her.

Cult

This description led the police to Robin Gecht, a 28-year old carpenter (who, bizarrely enough, had once worked for paedophile killer John Wayne Gacy). Gecht, as a teenager, had been accused of molesting his sister and had a long-term interest in satanism. At first, police had to release Gecht for lack of evidence, but after investigating further, they discovered that the previous year he had rented a room at a motel along with three friends – each of them with adjoining rooms.

The hotel manager said they had held loud parties and appeared to be involved in some kind of cult. Detectives then traced the other men, the Kokoraleis brothers, and Edward Spreitzer, a man of subnormal intelligence.

Satanic chapel

Under interrogation, Thomas Kokoraleis confessed that he and the others had taken women back to Gecht's place, to what Gecht called a 'satanic chapel'. There they had raped and tortured them, cutting off their breasts with a wire garrotte. He further alleged that they would eat parts of the severed breasts as a kind of sacrament, and that Gecht would masturbate into the breasts before putting them into a box. Kokoraleis claimed that he once saw 15 breasts in the box.

Police arrested the three men; Gecht was re-arrested. They searched Gecht's apartment and found the satanic chapel, though not the box of severed breasts. Both Kokoraleis bothers eventually confessed to their crimes, as did Spreitzer. Gecht, however, protested his innocence. After a drawn-out series of trials, Andrew Kokoraleis was convicted of murder and put to death in 1999. Thomas Kokoraleis was convicted of murder but only sentenced to life imprisonment, as a reward for his initial confession. Edward Spreitzer was sentenced to death but had his sentence changed to life imprisonment in 2002. In the absence of hard evidence linking him to the crimes, Robin Gecht was only convicted of the rape and attempted murder of Beverley Washington. He was sentenced to 120 years in prison, where he continues to maintain his innocence.

JERRY BRUDOS

For most of his 67 years, Jerome Henry Brudos was simply called 'Jerry', but he would become famous as 'The Shoe Fetish Slayer' and 'The Lust Killer'. Neither appellation quite covers what he was – for one, his fetishes went way beyond footwear. What is more, both nicknames suggest that Jerry's crimes extended no further than murder when in fact he was a torturer and a rapist, with an attraction toward necrophilia.

Brudos was born on 31 January 1939, in the small South Dakota town of Webster. Times were hard for his family. They had suffered under the weight of the Great Depression for nearly a decade. Not long after welcoming the new baby, they gave up on their farm and moved to Oregon, but the move did not bring the financial stability they had hoped for. Jerry's father, Henry, was forced to work at two jobs and he had little time to spend with the family.

When he was not at school, Jerry was usually with his domineering, stern mother, Eileen. It's strange that this is so – Eileen didn't like Jerry. She much preferred her eldest son, Larry, on whom she constantly doted.

Her resentment of Jerry can be traced back to his birth. As the mother of three sons she had desperately wanted her fourth child to be a girl, but Jerry had arrived instead. He grew up feeling that his mother was not happy about his gender.

Eileen's disappointment with Jerry's sex might explain a rather curious incident from his early life. At the age of five, he found a pair of elegant women's high-heeled shoes at the local dump. He began wearing them in secret around the house, but his mother soon saw what he was doing. She flew into a rage and then she insisted that he get rid of the feminine footwear. When she discovered that Jerry had not done as she requested, she doused the offending items in petrol and set them alight. Then she forced Jerry to watch as the forbidden footwear went up in flames.

Whatever Eileen's intention, it is likely that she only intensified her son's interest in women's footwear. In short, it was the attraction to the forbidden. Not long afterwards, Jerry was caught trying to steal his nursery school teacher's shoes.

By 1955 the Great Depression and the hardship it had caused seemed far away. The Brudos family had moved into an attractive middle-class home in a pleasant neighbourhood.

Now 16 years old, Jerry found himself living next door to a couple with three teenage daughters. He not only spied on the girls from the windows of his home, but he began stealing their underwear from the clothes line.

After the theft of the missing articles had been reported to the police, Jerry saw an opportunity to further his increasingly unusual desire for things feminine. He began by convincing one of the girls that he was working on the crime with the police and then he invited her over to discuss the case. When the girl appeared, Jerry invited her in and then he excused himself and left the room. He returned wearing a mask. Suddenly he held a knife to her throat and forced her to strip.

Once her clothes were on the floor, Jerry took a number of photographs before leaving the room. He reappeared just as his neighbour was about to flee. Before she could raise the alarm, he quickly explained that a masked man had locked him up. It was a bold story, a ridiculous story, yet the girl told no one about the bizarre and terrifying experience.

Unhealthy fantasies

Not long afterwards an emboldened Jerry began beating another girl after she had refused to strip for him. An elderly couple walking nearby heard the disturbance. The police were called, a report was made and an investigation began. They soon found Jerry's shoe collection, the stolen lingerie and the nude photographs he had taken of his neighbour.

Jerry was sent to the psychiatric ward at Oregon State Hospital, where he related his fantasies to the psychiatrists. One of them involved an underground prison. He dreamed of a place in which he could keep captured girls. That way, he would be able to have any girl he wanted, whenever he wanted.

The psychiatrists were not concerned by what they were hearing, because they believed that Jerry's dark sexual desires would pass with adolescence. The same psychiatrists determined that Jerry was borderline schizophrenic, yet after nine months at the hospital he was discharged. Tests revealed that Jerry was an intelligent person, yet he lacked motivation and self-discipline. When he graduated from high school he ended up very close to the bottom of his class.

Jerry gave no thought to university. Instead he looked for a job, but he found nothing.

Unusual requests

Having come to a dead end, he set his sights on a military career, but he was soon discharged as an undesirable recruit after sharing his sexual fantasies with an army psychiatrist. Forced to return home, he lapsed into his old habits. He not only began stealing shoes and underwear but he also went back to assaulting women. Taking things a stage further he tried to abduct one young woman, but when she lost consciousness Jerry stole her shoes instead.

By 1961 Jerry had become an electronics technician. While he was working at a local radio station he took up with an attractive girl named Ralphene. The 17-year-old liked the idea of dating a man who was five years her senior. At the age of 23, Jerry finally lost his virginity. It was not long before Ralphene became pregnant, so with considerable reluctance her parents agreed to a wedding.

The ceremony took place in the spring of 1962, but there was not much of a honeymoon. Ralphene soon discovered that her new husband was very controlling.

What is more, his requests were really peculiar. Jerry insisted that his bride do all her housework in the nude... except for a pair of high-heeled shoes, of course. Jerry also forbade Ralphene to enter his basement. Unbeknown to his wife, Jerry spent his time printing photographs of Ralphene wearing the articles of women's clothing that he had stolen over the years.

Ralphene was young and inexperienced when the couple were first married, so she went along with her husband's unusual requests, but as time went on she became more assertive. No longer was Jerry's wife willing to be photographed, no longer would she don the underwear he gave her. The housework was now done in an overall. She was a mother now, with another child on the way. Now that Ralphene was no longer an outlet for his sexual fantasies, Jerry turned inwards. He began wearing his collection of stolen women's underwear on a daily basis, often under his work clothes.

Things escalated dramatically one evening, shortly after the birth of his second child. Quite by chance Jerry spotted a very attractive woman walking down a street in Portland. He followed her to her apartment and then he stood and watched her windows. The hours went by, but Jerry did not move until he was certain that she had gone to sleep. He then broke in. The woman woke up just as he was in the process of stealing her underwear, so he jumped on the bed and raped her.

Frustrated by Ralphene's refusal to participate in his fantasies, Jerry took photographs of himself in women's clothing and then he left them around the house. When they were ignored, he retreated into his basement workshop. Jerry had already committed rape, but his sexual fantasies were about to manifest themselves in an even more violent fashion.

On 26 January 1968 he committed his first murder. His victim, 19-year-old Linda Slawson, was trying to fund her education as a door-to-door encyclopedia saleswoman.

When she approached Jerry in his garden he expressed great enthusiasm, so she willingly followed him into his basement so that she could continue her sales pitch. Once inside, she was clubbed on the head and strangled.

When he was certain that Linda was dead, he went upstairs, peeled some bills from his wallet and sent his family out to a local fast food restaurant. Once they had left, he began acting out his fantasies with the dead woman's body. But Jerry did not stop when his wife and children returned – in fact, he continued with his activities for several days.

He then dipped into his collection of shoes and women's underwear so that he could dress Linda's body in high heels and lingerie. Numerous photographs were taken, the articles of clothing would be changed and the cycle would be repeated. Jerry also had sex with Linda's body. After a few days of exhausting activity he took the corpse to the Willamette River and threw it from a bridge. Before doing so, he cut off one of Linda's feet with a hacksaw and placed it in the basement freezer. From time to time, Jerry would place a shoe on the severed foot and then masturbate. When the severed foot had almost rotted away, Brudos threw it into the river to join the corpse.

Jerry did not kill again for several months. In the intervening period he moved his family to Salem, Oregon's state capital. The new Brudos home was rather unattractive, but it did have one feature that appealed to the head of the household – a separate garage. Located off a narrow roadway, the structure would serve as Jerry's new workshop. It would be much more private than the basement.

Hung from a meat hook

On the evening of 26 November 1968 Jerry abducted Jan Whitney, his second murder victim. The family had not even settled in at that point. He had come across the young woman on Interstate 5 (I-5), after spotting her broken-down car. The vehicle could be fixed, or so he claimed, but first he had to return to his home to retrieve some tools. Jan went back to Salem with Jerry. Once there, Jerry raped and strangled her in the passenger seat of the family car.

During the next five days, Jan's body hung from a meat hook in Jerry's garage. He dressed the corpse, took photographs and committed acts of necrophilia, as before. Then he took a break by going off on a Thanksgiving weekend getaway with his wife and family.

While the Brudos family were away a freak accident very nearly exposed Jan's dangling corpse and with it Jerry's secret life. A car spun out of control and hit his garage with such force that it made a large crack in the wooden structure, which brought several police officers to the scene. Had they bothered to look through the damaged wall they would have seen Jan Whitney's hanging body.

The close call served to embolden Jerry. He thought he was so clever that he could do whatever he pleased without being caught. A few days after his return, Jerry disposed of Jan's corpse in the Willamette River. Before doing so he cut off her right breast, intending to use it as a mould for making paperweights. He would be frustrated in his attempts.

Linda Slawson's work had led her to approach Jerry, while Jan Whitney's murder was the result of a chance encounter – now, however, Jerry was ready to stalk his prey. Dressed in women's clothing, he hung around in a Salem department store parking garage and on 27 March 1969 he abducted his next victim. Jerry did not kill 19-year-old Karen Sprinker immediately. Instead he forced her to model various items from his collection of women's clothing. After he became tired of that game, he put a noose around her neck, raised her a few inches above the ground and left his garage workshop to join his family for dinner. When he returned, Karen was dead. He cut off both of her breasts in yet another attempt at making a paperweight and then he threw her into the Long Tom River.

Less than a month later, Jerry was hunting for a new victim. On 21 April he attacked another young woman, Sharon Wood, in a parking garage. A struggle ensued, Sharon bit Jerry's thumb and he ran. A few days later he tried again, this time choosing a much younger target. As 12-year-old Gloria Smith walked to school, he approached her with a fake pistol and began marching her to his car. Fortunately Gloria showed quick thinking by running to a woman who was working in her garden.

Fake police badge

Jerry had thought himself so clever, but he had now failed on two occasions. He had even been outwitted by a young girl. Clearly he needed more than an imitation pistol if his abductions were going to be successful. So Jerry went out and bought a fake police badge, which he used to abduct Linda Salee, his final victim. He approached the young woman in a Portland shopping centre car park and accused her of shoplifting. After meekly following his orders, Linda was driven back to his Salem garage where she was tied up. Jerry then had dinner in the house with his family. On his return, he was surprised to find that Linda had removed the ropes. The young woman was free and yet she had not fled, so Jerry tied her up a second time and suspended her from the ceiling. After undressing her and taking a series of photographs, he hanged her.

Linda was Jerry's fourth murder victim and yet the police had not linked the murders together. In fact, they did not even know that the women were dead. Jerry might have gone on killing for some time had it not been for an angler's discovery.

On 10 May 1969, roughly a month after Linda's murder, the man spotted her body floating in the Long Tom River. Two days later, police divers found Karen Sprinker's remains. They were just a few feet away from Linda's corpse.

Jerry was unconcerned when the news raced through the community. He was confident that nothing could link him to the bodies.

He was wrong.

When Jerry had tied the women up he had used an unusual knot, one that was often used by electricians when they pulled wires through a house. The knot would tie Jerry to the murders.

The police then visited the campus of Oregon State University, where Karen Sprinker had been a student. They were told stories about a peculiar man who had been seen roaming the campus. One young woman had even had a date with the man.

When he called again, the police were waiting. It was Jerry Brudos. A background check revealed Jerry's occupation and his history of attacking teenage girls, so detectives paid a visit to the Brudos home.

They noticed a piece of rope in Jerry's garage. It was identical to the one that had been tied around the two bodies that had been found in the Long Tom River. Recognizing the investigators' interest, the ever-bold Jerry offered them a sample. It later proved to be a perfect match.

The net tightens

Jerry could sense that the police were closing in, so on 30 May he made for the Canadian border, accompanied by his wife. The couple were spotted by the Oregon State Police. Although Jerry was arrested on the relatively minor charge of armed assault in relation to 12-year-old Gloria Smith, he became talkative in custody. He took great pleasure in providing very detailed accounts of the murders that he had committed. At the same time he showed no remorse, telling one detective that the women he had abused and killed were nothing more than objects to him. In fact, he went so far as to compare each of the dead women to a candy wrapper.

'Once you're done with them, you just discard them. Why would you not discard them? You don't have any more use for them.'

On 27 June, Jerry pleaded guilty to all of the charges that had been made against him. He received three life sentences amounting to at least 36 years in prison. Jerry became eligible for parole in 2005, but as the years passed and the date of his release approached it became increasingly clear that he would never again be a free man.

He died of liver cancer on 29 March 2006, at the age of 67.

ED GEIN

Ed Gein is far from the most prolific of serial killers. There are only two murders for which he was undoubtedly responsible, yet he occupies a peculiarly terrifying place in our collective psyche. Not only was he the inspiration for the murderer in Hitchcock's *Psycho*, but his crimes also inspired the *Texas Chainsaw Massacre* and the Buffalo Bill character in Thomas Harris' *The Silence of the Lambs*. So why does this inoffensive-seeming little man inspire such horror?

Household 'Decorations'

The simple answer is this: because of the things he kept in his kitchen and in his wardrobe. Things like bowls made of human skulls; a wastepaper basket made of human skin; a full breastplate made out of a woman's skinned torso; and even, perhaps most disconcertingly of all, a belt constructed entirely from female nipples. Not until the police raided Jeffrey Dahmer's apartment 30 years later would investigators find themselves in quite such a house of horror.

Ed Gein was born in La Crosse, Wisconsin, on 27 August 1906, the second son of Augusta and George Gein. Soon after his birth the family moved to a remote farm outside nearby Plainfield. His father George was a feckless drinker who worked as a tanner and carpenter, while Augusta was an extremely religious woman who dominated the family and ran a grocery in La Crosse.

Augusta drilled into young Ed and his older brother Henry the sinfulness of women and the utter evil of premarital sex (or by implication any kind of sex at all). She disapproved of her children having friends, not that there were any children nearby. Ed Gein grew up, unsurprisingly enough, a sexually confused loner, with a great fondness for escapist books and magazines. Even as an adult, Ed continued to have an isolated existence working on the farm alongside his parents and brothers. As long as that set-up continued, Ed appears to have been harmless enough. Things only really went off the rails when family members started to die off.

In 1940 George died, and his sons started to take on odd jobs in town to help make ends meet. Ed worked as handyman and even as a babysitter, and townspeople found him likeable and trustworthy. Then, in 1944, Henry died under what seem, with the benefit of hindsight, to be suspicious circumstances. Ed and Henry were fighting a fire in the nearby marshes when the two got separated and, when the fire cleared, Henry was found dead. What was odd was that his body was lying in an unburned area and there was bruising to his head. The cause of death, though, was recorded as smoke asphyxiation.

Grave Robbing

That left only Ed and his adored mother Augusta on the farm. Little more than a year later, however, she was dead too. She died of a stroke on 29 December 1945 following an argument with a neighbour. Ed's first response was to nail her bedroom door shut, leaving the room inside just as it was the day she died. His second response was to take up grave robbing. He became fascinated with human anatomy. He was particularly interested in reading about the first sex-change operation, undertaken by Christine Jorgensen, and even considered having a sex-change operation himself. Then, in consort with a disturbed local named Gus,

Ed Gein

he started visiting graveyards and taking souvenirs; sometimes whole bodies, more often selected body parts. He would scour the obituary column of the local newspaper in order to learn of freshly buried female corpses.

Resemblances

During these years, Gein started to manufacture his macabre household decorations, and eventually his grave-robbing expeditions failed to satisfy his strange obsession. In December 1954, a 51 year old woman called Mary Hogan disappeared from the bar she ran in Pine Grove, Wisconsin. There was blood on the floor and a spent cartridge was found at the scene. Gein was among the potential suspects but there was no hard evidence to connect him, and the police saw no reason to visit his home.

This was the first of only two murders that can certainly be credited to Gein. The next came three years later. Once again the victim was a woman in her fifties, and like Mary Hogan, she looked like Ed's mother. Her name was Bernice Worden and on 16 November 1957 she was abducted from her hardware store in Plainfield. Again, there was blood on the floor. This time, however, the police had a pretty good clue as to who was responsible. The victim's son told them that Ed Gein had asked his mother for a date, and another local resident recalled Ed saying he needed to buy some antifreeze from her store on the day she died. A receipt for antifreeze was found lying in the store and the police decided to pay Ed Gein a visit.

Bernice Worden's corpse was hanging from the rafters. Her head was cut off, her genitalia removed and her torso slit open and gutted. On further investigation they found her head turned into a makeshift ornament, and her heart sitting in a saucepan on the stove. They also discovered a pistol that matched the cartridge found at the scene of the Mary Hogan murder.

On arrest, Gein immediately confessed to the murders of Worden and Hogan as well as to his grave-robbing activities. A judge found Gein incompetent for trial and he was committed to a secure mental hospital. Meanwhile, his house was razed to the ground to prevent it from becoming the focus of macabre cults.

Soon after, Ed Gein's immortality was ensured when local writer Robert Bloch wrote a book called *Psycho*, inspired by the case, and Alfred Hitchcock picked it up for the movies. In 1968, Gein was once more submitted for trial but was again found insane. He ended his days in the mental hospital, dying of respiratory failure on 26 July 1984.

H. H. HOLMES

It is not correct, as is often claimed, that H. H. Holmes was America's first serial killer; both the Bloody Benders (a Kansas family of serial killers) and the Servant Girl Annihilator (the unidentified murderer of eight women in Austin, Texas in the 1880s) preceded him. He did, however, kill more people than the Servant Girl Annihilator and all the members of the Bender family put together. The claim that Holmes was the most prolific American serial killer of all time remains an issue of some debate.

The man who history remembers as H. H. Holmes was born Herman Webster Mudgett on 16 May 1860 in Gilmanton, New Hampshire. Nearly a century and a half later, the town numbers barely more than 3,000 inhabitants. It is perhaps most famous as having served as a model for Grace Metalious's Peyton Place, the setting for the 1956 novel of the same name.

Holmes grew up in an impoverished family with an abusive alcoholic father at its head. School provided only a partial escape. While an intelligent and handsome boy, he was also a frequent victim of bullying. He once claimed that, as a child, he had been forced by his classmates to touch a human skeleton. It was an event that appeared to haunt him for the rest of his life. Nevertheless, he sought to become a medical doctor and developed a fascination with anatomy. As an adolescent, this interest found expression in his killing and dismembering of stray animals.

At 16, he graduated from school and managed to get teaching positions – first in Gilmanton and later in nearby Alton, New Hampshire. It was there that he met Clara Lovering. The ardour between them was such that the two eloped. However, in marriage that same passion quickly dissipated and he soon abandoned his wife.

Still intent on a career in medicine, he attended the University of Vermont. It was, however, too small for his liking. In September 1882, he enrolled at the University of Michigan at Ann Arbor, which held what was considered to be one of the country's leading medical schools. Two years later, he graduated with what are best described as lacklustre grades.

After graduation, Mudgett adopted as his name the more distinguished sounding Henry Howard Holmes. He took up a position as prescription clerk in a pharmacy owned by a terminally ill doctor named Holton. He endeared himself to Holton's wife and customers. When the good doctor passed away, Holmes offered to buy the pharmacy, promising the newly made widow $100 a month. After signing over the deed, Mrs Holton subsequently disappeared; Holmes claimed she had settled with relatives in California.

Castle of Death

Under Holmes, the pharmacy thrived in the growing Englewood neighbourhood of Chicago. In 1887, he married Myrta Z. Belknap, a stunning young woman whom he had met during a business trip to Minneapolis. She remained unaware that Holmes had been married before – and that he had not obtained a divorce. In their third year of marriage, Myrta bore a daughter named Lucy. By this time she had already returned to the home of her parents. Though Holmes would never seek a divorce, the union was all but over.

Using the pharmacy as his base, Holmes continued to engage in a number of questionable business ventures he had begun several years before. However, his most notable achievement was the construction of a block-long, three-storey building on the site across the street from his pharmacy. Built over a three-year period, 'The Castle', as the locals dubbed it, included a ground floor which Holmes rented out to various shopkeepers. The upper two storeys Holmes kept for himself. A huge space, it was a confusing maze of over a hundred windowless rooms, secret passageways, false floors and stairways that led to nowhere. Some doors could only be opened from the outside, while others opened to reveal nothing but a brick wall. During construction, Holmes repeatedly changed contractors, ensuring that no one understood the design of the building or had any idea as to its ultimate purpose.

Beginning shortly after the completion of the Castle, and for the three years that followed, Holmes murdered dozens of women. He tortured them in soundproof chambers fitted with gas lines that enabled him to asphyxiate his victims. The corpses were sent down a secret chute to the Castle's basement. There, Holmes would dissect them, just as he had the animals he killed in his adolescence. They would be stripped of flesh and sold as skeleton models to medical schools. Some bodies were cremated or thrown in pits of lime and acid.

One of the first to die was Julia Connor, the wife of a jeweller to whom Holmes had rented a shop. After she came to Holmes with the news that she was pregnant with his child, the doctor murdered Julia and her daughter, Pearl.

Holmes saw great opportunity in Chicago's upcoming 1893 World's Columbian Exposition and made several modifications to the second storey of the Castle, transforming it into the World's Fair Hotel. The first guests arrived in the spring of 1893. Some returned home, others did not. With the high volume of guests, Holmes could be selective in choosing his victims. The fact that so many people were coming to the fair without any place to stay ensured that his activities went unnoticed.

One of those who remained alive was Georgiana Yorke, who became Holmes' third wife in January 1894. She believed Holmes to be a very wealthy man, with property in Texas and Europe. Indeed, he appeared to be quite prosperous. However, his debts had begun to catch up with him.

Running Out Of Time

After having been confronted by his creditors, he came up with a scheme which involved a man named Benjamin Pietzel. As a carpenter, Pietzel had worked on the Castle. Exactly how much he knew of Holmes' activities is a matter of some debate. What is certain is that Pietzel agreed to fake his own death in order to collect a large insurance claim. In the end, Holmes simply killed the man and kept all the money for himself. He then made off with three of Pietzel's children.

On 17 November 1894, having been on the road for nearly two years, Holmes was arrested in Boston. Initially, he was suspected of nothing more than fraud. However, an insurance agent's diligence in attempting to track down the three Pietzel children revealed that they had been killed in the cities of Indianapolis and Toronto. This news encouraged the police in Chicago to investigate Holmes' Castle. On 20 July 1895, all was revealed. The police spent a month investigating what some now called 'the Murder Castle' before, on 19 August, it was consumed by a fire of mysterious origin.

Exactly how many poor souls Holmes murdered is a mystery. The number has typically been estimated as being between 20 and 100. The authorities put the murder count at 27, committed in Chicago, Philadelphia, Indianapolis and Toronto. The police in Chicago noted that many of the bodies in the basement of the Castle had been dissected and burned to such an extent that it was difficult to determine precisely how many bodies it contained. At his trial, Holmes confessed to 27 murders.

Holmes was led to the gallows on the morning of 7 May 1896. As he watched the preparations for his hanging, he is reported to have said, 'Take your time; don't bungle it.' However, despite the hangman's care, Holmes died an agonizing death. For ten minutes after the trapdoor was sprung, his body twitched. He was officially pronounced dead after he had been hanging for 15 minutes.

DENNIS NILSEN

Dennis 'Des' Nilsen is one of the most perplexing of serial killers. He exhibited few of the conventional childhood signs of a future killer; he did not torture animals or play with fire. When he killed it was not in a sexual frenzy, but while his victims slept. He killed them, he famously said, so they would not leave. He was 'killing for company'. However, the fact remains that this mild-mannered civil servant was responsible for the violent deaths of at least 15 men.

Motivation

His case is fascinating not simply because it does not fit a pattern but also because, more than most other killers, Nilsen himself has tried to understand his own motivation. He helped the writer Brian Masters to write his biography and has written his own autobiography, as well as penning numerous letters to the press and researchers.

Dennis Andrew Nilsen was born in the Scottish port town of Fraserburgh on 23 November 1945 – yet another serial killer to be born during the post-war baby boom. His parents were Olav, a Norwegian soldier who had left Norway when the Nazis invaded, and Betty, who came from a religious Scottish family. His father was a heavy drinker who effectively deserted Betty from the very start. There was never a family home: Betty and Dennis remained at her parents' house and the couple were divorced in 1949.

The father figure in Dennis' life became his grandfather, Andrew Whyte. When Whyte died in 1951, it was a defining trauma in Dennis' life – all the more so because he was taken to see his grandfather's body without being told that he had died.

This unexpected sight of his grandfather's corpse is the event that Nilsen himself regards as having sown the seeds of his later sexual pathology.

In 1953, Nilsen's mother remarried and went on to have four other children. Understandably, she had less time for Dennis and he became a rather solitary child. In 1961, aged 16, he opted to join the army, to be a soldier like his absent father. He remained in the army until 1972, working for part of the time as a butcher in the Catering Corps. Dennis had no sexual experience as a teenager but was increasingly aware that he was attracted to men. During his last year in the army he fell in love with a fellow soldier. However, the man in question was not gay and did not return Nilsen's affections – though he did consent to Nilsen's request to film him while he pretended to be dead.

The end of their friendship was a great blow to Nilsen, who then left the army and trained to be a policeman – taking a particular interest in visits to the morgue. However police work did not suit him and after a year he left and found employment in a job centre in London's Soho, interviewing people looking for work.

Killing for Company

Soho was the hub of London's emerging gay scene at the time and Nilsen began to immerse himself in a new world of bar-hopping and casual pick-ups. However, whatever sexual gratification Nilsen got from this was not enough to counterbalance a terrible sense of loneliness. This abated for nearly two years, between 1975 and 1977, when he shared an apartment in north London with a man named David Gallichan. They were not, apparently, sexual partners, but they shared domestic duties and acquired a dog and a cat. However, temperamental differences drove them apart and in 1977 Nilsen asked Gallichan to leave the flat.

The loneliness returned and became unbearable for Nilsen. In December 1978 Nilsen picked up a young Irishman in a pub; Nilsen never even learned the young man's name. Later that night, as he watched his latest pick-up sleeping, and anticipated him leaving in the morning, Nilsen decided he could not bear to be left alone again. He strangled the young man using a necktie, then finished him off by drowning him in a bucket of water. He washed the corpse's hair and put him back into bed. Suddenly he had what he later called 'a new kind of flatmate'.

Realizing, after a while, that he had to do something with this corpse, Nilsen went out and bought an electric carving knife, but could not bring himself to cut up the body, so he ended up hiding the corpse under the floorboards where it remained for eight months until he took it out and burned it on a bonfire in his garden.

Ready to Kill Again

At the time he was sure he would be caught, but he was not, and so by the end of 1979 he was ready to kill again. This time, however, his intended victim, a young Chinese man called Andrew Ho, escaped and went to the police. The police, however, regarded the matter as a tiff between gay lovers and failed to press charges.

Just days later, he found his next victim, a Canadian called Kenneth Ockendon. This time, after strangling the man with an electric cord, Nilsen dissected the body, using the butchery skills he had acquired in the army. Then he flushed part of the body down the toilet while leaving other parts under the floorboards.

Over the next two years, Nilsen repeated the pattern ten more times. The young men he killed were generally transient drifters and rent boys; in only a few cases did Nilsen know their names. Each was strangled and dissected, the body parts flushed away or kept as trophies.

In October 1981 Nilsen decided to move house. Some sane part of his brain decided to move out of his garden flat and into an attic flat, in the hopes that this would make it harder for him to dispose of a body and thus would inhibit him from killing again. Before he left, he had one more bonfire in which he incinerated the last remains of his victims.

Over the next year or so, Nilsen succeeded in killing three more times. But finally his new living quarters did betray him. He had been flushing body parts down the toilet once more and this time the drains refused to co-operate. Another tenant in the house called in a company to unblock the drains. They found that the blockage was due to human flesh and soon traced the problem to Nilsen's flat. Nilsen was immediately arrested.

Once in custody, Nilsen stunned the police with an exhaustive confession. He was sentenced to life imprisonment.

PETER SUTCLIFFE

No one could quite believe that the softly spoken, scrupulously polite Peter Sutcliffe was the 'Yorkshire Ripper', responsible for the brutal murders of at least 13 women, plus seven others left hideously wounded. His wife Sonia could not, nor his parents, John and Kathleen. Nor, for a long time, could the police. After all, they had interviewed him no less than nine times in connection with the case before he was finally caught.

There was little in Peter Sutcliffe's childhood to point to his subsequent evil career as Britain's most notorious serial killer since Jack the Ripper. He was born in Bingley, Yorkshire, on 2 June 1946. He was much closer to his mother than his father, and was an effeminate child with little interest in sports or rough play. There was also a certain tension between his parents, his father suspecting his mother of having an affair. Conceivably, this may have inclined him to be suspicious of women.

Shy of Women

Certainly, Sutcliffe was shy of women and did not have a girlfriend until he was 19 and met Sonia, the daughter of Czech immigrants. They began to go out together and eventually married eight years later. Meanwhile, Peter worked at a series of jobs. For a while he was a gravedigger. He liked to steal trophies from the bodies he buried, and horrified his workmates with his persistent references to necrophilia. Evidently there was already something seriously disturbed about Peter Sutcliffe's fantasy life. This was also hinted at by his fondness for visiting a wax museum that specialized in macabre displays of dead bodies.

Peter and Sonia married on 10 August 1974. Shortly afterwards, in June 1975, he qualified as a long-distance lorry driver. Then he learned that, following a miscarriage, Sonia would not be able to have children. The following month, he carried out his first attack on a woman. He assaulted Anna Rogulskyj, hitting her over the head with a hammer and then slashing her body with a knife. She survived the attack, as did Sutcliffe's second victim, Olive Smelt. Both women were severely injured and utterly traumatized.

Trademark Injuries

Sutcliffe's next victim was unluckier. Wilma McCann, a Leeds prostitute he attacked in October 1975, was his first victim to die, killed by his trademark combination of hammer blows and knife wounds. However, police did not link this crime with the two previous attacks. Murders of prostitutes have traditionally been treated by both police and public with a lack of urgency. Thus, when Sutcliffe's next three victims, killed over an 18-month period, all turned out to be Leeds-based prostitutes, the general public was scandalized, but not yet terrified.

All that changed on 16 June 1977. This time, the victim was a 16-year-old schoolgirl named Jayne MacDonald. Distastefully, the papers referred to her as the first 'innocent' victim, but, by this time, the whole of the north of England was now on alert that the Yorkshire Ripper was a menace to all women.

Over the next three years, Sutcliffe killed eight more women and severely injured several more. Some were prostitutes and some were not. The crimes were carried out at various locations around the north of England. As the death toll increased, the Yorkshire Ripper, as he was now known, became the target of one of the biggest police investigations ever mounted in Britain.

Various clues were found. The Ripper had size seven or eight shoes; he drove a certain kind of car; he had type B blood; he left a new banknote at one crime scene that could be traced to the payroll of his employer. All this information pointed to Sutcliffe, which is why he was repeatedly interviewed by the police. Each time, however, he was so pleasant, and so plausible in his excuses, that the police let him go. The situation was not helped by numerous pieces of false information that were circulating about the Ripper.

The voice on a tape believed to be from him had a north-east accent that did not tally with Sutcliffe's way of speaking.

Finally Caught

Finally, however, the law caught up with Sutcliffe. On 2 January 1981, he was apprehended while sitting in a car with a prostitute in the south Yorkshire city of Sheffield. The policeman checked his car registration and found that the car had false number plates. He arrested Sutcliffe, though not before Sutcliffe had hidden a hammer and knife he had been carrying.

While in custody, Sutcliffe's history as a Ripper suspect surfaced. The arresting officer decided to go back to the crime scene, and found the weapons Sutcliffe had hidden. At this point, Sutcliffe realized the game was up and began to confess. His five-year reign of terror was at an end.

Sutcliffe was sentenced to life imprisonment on 13 counts of murder. Soon afterwards, psychiatrists pronounced him insane and he was transferred to Broadmoor. While in prison he has been attacked several times, culminating in a 1997 assault in which he lost the sight in one eye.

Sadistic Stranglers

Strangling is perhaps the most common and certainly the most intimate mode of murder, allowing the killer literally to squeeze the life out of the victim. Its intimacy has a particular appeal for the sexually motivated murderer, who often strangles victims to death while raping them.

Serial killers who strangle their victims to death almost always rape them, either before or after killing them. Killers motivated by money or by a more general misanthropic rage tend to use guns or knives, methods that distance them from their victim. By contrast, the strangler is a killer who revels in the intimate moment of murder.

This certainly holds true for the serial stranglers included here. The most famous of these is Albert de Salvo, the 'Boston Strangler'. De Salvo was a rapist whose desire to dominate women sexually eventually led him to strangle 11 women in the early 1960s. A decade before, serial killer Reginald Christie, also motivated by a hatred of women, strangled his wife and several prostitutes in London. These killers used their hands to murder their victims. In contrast, Kenneth Bianchi and Angelo Buono, the 'Hillside Stranglers', preferred a slightly less intimate form of strangulation (and mutilation), using a garrotte rather then their bare hands.

Of course, in many murder cases, strangulation takes place as the most immediate way of killing a victim, especially when no other weapon is at hand. However, for a small group of killers, it appears to be an integral part of their perverse pleasure in killing.

CARLTON GARY

Serial killers are conventionally motivated by sexual perversion or, occasionally, by money. It is perhaps surprising that, even in as divided a society as the United States, racial hatred has rarely been a motive for serial murder. In fact, for a long while, profilers maintained that serial killers only murdered within their own racial group. This may generally be true, but there are exceptions. One of them is Carlton Gary, the 'Stocking Strangler' (also known as the 'Chattahoochee Choker'), a black man who killed seven elderly white women during a nine-month reign of terror in his hometown of Columbus, Georgia. He is also thought to be the killer of two other elderly white women in Albany, New York.

Carlton Gary was born on 15 December 1952 in Columbus, Georgia. His father was a construction worker who wanted nothing to do with his son, and would accept no financial responsibility for the child. Gary only met his father once, when he was 12 years old.

Hatred

His mother was desperately poor and led a nomadic life. As a result, Gary was malnourished as a child, and was often left with his aunt or great aunt. Both women worked as maids for elderly, wealthy, white women. It has been conjectured that this may have led Gary towards the pathological hatred of older white women that manifested itself later. During his childhood, Gary suffered a serious head trauma in elementary school, when he was knocked unconscious in a playground accident. Head injuries are well known to be a common factor in the backgrounds of many serial killers.

In his teens, Gary became a heavy drug user, and between the ages of 14 and 18 he gathered a string of arrests for offences including robbery, arson and assault. He also acquired a wife, Sheila, and had two children. In 1970, he moved to Albany, New York, where he had plans to carve out a career as a singer, for which he showed some talent. In the meantime, he carried on with his criminal activities.

The Assaults

In May of that year, an elderly woman named Marion Brewer was robbed and attacked in her Albany hotel room. Two months later 85-year-old Nellie Farmer was robbed in her nearby apartment, and strangled to death. Following a third assault on an elderly woman, Gary was arrested. It was discovered that his fingerprints matched one left at the scene of the Farmer murder.

Gary admitted having taken part in a robbery but claimed that an accomplice, John Lee Mitchell, was responsible for the actual murder. The police believed him and charged Mitchell, despite no material evidence to connect him to the crime. Later, Gary recanted his statement and Mitchell was released on appeal; Gary meanwhile was charged with robbery, for which he was sentenced to a term in the Onondaga County Correctional Institution at Janesville, New York. He was paroled in 1975 and was a suspect in a series of rapes in Syracuse before being sent back to jail for a parole violation. He escaped from custody on 22 August 1977, and headed back home.

On 16 September, 60-year-old Ferne Jackson was raped, beaten and strangled to death with a nylon stocking at her home in the Wynnton district of Columbus. Nine days later 71-year-old Jean Dimenstein was killed in a similar fashion, as were 89-year-old Florence Scheible, murdered on 21 October, and 69-year-old Martha Thurmond, murdered on 23 October. Five days later, the killer now known to a terrified public as the Stocking Strangler struck again, raping and killing 74-year-old Kathleen Woodruff. This time, no stocking was left at the scene.

Wrong Man

Four months later, the Strangler struck again. On the night of 12 February 1978, the killer attacked Ruth Schwob, but she triggered a bedside alarm and her assailant fled. He went just two blocks down the road, before breaking into another house and raping and strangling 78-year-old Mildred Borom.

Police announced that they suspected a black man of the murders. Matters were complicated by a man calling himself the 'Chairman of the Forces of Evil', who threatened to murder selected black women if the Strangler was not stopped. This later turned out to be a black man trying to cover up three murders of his own by putting the blame on to white vigilantes. The Chairman was arrested on 4 April. Police suspected that he might also be the Stocking Strangler, but this hope soon faded when, on 20 April, the killer murdered his final victim, 61-year-old Janet Cofer.

Eight months later, following a robbery in Gaffney, Georgia, Carlton Gary was arrested. He confessed and was sentenced to

21 years in prison for armed robbery. He escaped from custody in 1983 and remained at large for over a year before being rearrested. New evidence came to light, including a gun that was traced back to Gary and a possible fingerprint match that led the police to believe that this armed robber was also the Stocking Strangler.

Gary was eventually arrested and charged with three murders. In August 1986, he was convicted of the crimes and sentenced to death. In January 2017 he sought a retrial in the light of discrepancies in the evidence against him as presented at the trial and recent DNA evidence.

KENNETH BIANCHI AND ANGELO BUONO

It is a common misapprehension that sexually motivated serial killers are all social misfits – twisted losers unable to find any other kind of gratification. The truth is rather more sinister. Plenty of serial killers are outwardly eligible men who have little trouble seducing women. The two men known as the 'Hillside Stranglers' are cases in point. Kenneth Bianchi was a good-looking young man in his mid-twenties, whose long-time girlfriend was pregnant at the time his murderous rampage began. His cohort, Angelo Buono, was no one's idea of good-looking but was nevertheless enormously popular with women. However, the two conspired together to torture, rape and murder 14 victims.

Adopted

Kenneth Bianchi was born on 22 May 1951 in Rochester, New York. His mother was a prostitute who immediately gave him up for adoption. Three months later he was adopted by the Bianchis. As a child he was given to daydreams and prone to fantasizing and lying. Despite a reasonably high IQ, he underachieved at school. In an effort to change this his mother sent him to a Catholic private school, but while he was there his father died and at 13 he had to leave because there was no longer enough money to pay the fees. Even so, Bianchi seemed to have absorbed his moral education; he was seen as a straight arrow at school, taking no part in the counterculture of the 1960s.

Immediately on leaving school he entered a brief marriage that ended when his wife left him after only eight months. This experience certainly left Bianchi embittered. He studied psychology briefly in college but then dropped out and started working as a security guard, using the job as an opportunity to steal items from the houses he was meant to be guarding. In 1975, his life drifting along, he decided to make a move. He headed for Los Angeles where an older cousin was now living. The cousin's name was Angelo Buono and he was to have a decisive and terrible influence on Kenneth Bianchi.

Family Values

Angelo Buono was also born in Rochester, New York, on 5 October 1934, 17 years earlier than Bianchi. His parents had divorced when he was young and he had moved to California with his mother, Jenny, in 1939. Buono was trouble from the start. From a young age, he had a precocious interest in sex. As a teenager he would boast to his classmates about raping and sodomizing girls. He stole cars and eventually ended up in reform school. In 1955 he briefly married a high-school girlfriend after she became pregnant, but left her almost immediately. He soon married again, to Mary Castillo, and had five more children with her, before she divorced him in 1964 due to his persistent sexual and physical abuse. The next year, he was married again, to a single mother of two called Nannette Campino. The couple had two more children together, until she finally divorced him in 1971 when, in addition to the abuse he visited on her, he raped her daughter.

During this time, Buono had established himself as an auto-upholsterer with his own business. Strangely, despite his unattractive physical appearance and his terrible record of abusive behaviour, women seemed magnetically drawn to him. He sported dyed hair and flashy jewellery; in essence he looked like a pimp – and this was just the career sideline he was planning on moving into when his cousin Kenny showed up from back east.

Kenny and Angelo hit it off from the start. Kenny already had a simmering resentment of women; Angelo showed him how to express it. He started by teaching his cousin how to impersonate a policeman in order to blackmail prostitutes for sex. Kenny was an eager student and happy to go along with Angelo's pimping plan. The pair met a couple of runaways, Sabra Hannan and Becky Spears, and put them out on the streets until first Becky and then Sabra succeeded in running away.

Meanwhile, Kenny was once again working as a security guard and had found a new girlfriend, Kelli Boyd, who had recently become pregnant. Kenny was disturbed by the loss of the pimping income that had enabled him to impress Boyd with his wealth. Together with Angelo, he decided to recruit some new girls. They found a prostitute named Deborah Noble who offered to help them out. However, when she tried to trick money out of them, they decided to teach her a lesson.

First Killing

Unable to find Noble they instead came upon her friend, a prostitute named Yolanda Washington, and decided to take their anger out on her. Whatever their initial intention, they ended up raping her, strangling her with a garotte and dumping her dead body in a cemetary. Evidently this first crime sent Bianchi and Buono over the edge. Their next victims were two more prostitutes, Judy Miller and Lissa Kastin, murdered over the next two weeks. Kastin's body was found on 6 November, but there was little public outcry: Los Angeles had too many murders for the deaths of three hookers to merit much attention.

All that changed later that month, during the week of Thanksgiving, when five more bodies were found on the Los Angeles hillside. None of these were prostitutes: these were middle-class girls, one of them only 12 years old. All had been abducted, raped and asphyxiated with the trademark garotte; in several cases there were signs of torture. Now Los Angeles was in a state of red alert too.

It was ten days until the deadly duo struck again. Their next victim was another prostitute. Kimberly Martin had gone to meet a client on 9 December; her dead body turned up on the hillside the next morning. Their next victim, Cindy Hudspeth, was found on 16 February; her raped and strangled body was found in the boot of her car, which had been pushed over a cliff.

The police continued their investigations but seemed to get nowhere. Los Angeles held its breath, but nothing happened. The months passed and the Hillside Strangler seemed to have retired. Perhaps it was simply down to fear on Bianchi and Buono's part; perhaps it was connected to the fact that Bianchi's girlfriend had given birth to their baby early in 1978, and he was caught up in domestic matters. Whatever the reason, the pair stopped killing – but only for a while.

Emerging Evidence

Later that year, Bianchi moved with his new family to Bellingham, Washington, and found work as a security guard. A year passed and then the murderous urge caught hold of him again. He lured two young women, Diane Wilder and Karen Mantic, to a house he was guarding, and raped and murdered them both. This time, however, Bianchi soon emerged as a suspect and was arrested. Once under arrest, further evidence started to emerge to connect him to the Hillside murders.

It was two years before the case finally came to trial, during which period Bianchi persuaded a serial killer groupie called Veronica Compton to carry out a murder for him, intending to suggest that the Strangler was still at large. The plot failed dismally and Compton herself was imprisoned.

Finally, the case went to court. Both Bianchi and Buono were found guilty and sentenced to life imprisonment. Buono died in prison from unknown causes in 2002. Bianchi continues to serve out his sentence.

REGINALD CHRISTIE

England may have given the world the definitive serial killer in Jack the Ripper but, after that Victorian monster vanished from view, relatively few serial murderers followed in his footsteps. Perhaps that is why the sordid life and crimes of Reginald Christie gained such a hold on the public imagination in the 1950s, even inspiring a feature film named, like Ludovic Kennedy's classic book on the case, 10 Rillington Place.

Reginald Christie lived for 15 years at the West London address of 10 Rillington Place, until his sudden departure in March 1953 – a departure that was explained when the new tenant found three dead bodies in a boarded-up wardrobe, one more under the floorboards and another two in the garden. The neighbours were reportedly stunned. Christie was not a well-liked man, being an officious, snobbish type, but he was no one's idea of a mass murderer.

Wrongly Hanged?

The address was already notorious. Just three years previously, another tenant named Timothy Evans – who had rented the top-floor flat while Christie and his wife had the ground floor – had been convicted of murdering his infant child and had been suspected of murdering his wife. Surely the same shabby little house could not have been home to two separate murderers? Or could it have been that Timothy Evans was wrongly hanged and that the real murderer was actually John Reginald Christie?

Reginald Christie was born near Halifax in Yorkshire on 8 April 1898. He had an authoritarian father and a mother inclined to overprotection. It was a combination that turned Reginald into an attention-seeking hypochondriac; he was to remain so throughout his life. One of his formative experiences was unexpectedly seeing his grandfather's dead body when he was eight years old (a very similar experience also had a profound influence on serial killer Dennis Nilsen).

Loner

Christie did not mix easily with other children and became something of a loner. In his teens he had a disastrous first sexual

Reginald Christie

experience with a girl who laughed at him when he failed to gain an erection. This was the start of his lifelong problem with impotence – one to which he was eventually to find a rather drastic solution.

Christie left school in 1913 and worked at various jobs before enlisting in the army in 1916, during the First World War. He served as a signalman and was sent to the front in 1918, when he suffered from the effects of a mustard gas attack. Following his wartime experiences, he had a nervous reaction that led to him claiming to be blind for several months, and being unable to speak for a longer period. Nevertheless, in 1919 he met Ethel Simpson, and married her the following year.

He found a job as a postman but was soon sacked and sent to prison for three months for stealing letters. Not long after his release, unable to get a job locally, he moved to London. Ethel remained with her family in Sheffield; their marriage had failed sexually, and she knew that Christie had been visiting prostitutes.

Over the next decade Christie disappeared into a lowlife London world of petty criminality and prostitution. He lived with a prostitute for a while and, in 1929, was sentenced to six months in prison after assaulting her with a cricket bat. He received another prison sentence in 1933 after he stole a car belonging to a priest he knew. While in prison this time, he wrote to Ethel and, evidently being very lonely, she agreed to come to London and live with him once he was released.

In 1938, the couple moved into Rillington Place in Notting Hill. Christie reinvented himself as a sober, respectable citizen, becoming a Special Constable during the war – however, he continued to frequent prostitutes behind Ethel's back.

Respectable Individual

Unbeknown to anyone, this now-respectable individual committed his first two murders during the war years. His first victim was an Austrian immigrant called Ruth Fuerst. He strangled her to death while raping her, an act that he found uniquely satisfying and was to practise several times more. His next victim was Muriel Eddy, a woman he met through work. He tricked her into inhaling carbon monoxide, and then, when she lost consciousness, he raped and strangled her. Both women were eventually buried in the back garden.

The end of the war seemed to halt Christie's killing spree for a while. The next murder with which he is associated did not occur until 1949. This time, the victim was Beryl Evans, the wife of the upstairs tenant Timothy Evans. There are several conflicting accounts of her death. The most likely one is that Christie pretended to be able to give her an abortion. He attempted to sedate her with gas and, when that failed, he knocked her unconscious and strangled her to death, before also murdering her baby daughter Geraldine, and then deliberately incriminating Timothy.

At the ensuing trial in 1953, the jury believed the apparently respectable Christie, rather than the illiterate Evans. Evans was found guilty and hanged; Christie was left to carry on his career of murder.

It was three more years before he struck again.

In December 1952 he told neighbours that his wife Ethel had gone back to Yorkshire. In fact he had strangled her and put her under the floorboards.

Over the next six weeks he lured three prostitutes to his house – Rita Nelson, Kathleen Maloney and Haroldina McLennan. He gassed, raped and strangled them, boarding them up in a cupboard. Then, with no money left for the rent, he simply walked out and began sleeping rough. Meanwhile, the new tenant at Rillington Place made a ghastly discovery. Soon, Christie's face was pictured in all the national newspapers as the UK's most wanted criminal.

It was not long before a policeman recognized and arrested him. In custody, Christie confessed to his crimes, though he never admitted to the murder of the infant Geraldine. His defence team had no alternative but to plead insanity. However, the jury were not persuaded and Christie was duly found guilty. On 15 July 1953 he was hanged.

ALBERT DESALVO

The case of the 'Boston Strangler' is one of the most enduringly mysterious in the annals of serial murder. What is known for sure is that between June 1962 and July 1964 11 women were murdered in the Boston area – all raped and strangled. Most people at the time assumed there was a single serial killer on the loose, and dubbed him the Boston Strangler. Others, including many on the police investigation, thought that there were two killers, because the first set of victims were all older women between the ages of 55 and 75, while five of the last six to die were women in their late teens and early twenties. These latter murders were also significantly more violent than the others. For this reason, some concluded that there was a first murderer fixated on older women (perhaps motivated by a hatred of his mother), followed by a copycat killer using the same modus operandi but preying on younger women.

However, all this speculation was quelled when, in early 1965, a man named Albert DeSalvo, who had recently been arrested for a series of rapes, confessed to all 11 murders, as well as some other killings that had not previously been attributed to the Strangler.

Physically Abused

Albert DeSalvo was born in Chelsea, Massachusetts, on 3 September 1931. He was one of six children born to Frank and Charlotte DeSalvo. Frank DeSalvo was a violent man who dealt out regular physical abuse to his family, and was jailed twice before Charlotte eventually divorced him in 1944. Albert became a troubled teenager, repeatedly arrested for breaking and entering, assault and other minor offences.

In 1948, aged 17, Albert joined the army and was stationed in Germany. While living there he met and married a German woman, Irmgard Beck, who came with him when he was transferred back to the States, to Fort Dix in New Jersey. At Fort Dix, DeSalvo was accused of molesting a nine-year-old girl but the matter was dropped when the mother declined to press charges. However, the affair resulted in him being discharged from the army in 1956.

Sexual Demands

At this point Albert and Irmgard, plus their baby daughter Judy, moved back to Massachusetts. Over the next few years DeSalvo worked a series of jobs, and was generally regarded as a likeable man by his fellow workers. Not all was well, though: he was arrested several times for burglary and there was considerable sexual tension between him and his wife. Irmgard was very unenthusiastic sexually after their daughter had been born with a hereditary disease and she was terrified of having another disabled child. Albert, meanwhile, demanded sex from his wife five or six times a day.

This manic sexual behaviour soon led DeSalvo into trouble. During the late 1950s reports began to come in from Massachusetts women about the 'Measuring Man': a man who claimed to be from a modelling agency and would persuade women to let him run his measuring tape all over their bodies. When DeSalvo was once more arrested for burglary, on 17 March 1960, he surprised police by confessing that he was the Measuring Man.

Due to the lack of violence involved in his crime, DeSalvo received a relatively lenient two-year sentence. With time off for good behaviour, he was released after 11 months. Far from teaching him a lesson, however, his time in prison seemed to have turned him into a more aggressive predator. Over the next two years he raped hundreds of women (300 by police estimates, 2,000 by his own exaggerated account), often carrying out more than one rape on the same day. He was known as the 'Green Man' rapist, since he often made his assaults while wearing green work clothes. These rapes were carried out during the same time period as the Boston Strangler killings, but the police made no connection between them at the time.

On 3 November 1964, DeSalvo was arrested on suspicion of being the Green Man rapist, after a witness gave the police a description that reminded them of the Measuring Man. DeSalvo promptly confessed and was sent to Bridgewater State Hospital for psychiatric observation. While he was there he confessed first to a fellow inmate, George Nassar, and subsequently to the police, that he was also the Boston Strangler.

The police were delighted to have the Strangler presented to them on a plate in this way. However, various problems remained. In particular, none of the witnesses who had seen the Boston Strangler, including his one surviving victim, were able to pick DeSalvo out of a police line-up. In the end DeSalvo, represented by the infamous lawyer F. Lee Bailey, made a deal with police that led to him receiving a life sentence for the Green Man rapes, but never being formally charged with the Strangler murders.

In November 1973, DeSalvo was stabbed to death by a fellow prisoner. However, his death failed to bring speculation to an end. Many people believe that DeSalvo only confessed to the killings as part of a deal with George Nassar, whereby Nassar would claim the reward for finding the Boston Strangler and would give half the money to DeSalvo's family to provide for them while he was in jail. Today, however, the consensus from experts who spent a substantial amount of time with DeSalvo, is that the man imprisoned as the Green Man rapist was indeed the legendary Boston Strangler.

MOSES SITHOLE

Moses Sithole is the most notorious serial killer to have terrorized South Africa in the years following the end of apartheid. He was convicted of 38 rape murders, committed in the period between January and October 1995. The killings were nicknamed the 'ABC Murders' after the initials of the three communities in which most of the killings were committed: Atteridgeville, Boksburg and Cleveland.

Apartheid

It was undoubtedly the experience of growing up under the apartheid system that helped turn Sithole into a murderer. The apartheid laws made it extraordinarily hard for families to live together, with men having to travel to find work, and women and children consigned to dismal homelands in remote corners of the country. Sithole was born in such circumstances in the early 1960s outside Johannesburg, but his mother soon gave up the struggle to raise him, and consigned him to a series of orphanages.

Apartheid-era South Africa did not bother itself too much with keeping tabs on its black population, so little independent verification about Sithole's early life exists. By his own account, he was arrested for rape during his teens – unjustly he claimed – and went on to spend seven years in prison. He later blamed this stint in prison for turning him into a murderer, explaining his crimes by saying that the women he murdered all reminded him of the woman who had falsely accused him of rape many years before.

However, the facts tell another story. To most people, Moses Sithole seemed to be a softly spoken, gentle individual. Unbelievably, at the time he carried out his crimes, Sithole was running an organization he had founded himself called Youth Against Human Abuse, devoted to the eradication of child abuse. Even as he campaigned to help others, however, his own method of dealing with the scars of his childhood was to take the lives of the innocent. Indeed, he used his apparent respectability as a means to attract his victims. All of them were young women he persuaded to meet him so that he could interview them for jobs with his organization. Instead he took them to remote fields, beat them, raped them and murdered them, generally strangling them with their own underwear. Afterwards he would often write the word 'bitch' on their dead bodies before dumping them.

The first cluster of killings occurred around the township of Atteridgeville, near Pretoria, a community that has, extraordinarily, been assailed by several serial killers over the years.

Methodical Killer

Sithole was a relatively well-organized killer and, after a while, moved the focus of his operations first to Boksburg, south-west of Johannesburg, and finally even further south to Cleveland. At this point, the killings began to attract national attention. President Nelson Mandela went to Boksburg in person to appeal for help. However, this did not produce the breakthrough the police needed. What did was the killer's own arrogance.

In October 1995, Sithole made an anonymous call to the Cape Town newspaper, the Star, and told them that the killings were his revenge for his unjust imprisonment. He went on to claim that he had killed 76 victims, twice as many as were known about. Finally, in order to prove that he was the killer, he gave directions to where one of the bodies had been left.

There were sufficient clues in the call for the police to narrow their inquiries down to the ex-convict and youth worker Moses Sithole, who had lately disappeared from his job. A tip-off then sent them to Sithole's hideout in Johannesburg. On being discovered there, he attacked the police with a hatchet, wounding one of them. In return he was shot and wounded, then arrested and taken to a hospital where his wounds were treated. He was found to be HIV-positive.

There was still little direct evidence to connect him to the murders, but when he was taken into custody he proved to be an inveterate boaster. Not only did he boast to his fellow prisoners about the number of murders he had carried out, but he was also inordinately proud of the fact that he had killed them all with his bare hands, using only their clothing to strangle them. Learning of this, the police equipped some of his fellow inmates with hidden cameras and recording devices, and they managed to record Sithole's boasts on tape. It was these tapes that provided the prosecution with much of its evidence when the case finally came to trial.

After various delays caused by Sithole's ill-health, he was finally convicted of 38 murders, 40 rapes and six robberies. On 6 December 1997 he was sentenced to 2410 years in prison. This was considerable overkill for a man who by now had full-blown AIDS, but the judge, an advocate of capital punishment, wanted to make a point. As of 2017, however, Sithole is still alive in Manguang Correctional Centre in Bloemfontein, and has reportedly taken a correspondence course in writing, so that he can tell his life story in his own words.

Skid-Row Slashers

Many serial killers operate at the lowest levels of society. The killers may come from different social backgrounds, from street vagrants to middle-class professionals, but very often their victims are chosen from the men, women and children at the bottom of the social pile. The reasons are obvious: if a killer murders a high-status woman, a huge manhunt will immediately be launched. If he preys instead on street prostitutes, the sorry truth is that he will probably kill half a dozen before anyone even notices.

Take the examples profiled here. Serial killer Robert C. Hansen picked up prostitutes from the skid row of Anchorage, Alaska, flew them out into the wilderness and butchered them there. No one noticed until one of them escaped and called the police. In the same way, for many years Carroll Edward Cole roamed the underbelly of American society, killing time and time again, mostly while both killer and victim were drunk out of their minds. As for Juan Corona, one of the most prolific of all serial killers, he found an even more invisible class of victim – the migrant workers on his California farm. Twenty-five of them were buried in his orchard and no one suspected a thing until a neighbour noticed a suspicious hole that had been dug on his land.

The terrifying truth is that, at any one time, there are many skid-row slashers operating across the world, taking the lives of people who will never be missed. Only in a society that values each individual equally, whether rich or poor, can we hope to stamp out this kind of serial killer.

JUAN CORONA

When Juan Corona was convicted of 25 murders in January 1973, he entered the history books as the most prolific serial killer in US history. Since then, however, his grisly record has been overtaken and Corona's name has become nearly as obscure as the man himself, who is suffering from dementia.

Successful Immigrant

Juan Corona was born in Mexico in 1934. Like many thousands of his compatriots he moved north to California to find work in the 1950s. Compared to most of his fellow Mexican immigrants he did well. Over the years he put down roots, married and had four children, establishing his own farm in Yuba City, just outside Sacramento in northern California. He specialized in providing labour for other farmers and ranchers in the area. In effect, he acted as a middleman between new generations of desperate immigrants – legal and illegal – looking for work in the fields, and their potential employers. The migrants would wait in lines in the early morning, and Corona would show up in a truck offering work.

It was a hard but settled life and it was only briefly disturbed when, in 1970, there was a violent incident at the cafe owned by Corona's gay brother Natividad. A young Mexican was savaged with a machete. The young man accused Natividad of being the attacker. Natividad promptly fled back to Mexico, and the case was soon forgotten.

Forgotten, that is, until the following year when, on 19 May 1971, one of Juan Corona's neighbours, a Japanese-American farmer who had hired some workers from Corona, noticed a hole that had been dug on his land. Suspicious, he asked police to investigate. On excavating the hole they found a body, which proved to be that of a drifter called Kenneth Whitacre. Whitacre had been stabbed in the chest and his head almost split in two by blows from a machete or similar cleaving instrument. Gay literature was found on the body, leading the police to suspect a sexual motive.

Four days later, workers on a nearby ranch discovered a second body, a drifter called Charles Fleming. At this point, the police started searching the area in earnest. Over the next nine days they discovered a total of 25 bodies, mostly in an orchard on Corona's land. They had all been killed by knives or machetes, following the same pattern: a deep stab wound to the chest and two gashes across the back of the head in the shape of a cross. Furthermore the bodies were all buried face up, with their arms above their heads and their shirts over their faces. In some, but not all, cases there was evidence of recent homosexual activity.

Frenzied Killing Rate

What was overwhelming was not just the number of victims, but the fact that none of the bodies had been in the ground for longer than six weeks. Whoever had killed them had been in the midst of an extraordinary orgy of murder, killing at a rate of more than one every two days. None of the dead had been reported as missing; indeed, four of the 25 were never identified at all; the rest were migrant workers, drifters and skid-row bums. Whoever had selected them for murder had clearly been a good judge of people at the bottom of the heap, well able to identify those who had fallen through the safety net.

The police quickly came up with a suspect: Juan Corona. To start with, all the bodies were buried on or near Corona's land. Secondly, two victims had bank receipts with Juan Corona's name on them in their pockets.

It was no more than circumstantial evidence, but the extraordinary scale of the crimes was enough to persuade the police to proceed, and Juan Corona was duly arrested and charged with the murders. His defence team tried to pin the blame on his brother Natividad, who had a history of violence, but failed to prove that Natividad was even in the country at the time. Overall, Corona's defence was spectacularly incompetent. At trial they failed to mention that Juan had been diagnosed schizophrenic in 1956, which prevented them from mounting a defence of insanity. Even so, the lack of direct evidence meant that the jury deliberated for 45 hours before finding Corona guilty. He was sentenced to 25 terms of life imprisonment (the death penalty not being available in California at the time).

Juan Corona continued to protest his innocence and he was allowed a retrial in 1978 on the grounds that his previous defence had been incompetent. Even with competent defence, however, Corona was again found guilty. While in prison he was the victim of a serious attack by a fellow inmate, in which he lost an eye. He is currently held in Corcoran State Prison along with Charles Manson. However, while Manson remains the focus of a gruesome cult following, Corona is largely ignored, and can still be seen mumbling to himself in the prison courtyard – like his victims, another forgotten man.

ROBERT C. HANSEN

It sounds like the stuff of pulp fiction – a serial killer who abducted his victims, set them loose in the Alaskan wilderness, then hunted them down with knife and rifle. Robert Hansen made it a nightmare reality for the dozen or more women he plucked from the sleazy Tenderloin district of Anchorage, Alaska, between 1973 and 1983. Described by one of the women who escaped his clutches as looking like the archetypal nerd, the diminutive, acne-scarred Hansen appears to have been motivated to kill by little more than a base desire to get back at the world in general, and women in particular.

Resentment

Born in Pocahontas, Idaho, on 13 February 1939, Hansen's father, Christian, was a Danish immigrant who ran his own bakery. A strict disciplinarian, he soon had his son working in the bakery at all hours. This did not help Robert's social life as a teenager; neither did the young man's acne, or his stammer. His was not a happy all-American adolescence and resentment of his lot evidently festered.

After Robert left school he carried on working for his father, while also signing up for the army reserves. In 1960, he married a local girl. However, his marriage seems to have provoked him into making his resentment overt: shortly after he burned down part of the local high school. He was arrested, found guilty and sentenced to three years in prison. His wife responded to discovering this unsuspected side of her new husband by divorcing him.

New Start

Shortly after his release from prison, Hansen remarried and spent the next few years moving around the States. In 1967, the couple decided to make a new start, and headed for America's last frontier: Alaska. They settled in the main town of Anchorage and, for the first time, Hansen seemed to find a place where he could fit in. He had used his time in the army reserves to become an expert marksman and was now able to put these skills to use, gaining a reputation as a leading outdoorsman.

Somewhere along the way, though, killing wild animals failed to fulfil Hansen's need for revenge. The year after the last of his record-breaking animal kills, he was arrested for the attempted rape of a housewife and the actual rape of a prostitute. The rape of prostitutes not being taken too seriously, he only served six months in prison.

According to his own confession, from 1973 onwards Hansen developed a routine whereby he would pick up prostitutes and topless dancers from Anchorage's Tenderloin district, fly them out into the wilderness and rape them. If they submitted to his sexual whims, he let them live, taking them back to Anchorage with the threat that if they reported what had happened they would be in big trouble. He murdered those who did not comply; setting them loose in the wilderness, giving them a head start, then hunting and killing them.

His activities went on entirely unnoticed until 1980: Anchorage, during the 1970s oil boom, was a wild and dangerous town, where the law struggled to make its presence felt and people came and went unpredictably all the time. In addition, there was plenty of wild country where Hansen could hide the bodies of his victims.

In 1980, however, the bodies of two young women did come to light. One, found by construction workers, has never been identified. The second was a topless dancer named Joanna Messina. At the time the police were unable to find any leads. Nor did they come any closer to finding a suspect when, two years later, the body of another topless dancer called Sherry Morrow was found by hunters in a shallow grave near the Knik River. By now, the police suspected they were dealing with a serial killer, but they had nothing to connect that theory with the convicted rapist Robert Hansen.

Respected Citizen

Far from being a suspected murderer, Hansen had by now become a well-to-do respected citizen. He had claimed a large insurance settlement following a faked break-in at his house, and had used the money to start his own bakery. He now lived in a pleasant house with his wife and two children, and even had his own small private plane.

In June 1983, all that changed. A trucker picked up a prostitute running down the road with a pair of handcuffs trailing from one wrist. He took her to the police station, where she explained that she had been picked up by a client who had taken her to his house, raped and brutalized her, then taken her to his private plane. She had managed to escape at the last minute, and was convinced that, if she had not run, the man would certainly have killed her. She led the police first to the house and then to the light aircraft from which she had escaped. Both belonged to Robert Hansen.

Hansen denied everything. He produced an alibi, claiming to have spent the evening in question with two friends. With no more evidence than the unsupported word of a prostitute, the police decided not to press charges.

Three months later, however, another body was found, that of Paula Golding. The police task force called in FBI serial-killer expert John Douglas, and they decided to have another look at Hansen. Under questioning, Hansen's friends admitted that the alibi was false. Hansen's house was searched and the police found weapons used in the murders, plus IDs taken from the dead girls. After some initial resistance, Hansen made a deal whereby he would only be charged with four murders, and would serve his time in a federal prison. In return for this he confessed to many other murders, for which he was never charged. He took state troopers on a tour of the wilderness, in the course of which they were able to recover 11 bodies, several of which remain unidentified.

On 18 February 1984, Hansen was convicted of murder and sentenced to life plus 461 years.

FRITZ HAARMANN

Fritz Haarmann was one of the first serial killers to hit the headlines in modern times. He confessed to the murders of at least 27 young men and boys in the town of Hanover, Germany, between 1918 and 1924. What made Haarmann uniquely terrifying was the mixture of frenzy and orderliness that characterized his crimes. He would kill his victims in a savage onslaught, biting through their windpipes as he raped them. Then, with considerable care, he would remove their clothes and sell them, dismember the bodies, dispose of the bones, and finally cook the flesh and sell it on the black market as pork. If that seems hard to believe, one should remember that Germany in the years after the First World War was on the brink of starvation; food was food, and people at that time did not ask too many questions as to its provenance.

Mother's Favourite

Fritz (Friedrich) Haarmann was born on 25 October 1879 in Hanover, the sixth child of impoverished parents. His father was a drunk and a womanizer; his mother was older than her husband, 41 at the time Fritz was born, and in poor health. Fritz, the baby of the family, was his mother's favourite and he constantly sided with her against his father. As a child he preferred dolls to boys' toys. More worrying at the time was a fondness for frightening people, particularly his sisters. He liked to play games that involved tying them up or scaring them by tapping on their windows at night.

Fritz's mother died when he was 12 and his feuding with his father intensified. After school, he became apprenticed to a locksmith. When that did not work out he was sent to military school. After six months there, he was sent home because he seemed to be suffering from epileptic fits. Back in Hanover, he took to molesting children. Complaints were made, and Haarmann was examined by a doctor, who sent him to the insane asylum. This was a deeply traumatic experience for Haarmann. He eventually escaped and fled to Switzerland, before returning to Hanover in 1900. By this time, he appeared to be a reformed character. He married a woman named Erna Loewert and seemed ready to settle down.

When Erna became pregnant, Fritz left her, joined the army and became involved in petty crime. He was soon arrested for burglary, pick-pocketing and small-scale cons. In 1914 Fritz was convicted of a warehouse burglary and sent to prison for his longest stint yet, enabling him to see out the First World War from his prison cell. On release in 1918 he found himself in a poverty-stricken society as Germany struggled to recover from the war.

Crime was flourishing as people desperately sought means of survival. This was the ideal environment for Haarmann. He immediately joined a smuggling ring and simultaneously became a police informer, managing to profit from both sides at once.

Post-War Crimes

A salient feature of the post-war years was the number of homeless and displaced people milling around the city. Many of them resorted to prostitution, so it was easy for Haarmann to pick up boys and youths. In particular he liked to frequent the railway station and find likely prospects there. Often he would introduce himself as 'Detective Haarmann' and use that pretext to get the boys to go with him. At one time, he had been satisfied with sexual abuse, but now his sickness had deepened and he needed to kill his victims to satisfy his lust.

One of his first victims was named Friedel Rothe. Rothe's parents found out that their son had gone with 'Detective Haarmann' and the police went round to Haarmaan's apartment but failed to notice the boy's severed head, hidden behind the stove. Shortly afterwards, Haarmann received a nine-month prison sentence for indecency. On release he met a young homosexual called Hans Grans. They became lovers and moved in together.

Next they became business partners, trading on the black market as Fritz continued to act as a police informer. Over the next couple of years their business began to include a gruesome new sideline: selling the clothes and cooked flesh of Haarmann's victims.

For the most part the pair's victims were not missed. Even when they were, the authorities seemed to make elementary blunders in following up clues: the parents of one victim told the police they suspected Grans of having been the murderer, but Grans was in prison at the time; however, Haarmann was never investigated, even though he visited the parents pretending to be a criminologist and laughed hysterically as they told him of their fears. Another time, a suspicious customer took some of Haarmann's meat to the authorities for examination; the police expert duly pronounced it to be pork. It seems that, as long as the murders were confined to a homosexual netherworld, people in general preferred to look the other way.

All that changed in May 1924 when several human skulls were found by the River Leine. At first, the authorities tried to calm the public's fear, suggesting that this was some kind of macabre joke, the skulls having been left there by grave robbers. However, when, on 24 July, children found a sack stuffed full of human bones, there was no stopping the panic. In all the police found 500 bones belonging to at least 27 bodies.

The police investigated all the local sex offenders, among them Fritz Haarmann, but still found no evidence to connect him to the apparent murders. In the end it was Haarmann's own arrogance that led to his downfall.

For some reason – conceivably to stop himself from committing another murder – he took a 15-year-old boy to the police to report him for insolent behaviour. Once under arrest, the boy accused Haarmann of making sexual advances. Haarmann was arrested and his flat searched. The police found garments belonging to missing children, some of them bloodstained. Haarmann at first explained them away by saying that he was a dealer in used clothing and that he had no idea where the blood had come from. However, after a week in custody, under questioning, Haarmann finally confessed to the murders. He took detectives to a number of sites around Hanover where he had buried further bodies, seeming to take pride in his crimes. His testimony only varied when it came to the role of Hans Grans, whom he alternately blamed and exculpated.

When the case came to court, Haarmann was tried and sentenced to death. The jury decided that Grans was no more than an accessory after the fact and sentenced him to 12 years in prison. Haarmann appeared to enjoy his trial, conducting his own defence, smoking cigars and complaining about the presence of women in the courtroom. It was his final act of bravado, however.

On 25 April 1925 he – like so many of his victims – was put to death by beheading.

CARROLL EDWARD COLE

One of the few serial killers known to have the IQ level of a genius is Carroll Edward Cole. Paradoxically, however, he turned out to be the absolute model of the disorganized killer. When Cole killed, there was no pattern or logic to his crimes; there were no cryptic clues left behind, or crosswords puzzles sent to the police. Most of the times Eddie Cole murdered, he was too drunk to remember anything about it. The fact that he was allowed to roam free for so long and kill so many people is sad testament to the incompetence of the legal and medical authorities.

Carroll Edward 'Eddie' Cole was born on 9 May 1938 in Sioux City, Iowa, the second son of LaVerne and Vesta Cole. His sister was born in 1939, and soon afterwards the family moved to California, where LaVerne found work in a shipyard. Not long after that LaVerne was drafted to fight in the Second World War.

Bullying Mother

While his father was away, Eddie Cole's mother started having affairs. Sometimes she would take her son with her, and afterwards threaten and beat him to ensure that he did not tell his father. Vesta was a cruel bully, especially in her treatment of her son. She dressed him as a girl and made fun of him. When Carroll went to school, he was teased about his name by his schoolmates, and became increasingly angry and withdrawn. He claimed (in an autobiography he wrote while in prison) that when he was nine years old he drowned one of his tormentors, a fellow nine-year-old called Duane, but at the time the police regarded the incident as an accident.

In his teens, Carroll drifted into petty crime. He was regularly arrested for drunkenness and minor thefts. After high school he joined the army but was soon discharged after stealing some pistols. By this time, he was showing signs of mental deterioration. In 1960, he attacked two couples parked in cars in a lovers lane. Soon afterwards, he called the police in Richmond, California, where he was living, and told them that he was plagued by violent fantasies involving strangling women.

Psychiatric Help

The policeman he spoke to advised him to get psychiatric help; Cole spent the next three years in and out of mental institutions. At the last of these, Stockton State Hospital, a Dr Weiss wrote: 'He seems to be afraid of the female figure and cannot have intercourse with her first but must kill her before he can do it.' Despite this apparently damning diagnosis, Weiss approved Cole's release in April 1963.

On release, Cole drifted east to Dallas, Texas, where his brother Richard was living. There he met and married Billie Whitworth, an alcoholic stripper. Not surprisingly, this relationship failed to cure him of his violent feelings towards women. After two acrimonious years, the marriage ended when Cole burned down a motel after convincing himself that Whitworth was having sex with men there. He was imprisoned for arson.

On release, Cole attempted to strangle an 11-year-old girl in Missouri. He was arrested for the crime and sentenced to five years in prison. After serving his sentence, he was released again and ended up in Nevada, where he attempted to strangle two more women. Once again, he turned himself in to the psychiatric services. There, the doctors noted his murderous fantasies but still saw no reason to detain him and he was given a ticket back to San Diego, California.

First Three Victims

In San Diego he murdered for the first time as an adult. He killed three women there, each of whom he had picked up in a bar, had sex with and then strangled. He later claimed that they had all proved themselves unfaithful to their husbands, and so reminded him of his adulterous mother.

These killings set the template for the next ten years. Cole drifted: in each new place he strangled women, generally in a drunken stupor. In the case of a woman he murdered in Oklahoma City, he claimed he came out of an alcoholic blackout to find slices of his victim's buttocks cooking on a skillet.

By 1979, Cole was back in San Diego, married again to another heavy-drinking woman. While there, he murdered a woman called Bonnie Sue O'Neill and left her body outside his workplace. Still the police failed to interview him. Soon after that, he murdered his wife. This time, there was a documented history of how he had threatened to kill her. A neighbour found him drunk, digging a grave underneath the house. The neighbour called the police, who found Cole's wife's body in a closet in his house. Extraordinarily, they decided that she had probably died of alcohol poisoning and pressed no charges against Cole.

Cole then left San Diego and went back on the road. He killed another woman in Las Vegas, and then returned to Dallas, where he strangled three more women during November 1980. Cole was a suspect in the second of these killings and was actually found on the scene of the third murder. He was arrested and held in custody. The police then came to the conclusion – once again – that the victim had probably died of natural causes, and were about to let him go. However, before they could do so, Cole confessed – not just to this murder but to his whole history of killing.

On 9 April 1981, Cole was convicted of three of the murders committed in Texas. He was sentenced to life imprisonment in Huntsville Prison. In 1984, his mother died, and his attitude seems to have changed. Soon afterwards, rather than serve out his sentence, and look forward to a possible parole, he agreed to face further murder charges filed in Nevada, even though he knew these could involve the death penalty.

In October 1984, Cole was indeed sentenced to death in Nevada. Anti-death penalty campaigners tried to have his sentence commuted but Cole wanted none of it. When the sentence was passed, he said 'Thanks, Judge.' In December 1985, he was executed.

ROBERT PICKTON

When Robert Service first cast his eyes on British Columbia, the poet described what he saw as being 'something greater than my imagination had ever conceived.' Canada's westernmost province is known for its natural beauty. Robert Pickton saw these wonders on a daily basis, but his immediate surroundings were much less attractive.

Pickton lived on a pig farm, a muddy, run-down 17-acre parcel of land in Port Coquitlam that he and his siblings had inherited from their parents.

On the occasions that he left his home, Pickton could often be found 20 miles away hunting down the drugged and desperate in Vancouver.

For runaways, the homeless and those who are simply down on their luck, British Columbia's biggest city holds an understandable allure.

Nestled by the warm Pacific Ocean, it enjoys a much milder winter than any other major Canadian city. For the drug addict, there's a steady supply of illegal narcotics flowing through its port. For those who still dream of sudden fame, there is fantasy to be found in the city's healthy film industry; 'Hollywood North' is just one of Vancouver's many nicknames.

Sadly, Vancouver is also by far the most expensive city in Canada; in North America it is surpassed only by Manhattan proper. Real estate is at a premium, and rental units are expensive and hard to come by. This city, with the highest concentration of millionaires in North America, is also home to the poorest neighbourhood in the country. Haunted by glorious buildings, reminders of long-gone days as a premier shopping district, Vancouver's Downtown Eastside is a blight on the utopian landscape. The banks disappeared years ago, as did the well-stocked department stores. The few shops that aren't boarded up house lowly pawnbrokers. Outside their doors, and in the blocks that surround, prostitutes – some as young as 11 years old – ply their trade.

Monstrous appetites

Pickton did not prey on children. It's thought that his first victim was a 23-year-old woman named Rebecca Guno, who was last seen on 22 June 1983. She was reported missing three days later – a very short time period compared to the many that followed. The next victim, Sheryl Rail, was not reported missing for three full years. The lives of Guno and Rail were just two of the six Pickton is known to have taken in his first decade of killing. With as much as 28 months separating one murder from the next, the pig farmer had no clear pattern. These early erratic and seemingly spontaneous killings enabled Pickton to pass under the radar. It wasn't until the closing years of the millennium that speculation began to surface that a serial killer just might be at work on the seedier streets of Vancouver. By then Pickton had picked up the pace; it's believed that he killed nine women in the latter half of 1997 alone.

The next year, the Vancouver Police Department began reviewing cases of missing women stretching back nearly three decades. By this time, talk of a serial killer was a subject of conversation in even the most genteel parts of the city, and still authorities dismissed speculation.

When one of their own, Inspector Kim Rossmo, raised the issue, he was quickly shot down. 'We're in no way saying there is a serial murderer out there,' said fellow inspector Gary Greer. 'We're in no way saying that all these people missing are dead. We're not saying any of that.'

The police posited that the missing women had simply moved on. After all, prostitutes were known to abruptly change locations and even names. Calgary, 600 miles to the east and flush with oil money, was often singled out as a likely destination.

Years later, veteran journalist Stevie Cameron would add this observation: 'There were never any bodies. Police don't like to investigate any case where there isn't a body.'

Even as the authorities dismissed the notion of a serial killer, Pickton continued his bloody work. Among those he butchered was Marcella Creison. Released from prison on 27 December 1998, she never showed at a belated Christmas dinner prepared by her mother and boyfriend. Sadly, 14 days passed before her disappearence was reported.

The waters were muddied by the fact that some of the women who had been reported missing were actually found alive. Patricia Gay Perkins, who had disappeared leaving a one-year-old son behind, contacted Vancouver Police after reading her name on a list of the missing. One woman was found living in Toronto, while another was discovered to have died of a heroin overdose. However, the list of missing women continued to grow, even as other cases were solved.

Accepting, for a moment, that there was a serial killer on the loose, where were the police to look? There was, it seemed, an embarrassment of suspects – dozens of violent johns who had been rounded up on assault charges during the previous two decades.

However, Robert Pickton was not among them. Should he have been?

In 1997, Pickton got into a knife fight with a prostitute on his farm that resulted in both being treated in the same hospital.

Nurses removed a handcuff from around the woman's wrist using a key that was on Pickton's person. He was charged with attempted murder, though this was later dismissed.

In 1998, Bill Hiscox, one of Pickton's employees, approached police to report on a supposed charity, the Piggy Palace Good Times Society, that was run by Robert and his brother Daniel. Housed in a converted building on the pig farm, Hiscox claimed that it was nothing but a party place populated by a rotating cast of prostitutes.

It wasn't the first police had heard of the Piggy Palace Good Times Society. Established in 1996 to 'co-ordinate, manage and operate special events, functions, dances, shows and exhibitions on behalf of service organizations, sports organizations and other worthy groups', it had continually violated Port Coquitlam city bylaws. There were parties – so many parties – drawing well over 1,000 people to a property that was zoned as agricultural.

The strange goings on at the Piggy Palace Good Times Society might have been a concern, but Hiscox's real focus had to do with the missing women. The Pickton employee told police that purses and other items that could identify the prostitutes would be found on the pig farm.

Police visited the Port Coquitlam property on at least four occasions, once with Hiscox in tow, but found nothing. Robert Pickton would become nothing more than one of many described as 'a person of interest'.

Mission to murder

The years passed, women kept disappearing, and still the notion of a serial killer at work in the Downtown Eastside was dismissed.

By 2001, the number of women who had gone missing from the neighbourhood had grown to 65 – a number that police could no longer ignore. That April, a team called 'The Missing Women Task Force' was established. The arrest of Gary Ridgway seven months later by American authorities brought fleeting interest. Better known as the 'Green River Killer', Ridgway killed scores of prostitutes in the Seattle area, roughly 150 miles south of Vancouver. The many murders coincided with the disappearances of the missing women, but it quickly became clear that Ridgway had had nothing to do with events north of the border. The Missing Women Task Force looked into other American serial killers, as well, including foot fetishist Dayton Rogers, 'The Malolla Forest Killer', who had murdered several prostitutes in Oregon.

Despite the newly established task force, prostitutes continued to disappear. No one foresaw the events of February 2002.

Early in the month, Pickton was arrested, imprisoned and charged with a variety of firearms offences, including storing a firearm contrary to regulations, possession of a firearm without a licence and possession of a loaded restricted firearm without a licence. In carrying out the search warrant that led to the charges, police uncovered personal possessions belonging to one of the missing women.

Pickton was released on bail, but was kept under surveillance. On 22 February, he was again taken into custody – this time to be charged with two counts of first-degree murder in the deaths of prostitutes Serena Abotsway and Mona Wilson. The pig farmer would never again experience a day of freedom.

The Pickton farm soon came to look like something out of a science-fiction film. Investigators and forensics specialists in contamination suits searched for signs of the missing women. Severed heads were found in a freezer, a wood chipper contained further fragments, and still more were found in a pigpen and in pig feed. These were easy finds; a team of 52 anthropologists were brought in to do the rest, sifting through 14 acres of soil in search of bones, teeth and hair. Their diligence brought over 10,000 pieces of evidence – and, for Pickton, a further 24 counts of murder.

But to the citizens of Vancouver, particularly the friends and families of the missing women, the breakthrough had come far too late. In place of praise came criticism. How was it that the police had found nothing at all suspicious when they'd visited the farm just a few years earlier? Serena Abotsway, Mona Wilson and several other women whose body parts were found on the farm had disappeared after those initial searches. Might their lives have been spared?

We might add to these questions: What do we now make of Robert Pickton? A decade after he made headlines as Canada's most prolific serial killer, his picture is still coming into focus.

Pickton promised prostitutes not only cash, but drugs and alcohol, if they would only come to Piggy Palace. It's thought that he would almost invariably accuse each of his victims of stealing. He bound each woman, before strangling them with a wire or a belt. Pickton would then drag his victim to the farm's slaughterhouse, where he would use his skills as a butcher.

Some remains he buried on the farm, while others were fed to his pigs. Still more was disposed of at West Coast Reduction Ltd, an 'animal rendering and recycling plant' located well within walking distance of Main and Hastings, the worst corner in the country. In fact, dozens of prostitutes strolled the streets in the shadow of the plant. Eventually, the remains would find their way into cosmetics and animal feed.

Testing found the DNA of some victims in the pork found on the farm. The meat processed on the farm was never sold commercially, though Pickton did distribute it amongst friends and neighbours.

'Nailed to the cross'

It took nearly five years and $100 million to prepare the case against Pickton. The pig farmer denied his guilt to all but one person: a police officer who had been posing as a cellmate. The pig farmer's words were caught by a hidden camera: 'I was gonna do one more, make it an even 50. That's why I was sloppy. I wanted one more. Make... make the big five O.'

Pickton seemed to acknowledge that he was stuck, that there was no way he would be found not guilty. 'I think I'm nailed to the cross,' he told the bogus cellmate. 'But if that happens there will be about 15 other people are gonna go down.'

The statement only added to suspicions that the remains found on the pig farm weren't solely Pickton's work. Yet, on 22 January 2007, when the pig farmer finally had his day in court, he went alone.

The trial proceeded on a group of six counts that had been drawn from the 26 that Pickton faced. As explained by Justice James Williams, the severing had taken place in the belief that a trial dealing with all 26 might take as long as two years to complete, and would place too high a burden on the jury.

As it turned out, Pickton's trial on the six charges lasted nearly 11 months, and was the longest in Canadian history. Pickton, who had pleaded not guilty on all counts, sat barely paying attention as 128 witnesses took the stand.

That he was found guilty came as a surprise to no one, though the details of the verdict were unexpected. On 9 December 2007, after nine long days of deliberation, jurors found Pickton guilty only of six counts of second-degree murder. The men and women were not convinced that Pickton had acted alone.

Robert Pickton was sentenced to life in prison. Though he will be eligible for parole after 25 years, it is unlikely to be granted.

Vampire Killers

The vampire has one foot in myth, the other in bloody reality. On one level, vampire killers are fantastical monsters, like werewolves and zombies. However, it is in the power of ordinary humans to enact these monsters' exploits, at least as far as drinking blood goes.

Sixteenth-century Hungarian countess and serial killer Elizabeth Bathory was said to be a vampire; her murderous exploits are part history, part myth. It was Bram Stoker's 1897 novel *Dracula* that established the modern image of the vampire killer as the most seductive, most elegant of monsters. A host of horror films since then have fixed in our minds the image of the sleek killer in a dinner jacket, revealing his fangs only when it is much too late for his victims to escape.

Real-life vampires, however, tend to be less than elegant creatures. They are often lonely, inadequate men, enraged by the world, whose actions are just part of a killing frenzy. The psychology of their bizarre blood-drinking ritual is complex, but as with the cannibal killers, it horrifies us, for here we see the breaking of another deep, ancient human taboo.

BELA KISS

Very little is known about the early life of Bela Kiss, one of the most horrifying serial killers of all time. His story only comes fully into focus with the beginning of his career of murder, as a young man apparently searching for a wife. A handsome man with blue eyes and fair hair, Kiss was very attractive to women, not only because of his good looks, but also because he was educated, intelligent and well mannered. However, when his crimes came to light, it emerged that Kiss was a lady killer in a more literal sense. He murdered over 20 women and pickled their bodies in alcohol, inside large metal drums that he hid in his home and around the countryside nearby. Perhaps most horrifying of all, he actually managed to get away with it.

Barrels

In 1912, Bela Kiss was living in the village of Czinkota, just outside Budapest in Hungary. He shared a house with his housekeeper, an elderly woman named Mrs Jakubec. Although well liked in the village, Kiss was not on intimate terms with any of his neighbours. A single man, he had a series of relationships with several attractive young women who often came to the house, but who were never introduced to the housekeeper or to any of his neighbours. Kiss also collected metal drums, telling the local police that they were for storing gasoline, which was likely to be in short supply in the future because of the impending war.

In 1914, Kiss was called up into the army. While he was away, soldiers went to his house to look for the extra supplies of gasoline he was known to have kept there. They found the drums and opened them. Instead of gasoline, inside each drum they found the dead body of a woman who had been strangled and whose body had then been preserved in alcohol. A further search through Kiss' papers revealed dozens of letters from the women, who had visited the house after replying to his newspaper advertisements for a wife. Kiss lured well-to-do, attractive women by correspondence, promising to marry them and often divesting them of their savings in the process. He then invited them to his home. Once there, he would strangle them, pickle their bodies in alcohol and seal them in the metal drums. The bodies also had puncture marks on their necks and their bodies were drained of blood. Bela Kiss was not just a murderer, but a vampire too.

Why he chose to preserve the bodies in this way nobody knows to this day. It was obviously a risky thing to do. Firstly, the drums were big and hard to hide; secondly, the bodies inside were so perfectly preserved that in some cases even the labels on their clothing could be read. Surely Kiss must have known that if ever the drums were opened, his crimes could easily be traced.

Changing Identity

Several local women who had gone missing were discovered in the drums, along with many others whose absence had not been missed. Kiss had repeated his crimes again and again, with a series of innocent, unsuspecting victims, using a false name, 'Herr Hoffmann'. Until the discovery of the bodies, the connection between Bela Kiss and 'Herr Hoffman', who was wanted for questioning in regard to the disappearance of two widows with whom he had corresponded, had never been made.

With the advent of war, Kiss found a perfect way to escape detection: he faked his own death. He assumed the identity of an army comrade who had been killed in combat, switching his papers with those of the dead man. However, his plan was foiled when, in the spring of 1919, he was spotted in Budapest by someone who had known him from his earlier days. Police investigated, and found out about the fraud, but were still unable to catch up with him. Later, a soldier called Hoffman boasted to his comrades of his prowess as a strangler; but once again, when police tried to find Kiss, the trail went cold.

Many years later, Kiss was apparently spotted in New York by a homicide detective called Henry Oswald, renowned for his ability to remember faces. By this time, Kiss would have been in his late sixties. Oswald pursued Kiss but lost him among the crowds of Times Square. A few years later, Kiss was again seen in New York, this time working as the janitor of an apartment block; but he escaped police and was never apprehended.

Nobody knows how or when Bela Kiss died. The true number of his victims is also unknown. Did he cease killing women when he went on the run, or did he continue his hideous crimes undetected? How many women who went missing at that time in Hungary could have been lured to their death by Bela Kiss? These are questions to which we will never know the answers.

JOHN GEORGE HAIGH

Arguably Britain's worst serial killer since Jack the Ripper, John George Haigh the 'Acid Bath Murderer' remains something of an enigma. Was he a calculating swindler who murdered for profit? Did he deliberately portray himself as a crazed lunatic who needed to drink human blood so that he could plead insanity? Or was he indeed a modern-day vampire?

John Haigh was born on 24 July 1909 in Stamford, Yorkshire, in the north of England. Soon after his birth, his parents, John

Robert and Emily, moved to Outwood, near the larger town of Wakefield. They were both members of the Plymouth Brethren, an ultra-puritanical Christian sect, with a hellfire ideology based on sin and punishment.

Background

The family seems to have been settled enough, but religion dominated Haigh's childhood. His father often showed him a scar that he said was a punishment from God for committing a sin. The young Haigh at first lived in fear of receiving such a mark himself, but when he did sin and received no such mark, he began to develop the profound cynicism that would characterize his adult life.

On leaving school, Haigh worked briefly as a car mechanic. Although he loved cars, he had a lifelong aversion to dirt (later he would habitually wear gloves to avoid contamination). He soon left the job and worked briefly as a clerk before finding a career in which he was able to exploit an already well-developed ability to embellish the truth: he became an advertising copywriter. He did well at the job and bought himself a flash Alfa Romeo car. But before long he was sacked after money went missing.

In 1934 he met and married Beatrice Hammer. Four months later he was convicted of fraud for a scam involving hire-purchase agreements, and sent to prison. While he was there, Beatrice gave birth to a child who she immediately gave up for adoption. On his release, Haigh left Beatrice and then simply ignored her, acting as if he had never been married.

Prison seemed to have shocked Haigh back on to the straight and narrow. He started a dry-cleaning company that prospered until his partner in the business died in a motorcycle accident, and business began to decline with the coming of war. Haigh then moved to London where he worked in an amusement arcade, owned by a man named Donald McSwann. A year later, he struck out on his own with a scam that resulted in him being sent to prison again, this time for four years. In prison he talked a lot to his fellow inmates about committing the perfect crime. An imperfect understanding of the law allowed him to develop the notion that if the police could not find a body, then the killer could not be convicted of murder. He decided that the best way to effect this would be to dissolve a body in acid. He experimented in the prison workshops, managing to dissolve a mouse in acid.

Life After Prison

Once back in the community, he put his plan into action. He met up with McSwann, luring him to a workshop that he was renting. He then killed him and, with some difficulty, dumped his body into a large barrel of acid that he had prepared for the purpose. The plan worked perfectly and Haigh was able to tip the last sludgy remains of his friend down a drain. McSwann's parents were suspicious but Haigh managed to fob them off with the story that McSwann had fled to Scotland to avoid being drafted to fight in the war.

When the war ended and McSwann failed to return, his parents became more suspicious. Haigh took drastic action. He lured the parents to the workshop and murdered them both, just as he had killed their son. He then forged letters to enable him to sell off their substantial estate. For the next three years he lived off the money he had received. Thanks to his gambling habit, however, the money ran out and he had to look around for new victims.

He found a couple called Archie and Rosalie Henderson, who met the same fate as the McSwanns and once again Haigh managed to get his hands on their estate. However, it took him less than a year to get through their money. By February 1949 he was unable to pay the bill at the hotel he was living in, a place called the Onslow Court, popular with rich widows. He persuaded one of the widows, Olivia Durand-Deacon, that he had a business plan she might be interested in. She agreed to come with him to his new workshop, located next to a small factory in Surrey, just outside London. Once there he shot her in the head, removed her jewellery and fur coat, and dumped her in an acid bath.

Within two days a friend of Mrs Durand-Deacon alerted the police and mentioned that she had been planning to meet Haigh. Haigh claimed that she had never arrived at the meeting, but his manner was suspicious and they decided to investigate further.

They learned of his workshop in Surrey and obtained a search warrant. They found several clues to suggest that Mrs Durand-Deacon had been there, and then obtained evidence from a local shopkeeper, who identified Haigh as the man who had sold him the widow's jewellery. They duly brought Haigh in for questioning.

The Defence

Once in custody, Haigh boasted that Mrs Durand-Deacon would never be found because he had dissolved her in acid, believing that without her body they would be unable to charge him. In fact, once the police went back and dredged through the hideous sludge in the bottom of the acid bath, they found several pieces of human bone and part of Durand-Deacon's dentures.

The game was clearly up for Haigh, who now switched his tactics. Clearly aiming to plead insanity, he confessed to the murders of the McSwanns and the Hendersons, as well as three other murders of unidentified victims. He claimed that the motives were not financial but that he was tormented by dreams that dated back to his religious childhood. These dreams apparently gave him an unquenchable thirst for human blood – that he sucked up through a drinking straw. It was generally believed that he had added a confession to the three mystery victims because the motivation for the murders of his actual victims was so clearly financial.

The defence found a psychiatrist to attest to Haigh's insanity, but the jury was not convinced, and he was found guilty of murder and sentenced to death by hanging. The sentence was carried out at Wandsworth Prison, London, on 6 August 1949.

ALI REZA KHOSHRUY KURAN KORDIYEH

Serial killers generally flourish in the cities of the West, above all in the United States. In western Europe, the phenomenon is well known, and has become more so in Russia and South Africa in recent years. Therefore, for a serial killer to strike in the heart of the Islamic state of Iran was something quite unprecedented.

Ali Reza Khoshruy Kuran Kordiyeh was 27 when he was arrested in 1997 after killing at least nine women, including a mother and her ten-year-old daughter. Little is known of Kordiyeh's early life except that he was arrested once before, in 1993, when he was charged with kidnapping and rape. At that time he managed to escape from the police as he was being escorted to the court for trial. He proceeded to lie low for the next four years before starting his final rampage.

The Method

Kordiyeh's modus operandi was simple. He pretended to be a taxi driver and cruised around Iran's capital, Teheran, looking for potential victims. Once he had lured a woman into his car, he raped and stabbed her repeatedly, as many as 30 times in some instances. Once she was dead he covered her body in gasoline and set her on fire, in an attempt to destroy any incriminating evidence.

As the number of Kordiyeh's crimes escalated, the city began to live in terror of the man the press were now calling the 'Teheran Vampire'. For a while the police had no clues at all, until two women on separate occasions managed to escape his clutches and were each able to give a description of their attacker to the police.

A short while later, Kordiyeh was picked up by the police while acting suspiciously in a shopping mall. His resemblance to the photofit of the Teheran Vampire was noticed. The police then examined his car and found bloodstains. Under questioning, Kordiyeh confessed that he was indeed the Vampire, though he gave no indication as to what lay behind his crimes.

The Punishment

Kordiyeh's trial was shown live on Iranian television and became a public sensation. He was sentenced to death by hanging, to be preceded by 214 lashes. The sentence was to be carried out in public, in a square in the Olympic Village district of the city, near where many of the murders had been carried out. The people of Teheran turned out in their thousands for the event, creating huge traffic jams in the rush to be there for the public execution at dawn on 12 August 1997.

Before the execution, a cleric told the assembled crowd, estimated to have been as many as 20,000 strong, that 'innocent blood will always be avenged; this is punishment for the criminal, but for us witnesses it is a lesson to be learned.' Then Kordiyeh was brought out to face his death. First, he was thrown face down on to a bench and male relatives of the victims took turns to deal out the 214 blows, using a heavy leather belt. At this point, the crowd had to be restrained from joining in and actually beating Kordiyeh to death. Then the semi-conscious Kordiyeh was hauled up and attached to an improvised gallows, a giant yellow construction crane that lifted his body high into the air as he died. His last words were: 'I borrowed money from no one and I owe none to anyone. I ask God for forgiveness for what I did.'

If this brutal execution was meant to dissuade others from following in Kordiyeh's footsteps, it was not successful. A few months later another Teheran cab driver was arrested by the police after an attempted rape. He told them that 'I'm going to be the next Teheran Vampire.' The same year, Ahmad Taqiabadi was tried in the southern Iranian city of Shiraz for kidnapping 12 children, raping six of them, and killing three people. Kordiyeh's public execution did not have the desired effect, and the hitherto unknown serial killer phenomenon began to be seen in Iran as in other parts of the world.

DEAN CORLL

When the police discovered 27 bodies buried in three separate sites around Houston during August 1973, Dean Corll, 'the Candy Man', shot to the top of the United State's serial killer list in terms of actual bodies recovered. Corll would eventually cede his position to John Wayne Gacy, another sadist with a gruesome record of murdering teenage boys. Corll may not have gained the infamous reputation that later murderers like Gacy and Jeffrey Dahmer have since attracted, but for pure evil he must rank among the most depraved of all serial killers.

Dean Corll was born on 24 December 1939, in Fort Wayne, Indiana. His parents, Arnold and Mary, had a violently combative relationship and divorced when Dean was six, leaving Mary to raise Dean and his brother, Stanley. However Arnold and Mary's relationship continued; they remarried in 1950 when Dean was 11, and moved to Houston in 1950, splitting up again soon after.

The Candy Man

During the 1950s, Mary Corll started a small business making pecan candies. Dean helped her with this enterprise and, by the early 60s, it had expanded into a fully fledged business. Dean would make the candy at night in their converted garage, and go to work at Houston Lighting and Power by day. Around this time he became well known around the area for giving free samples to children, and so acquired the nickname 'the Candy Man'.

In 1964, Corll was drafted into the army, but left after a year on a hardship discharge, in order to help his mother run the candy business. They carried on working together until 1969 when his mother moved to Colorado, and Corll went back to training as an electrician.

What his family did not realize was that Corll had begun to live a secret life. His time in the army had ignited his homosexual impulses, and he had started to lead an active if unacknowledged homosexual life. He was particularly attracted to teenage boys and his taste was for bondage, with an ever increasingly sadistic bent. He would host parties, offering drink and dope and glue for sniffing in an effort to attract teenage boys and get them sufficiently high to let him do what he wanted with them. During 1970 he stuck up a relationship with two boys, Elmer Henley and David Brooks, who were ready and willing to help him take his fantasies to the next stage.

The Accomplices

David Brooks was born in Beaumont, Texas in 1955. His parents were divorced in the early 1960s, when David was only five years old. Elmer Henley was a school dropout who suffered from acne and had a drink problem.

By Henley's account what happened next was that Corll offered the boys money, $200 a time, to bring him young boys, not just to have sex with, but to torture and to kill. However, there is little evidence that money ever changed hands, and it seems likely that Henley made up this story. The more likely scenario is that Brooks and Henley willingly took part, not only in the abusive sex that was happening in Corll's apartment, but in the subsequent murders too.

According to Brooks, Corll's first murder took place some time in mid 1970. The victim was a hitchhiking college student called Jeffrey Konen. In December 1970 he murdered 14-year-old James Glass and 15-year-old David Yates on the same day. In January 1971, he murdered a pair of brothers, Donald and Jerry Waldrop. On another occasion, he killed a boy called Billy Baulch, and then waited a year before abducting and killing Billy's brother, Mike. Most of Corll's victims were in their teens; however, one, a boy who lived across the street from Corll, was just nine years old.

Horrifyingly, many of these young people were friends of Henley and Brooks; kids who were happy to accompany their buddies to a party, only to find themselves plied with alcohol until they became insensible. They would wake up attached to one of Corll's custom-made torture racks before finally being killed in a violent frenzy that would often culminate in Corll biting off their genitals and simultaneously drinking their blood.

Corll's career of evil scarcely attracted the notice of the police. Some of the parents of the missing boys tried to get the police to investigate, but they mostly met with shameful indifference.

However, on 8 August 1971, after three years of slaughter, Elmer Henley brought a teenage girl to one of Corll's parties. Corll did not like that at all; these were strictly male-only affairs. He plied the teenagers with drinks until they passed out, and when they came round, all of them were tied up, including Henley himself. Henley, of course, knew what was likely to happened next. He persuaded Corll to release him, saying that he would rape and kill the girl for Corll's delectation. Corll agreed, and let his guard down long enough for Henley to pick up Corll's gun and shoot Corll dead.

Self Defence?

Henley then called the police. When they arrived, he told them that he had acted in self-defence and that Corll was a murderer. At first, the police were dubious: as far as anyone knew Corll was a respectable citizen. However, the sight of his torture racks was enough for them to allow Henley to take them to a boathouse that Corll had rented in southwest Houston. There, they found 17 buried bodies. A drive to Lake Sam Rayburn led them to four more graves; six others were found on the beach at High Island, making a total of 27 dead. Henley insisted that there were at least two more corpses in the boat shed, plus two more at High Island, but police called off the search. Cynics have suggested that this was because as soon as they had unearthed enough corpses to break Juan Corona's record of 25, they lost interest.

Brooks and Henley both attempted to shift blame on to each other and on to the late Dean Corll. Henley was sentenced to life imprisonment in August 1974 and Brooks received the same sentence in March 1975.

PETER KÜRTEN

'Just you wait a little while,
The nasty man in black will come.
With his little chopper,
He will chop you up!'

So begins *M*, the first sound film by the great German director Fritz Lang. The speaker is a young girl who is playing a schoolyard game. Although she is not seen again in the film, one presumes that she remains quite safe. The same cannot be said for another character, a schoolgirl named Elsie Beckmann, who soon falls victim to a serial killer of children. The murderer is portrayed by Peter Lorre, and the character he plays, Hans Beckert, is thought to have been based on a man named Peter Kürten. Lang always denied that he'd used Kürten as a model – and it must be said that there are great differences between the two, the foremost being that Kürten's crimes were so much more horrific than anything that had been portrayed on film.

Born on 26 May 1883 at Müllheim, Germany, the man who has come to be called the Vampire of Düsseldorf was the third of 13 children. Raised in poverty, as a child Kürten witnessed his alcoholic father's repeated sexual assaults on his mother and at least one of his sisters. He himself suffered through years of vicious beatings by the head of the household. Kürten turned to petty crime and several times attempted to run away from home.

Dog Torturer

Late in life, Kürten claimed that as a child he had actually murdered two young friends while swimming in the Rhine, holding each under water until they drowned. He also claimed to have befriended a local dog-catcher, who taught him how to masturbate and torture the dogs they caught together. It is thought that during this period he also engaged in bestiality.

In 1894, the family moved to Düsseldorf. He continued in his petty thievery and was soon serving the first of what would be a series of 27 short prison sentences. In fact, Kürten would spend most of his life incarcerated in one institution or another. While in custody he would make a point of committing minor offences in order to be placed in solitary confinement. Once alone, Kürten would dream of mass murder – he found these fantasies sexually stimulating. For a time, beginning in 1899, he lived with a masochistic prostitute who was twice his age.

On 25 May 1913, Kürten committed his first provable murder during what would otherwise have been a routine burglary. His victim, a 13-year-old girl named Khristine Klein, was strangled and sexually assaulted. She died after Kürten cut open her throat. The next day, he sat drinking in a café across the street from

Perter Kürten

the murder scene, reading descriptions in the newspaper, and eavesdropping on the conversations going on about him.

In addition to murder and stealing, Kürten had for many years been committing acts of arson. It was the sight of destruction, including that of human life, which excited him to the point of climax. His 1921 marriage had no erotic appeal. He would later say that the union had been made for companionship alone.

For many years, it seems that arson and quite likely rape satisfied his desires. This changed suddenly and dramatically on 8 February 1929 when he sexually assaulted and killed an eight-year-old named Rosa Ohliger. Found the next day beneath a hedge, the body of the dead girl bore 13 stab wounds. Kürten had doused the corpse with gasoline and set it alight – an act that brought him to orgasm.

Five days later he grabbed a woman off the street and stabbed her 24 times. Incredibly, she survived the assault. Kürten found that visits to the scene of the crime would stimulate him sexually.

The next victim, a 45-year-old mechanic, was killed on 18 February. Kürten had stabbed the man 20 times, including several times to the head.

There followed six months of what seems to have been inactivity, during which a mentally handicapped man named Strausberg confessed to Kürten's crimes. He was committed to an asylum.

On 21 August, Kürten resumed his attacks in dramatic fashion, stabbing three people out walking through the Düsseldorf suburb of Lierenfeld. Two nights later, he came upon two girls, five-year-old Gertrude Hamacher and her 14-year-old foster sister Louise Lenzen, walking home from the annual fair in the town of Flehe. Kürten asked Louise to get him some cigarettes, and sent the girl, money in hand, back to the fairground. While Louise was away, he strangled Gertrude and cut her throat. When Louise returned from the errand, she was strangled and decapitated.

The next day, he propositioned a servant girl named Gertrude Schulte. When she replied that she'd rather die than have sex with him, Kürten stabbed her, saying: 'Die then.' Schulte survived and was able to provide an accurate description of her assailant.

Kürten then, inexplicably, put down his knife. His next victims were both beaten to death: a young girl named Ida Reuter in September, and another servant girl, Elizabeth Dorrer, in October. Two other women were also beaten, both with a hammer, but survived.

On 7 November, he abducted a five-year-old girl named Gertrude Albermann. The two-day search for the missing girl came to an end after Kürten sent a detailed letter to a local newspaper in which the location of the girl's body was revealed. She had been stabbed 35 times.

It would prove to be Kürten's final murder.

More hammer attacks, none of them fatal, took place during the months of February and March 1930. Then, on 14 May, he encountered Maria Budlick, yet another servant girl. She had travelled from Cologne to Düsseldorf in search of work. On the railway platform she met a man who offered to show her the way to the local hostel. As Budlick walked with the man she was reminded of newspaper stories she'd read about murders in Düsseldorf and refused to go any further. An argument ensued, only to be broken up by the arrival of another man: Peter Kürten.

Budlick accompanied the man she thought of as her rescuer to his home, where she was fed. Kürten then led the girl into the local woods and raped her.

Although he had been certain that Budlick would not be able to lead police to his home, within days Kürten realized he'd been wrong. Finding he was under police surveillance, he confessed all his crimes to his wife and urged her to turn him in for reward money. After some reluctance – she had proposed a suicide pact – Kürten's wife agreed. He was arrested on 24 May.

While in prison awaiting trial, Kürten relayed details of his life and crimes to German psychologist Karl Berg. With great clarity, the murderer dictated vivid accounts of a total of 79 crimes, which he numbered and presented in chronological order. Berg would later use the interviews as the foundation for his 1932 book on Kürten entitled Der Sadist.

In April 1931, Kürten was put on trial for nine murders and seven attempted murders. He pleaded not guilty, stating that his confession was only an attempt to secure a lucrative reward for his wife. However, as the trial progressed, he changed his plea to guilty and, as he had with Berg, began to talk openly and with great detail about his crimes.

M leaves the viewer with an ambiguous ending. Hans Beckert, the Lorre character, is about to receive his sentence, but the film finishes before it is pronounced. Will Beckert be sentenced to death or will he be found insane? Peter Kürten's fate is much more clear. Found guilty, on the morning of 2 July 1931, he was executed in Cologne by guillotine. His final wish was that he might remain alive long enough to hear the blood flowing out of his severed head.

Bibliography

Paul Begg, *Jack The Ripper: The Facts*, London: Robson, 2004

Gordon Burn, *Happy Like Murderers*, London: Faber and Faber, 1998

Oliver Cyriax, *Crime: An Encyclopedia*, London: Andre Deutch, 1993

Carol Anne Davis, *Women Who Kill*, London: Allison & Busby, 2002

Elliott Leyton, *Hunting Humans*, New York: Seal, 1987

Brian Masters, *Killing for Company*, London: Jonathan Cape, 1985

Charles A. Moose, *Charles Fleming, Three Weeks in October*, New York: Dutton, 2003

Michael Newton, *The Encyclopedia of Serial Killers*, New York: Facts on File, 2000

Ann Rule, *The Stranger Beside Me*, New York: Norton, 1980

Harold Schechter, *The Serial Killer Files*, New York: Ballantine, 2003